L. Fi

Toward a Science of Mankind

TOWARD A SCIENCE
OF MANKIND

Laura Thompson

LABORATORIES OF ANTHROPOLOGY
UNIVERSITY OF NORTH CAROLINA

McGRAW-HILL BOOK COMPANY, INC.

New York   Toronto   London   1961

TOWARD A SCIENCE OF MANKIND

64425

To the very special friends whose encouragement
and generosity have facilitated this endeavor

Preface

> One of the greatest needs of the social sciences is
> for the development of skilled practitioners who
> can use social data for the cure of social ills as
> doctors use scientific data to cure our bodily ills.

This deceptively simple statement by Pendleton Herring (1947,
p. 5) sets forth one of the most challenging problems of
our time. Many observers believe that the social sciences will
never be able to develop such a body of knowledge, skills, and
practitioners. Others, suspending judgment, sit back in a com-
fortable seat to wait and see. Still others are casting their lot
with a band of explorers from many disciplines who are collecting a body of empirical data, formulating generalizations, and
developing clinical skills designed to advance the study of mankind in the direction of a mature, unified science.

I count myself among those students of man who believe
that the development of such a science of mankind is not only
possible, but imminent. While appreciating other points of
view, I assume that a major goal of the student of man today is
to develop such a science. By this I mean that the goal is to
advance our knowledge of mankind to the point where it has
sufficient predictive value that we may apply it systematically
to social problems of global scope.

Professional cultural anthropology demands from its students a dedicated, lifelong effort to understand and compare the lifeways of culturally unique human groups. The professional anthropologist works as far as possible by firsthand observation and analysis. He goes out again and again to study the habits, customs, attitudes, and values, as well as the languages and physical types, of little-known peoples wherever they may be found. For long periods, he lives among his subjects of study in unfamiliar, difficult, and often dangerous conditions. This he does to gain empirical knowledge about man. He seeks new insights into the nature of human groups as creators of cultures. Because of this face-to-face approach, anthropology is more a way of life than a professional career.

I regard myself especially fortunate in being a woman in this profession. A woman anthropologist is ordinarily under less pressure for immediate results, in professional terms, than most men in the field. A woman can, not without certain strains, of course, pursue her studies unhampered by many of the restrictions and compulsions for success, careerwise, which beset most scientists in our society.

I have been prodded and pushed, however, by a still more severe taskmaster. This is an awareness of the urgent need for an adequate conceptual base and fruitful methodology for the practice of a mature applied science of mankind. Virtually all my research has been oriented toward this area of problem. In exploring it, I have, to a large extent, formulated my own field problems, organized my own field expeditions, and selected as field laboratories isolated communities which I considered most favorable to the elucidation of these field problems.

Since my first expedition to the Lau Islands, Fiji (1933–1934), I have been interested in applied anthropology. In *Fijian Frontier* (1940a) I attempted to present the field findings from this project in a form useful to administrators interested in the government and economic development of peoples in dependency political status. As pointed out by Bronislaw Malinowski in his introduction to the book, *Fijian Frontier* pioneered in applied anthropology. The field it attempted to explore is now known as "administrative anthropology." The book's favorable reception by British colonial administrators, and by others with similar interests, encouraged me to pursue other studies along these lines.

My second field expedition was to Guam, an American outpost in the Marianas Islands (1938–1939). It was undertaken at the invitation of the island's naval governor. He requested an evaluation of the local educational system and sought suggestions for improving the schools so that they might meet native needs more effectively. *Guam and Its People* (1947a) was a product of this project. It pioneered in the field now known as "educational anthropology."

My third field project (1940–1941) was an attempt to elucidate Hawaii's complex cultural picture in a way helpful to territorial school administrators and teachers. The findings were incorporated in the final report of the project as a whole, called *Community Survey of Education in Hawaii* (1941, p. 126–142).

The next field job (1942–1945) was among American Indians of the United States. I served as coordinator of the Indian Education, Personality, and Administration project, an extensive multidiscipline project, which is described in Chapter 4. It yielded findings relevant to all the subdivisions of present-day applied anthropology: administrative, educational, psychiatric, medical, and industrial. The coordinator's duties included helping to design the research, testing the methodology in a pilot field survey, and supervising the field workers. They also involved helping to work out the method of analysis of the field findings, helping to formulate the findings from one tribe (Thompson and Joseph, 1944), applying the processed findings from one tribe, by means of a pilot analysis, to elucidate the tribe's practical administrative problems (Thompson, 1950b), and writing the final report of the project (Thompson, 1951b).

As I lived through these experiences, I focused my studies more and more on the applied anthropologist's area of problem. I concluded that if anthropology were ever to yield a genuine applied science, applied anthropologists would have to develop a deductive working hypothesis regarding the na-

ture of culture and cultural dynamics—a hypothesis adequate
to the need to predict the behavior of local communities in solving community-wide practical problems.

I searched the literature in the social sciences, the psychic
disciplines, biology, philosophy, and semantics for such a theory.
In an attempt to solve actual clinical problems in applied
anthropology assigned me by administrators, I experimented
with several deductive hypotheses. For example, in trying to
elucidate the community-welfare problem of the Hopi Indians,
as part of my assignment in the IEPA project mentioned above,
I attempted to analyze the processed findings of the fieldworkers
in *The Hopi Way* (1944), according to the model proposed
by F. S. C. Northrop (1947). The results, embodied in *The
Hopi Crisis* (1946), I rejected as unsatisfactory from the viewpoint of an emerging science of mankind in its applied phase.

Eventually, by a process of experimentation, trial, and
error on the actual clinical problems themselves, I arrived at
a deductive working hypothesis regarding the nature of culture,
community, and personality in cosmic setting, which I judged
did solve the problematic situation in a manner consistent with
the cannons of a mature science in its applied phase. The
analysis, applied to the findings of the project in relation to
the Hopi community-welfare problem, was presented in *Culture
in Crisis* (1950b). But this analysis emerged only after the
materials had been reprocessed and rewritten seven times.

Owing to space limitations, I could not include the entire
working hypothesis, together with the basic assumptions underlying it and the concepts embedded in it, in *Culture in Crisis.*
That volume was devoted primarily to elucidating the practical community-welfare problems of a specific Indian tribe.
Under the circumstances, the clinical application of the theory
had first priority. Moreover, as in most clinical disciplines so
also in applied anthropology, practice preceded theory. The
time was not ripe for such a theoretical presentation.

I believe that now the time is ripe, and hence I am attempting, for the first time, to present the theory as a whole

in this volume. Several parts of it have been published during the last fifteen years, but no attempt has been made before to show their interrelationships in a consistent model of community, culture, and personality in the context of the cosmos. To clarify the position of this hypothesis in the history of anthropological theory, I have tried to set it in historical perspective and to compare it with other hypotheses currently in use, especially among applied anthropologists.

This book, therefore, is a frankly theoretical treatise. It presents a deductive working hypothesis, which is the product of a long period of germination and growth. The hypothesis has emerged from empirical field research and clinical testings in a number of culturally diverse communities. But no attempt is made here to validate the hypothesis, or to relate it systematically to the field findings from whence it sprang, except by reference to the published accounts of those findings. These are, I regret, frequent, but I believe they are necessary, in the interest of clarity. Other illustrations and case studies which elucidate the text have been chosen from a large body of available reports. I have related some of my field findings to the generalizations which emerged therefrom in a separate study, *Peoples I Have Known,* presented on educational television in the spring of 1960, and now being prepared for publication.

I also have research projects designed to test the validity of the working hypothesis under way. For the first testing operation, I selected Iceland, an isolated island community which affords the anthropologist nearly ideal testing conditions. The findings of my field expeditions to Iceland in 1952 and 1960 will be published in due course. A field trip to the Lower Saxons in 1960 and management-consultant work in industry in 1957 have furnished other testing opportunities.

I am aware, of course, that, among my colleagues in the United States, to write a theoretical book is believed to invite the kiss of death. And besides, an applied anthropologist is not supposed to need much theoretical grounding. I hope to show, however, that good applied anthropology, in its present stage of development, needs not only a thorough theoretical foundation on the part of the practitioner, but a framework that can weather the crucial clinical test (Thompson, 1959).

With the development of a mature applied anthropology, anthropologists will have turned a corner in the development of their discipline. Without the clinical test, which applied anthropology uniquely affords, anthropologists can relax in the comforting notion that, as in the humanities, consensus is the only available means of evaluating the results of research. But with the development of applied anthropology, a new conditioning factor is added. Culture change becomes the unquestioned focus of concentration, and the prediction of change, with the degree of precision requisite to solve a given practical problem, becomes the anthropologist's key skill. Thus, applied anthropology affords the proving ground for anthropological theory as well as the empirical test for the crucial skill of the genuine scientist, namely, prediction.

As will be apparent to the reader, the hypothesis set forth in this volume is not really new. It embodies, in slightly altered form, familiar ideas from many sources. I regret that, for obvious reasons, only a fraction of my intellectual debt can be acknowledged here.

I have been especially influenced, I believe, by Alfred N. Whitehead, Kierkegaard, John Dewey, and F. S. C. Northrop; by Bronislaw Malinowski and Ruth Benedict; by A. L. Kroeber and R. H. Lowie; by Dorothy Lee and Benjamin Lee Whorf; by Richard Thurnwald, Raymond Firth, Paul B. Sears, and Karl Polanyi; by Earnest Hooton, Bernard Glueck, Sr., Alice Joseph, Gardner Murphy, and John Collier. And, of course, by Charles Darwin. To all these mentors, I am very grateful.

I am deeply indebted to the members of sixty-four multidisciplinary seminars at the University of Chicago's Committee on Human Development, where was thrashed out the method of analysis of the field findings of the Indian Education, Personality, and Administration project. I also owe a great debt to the members of twelve multidisciplinary seminars, who, under the chairmanship of Roy R. Grinker, attempted to develop a unified theory of human behavior. We met regularly over a period of six years at the Michael Reese Hospital's Psychosomatic and Psychiatric Research and Training Center in Chicago.

Participation in these seminars convinced me that progress in the direction of a mature, unified science of mankind requires the cooperative efforts of many different kinds of scientists—biological, social, and physical—as well as specialists in philosophy, mathematics, and the humanities. It also demands that the student of mankind possess a multidiscipline facility. Obviously, no one person can master all the skills and knowledge and have the insight required for an enterprise of such magnitude. But little by little, through the joint efforts of many different kinds of workers, a genuine science of mankind may emerge.

I offer this book in the hope that it may contribute to this common effort. My aim is not to convince, convert, or otherwise persuade my readers of the validity of my position. Ideas in themselves, of course, are not coercive. My purpose is rather to formulate and clarify that position to the best of my ability. Further research will determine its usefulness as a research tool, irrespective of personal opinion or consensus.

I am only too conscious of the shortcomings of the present effort. Its greatest weakness may be its failure to spell out in detail the link between the two basic subdivisions of anthropology: cultural anthropology and physical anthropology. Such relationships are merely suggested. But I hope that others, far better qualified for the task, will fill in this and other gaps.

Perhaps a warning should be given here that parts of this book will appear unorthodox to many readers. The long search toward the goal has led me into areas of problem not generally regarded as strictly the province of the anthropologist. But I hope that the shortcomings of the book will be countenanced as an effort to face urgent, but difficult, human problems of our age with integrity.

Laura Thompson

Acknowledgments

It is a pleasure to express my appreciation to the following individuals for help in preparing this book: Edwin H. Bryan, Jr., Alfred E. Emerson, Kenneth P. Emory, John Gillin, Dorothy Lee, Kenneth Leisenring, and David Riesman for reading parts of the manuscript; Martin G. Silverman for research assistance; and Virginia Andrews for secretarial assistance.

I am very much indebted to Joffre Coe and the staff of the Laboratories of Anthropology of the University of North Carolina for the use of office space and research facilities. I thank the Directors of the Rockefeller Foundation, and the Committee on Faculty Research and Professional Development, North Carolina State College, for grants to facilitate field work designed to test parts of the present working hypothesis.

I am grateful to the following publishers, journals, editors, and authors for permission to quote from or reproduce the items listed here: *The American Anthropologist* and A. I. Hallowell, "Myth, Culture and Personality," 1947; *The American Journal of Sociology,* University of Chicago Press, "Culture, Genuine and Spurious" by Edward Sapir, 1924; The Beacon Press, Boston, *Knowing and the Known* by John Dewey and Arthur F. Bentley; The Board of Editors of *American Scientist* and Paul B. Sears, "Integration at the Community Level," 1949; Cambridge University Press, New York, *The Directiveness of Organic Activities* by E. S. Russell; and *Man on His*

Nature by Charles Sherrington; The Chicago Natural History Museum and Alexander Spoehr, *Marianas Prehistory; Archaeological Survey and Excavations on Saipan, Tinian, and Rota;* Columbia University Press, New York, *Papago Indian Religion* by Ruth Underhill; Cornell University Press, Ithaca, N.Y., materials by Clyde Kluckhohn in *Adaptation,* John Romano, editor; Alfred E. Emerson, University of Chicago, *Proceedings of the Conference on a Unified Theory of Human Nature,* Michael Reese Hospital, Chicago, March, 1954; The Free Press, Glencoe, Ill., *Social Anthropology* by E. E. Evans-Pritchard; and *A Natural Science of Society* by A. R. Radcliffe-Brown; Harper and Brothers, New York, *New Bottles for New Wine;* Harvard University Press, Cambridge, Mass., *Space, Time and Architecture: the Growth of a New Tradition* by Siegfried Giedion; William Heinemann, Ltd., London, *Mutual Aid: a Factor of Evolution* by P. Kropotkin; Holt, Rinehart and Winston, Inc., New York, *The Unitary Principle in Physics and Biology* by Lancelot Law Whyte; and *The History of Ethnological Theory* by Robert H. Lowie; Houghton Mifflin Company, Boston, *Client-centered Therapy* by Carl R. Rogers; Macmillan and Co., Ltd., London, and St. Martin's Press, Inc., New York, *The Dynamics of Morals* by R. Mukerjee; Methuen & Co. Ltd., London, *Space, Time and Matter* by Hermann Weyl; W. W. Norton & Company, Inc., New York, *Neurosis and Human Growth* by Karen Horney; Rutgers University Press, New Brunswick, N.J., *Nature and Human Nature; Man's New Image of Himself* by Lawrence K. Frank; *The Scientific American,* "Turbulence in Space" by George Gamow, 1952; Charles Scribner's Sons, New York, *The Nature of Natural History* by Marston Bates; Sedgwick and Jackson, London, *Animal Ecology* by Charles Elton; Charles C Thomas, Publisher, Springfield, Ill., and M. K. Opler, *Culture, Psychiatry and Human Values;* University of Chicago Press, Chicago, *The Folk Culture of Yucatan* by Robert Redfield, 1941; and *George Ellett Coghill, Naturalist and Philosopher* by C. Judson Herrick, 1949; University of Chicago Press and the Bureau of Indian Affairs, *The Desert People* by Alice Joseph et al.; University of Illinois Press, Urbana, Ill., *Theory of Culture Change* by Julian H. Steward; The University of Minnesota Press, Minneapolis, Minn., *The People of Alor* by Cora DuBois, 1944; The University of North Carolina Press, Chapel Hill, N.C., *A Scientific Theory of Culture and Other Essays* by Bronislaw Malinowski; The Viking Press, Inc., New York, *The Biology of the Spirit* by Edward W. Sinnott; The University of Wales Press, Cardiff, and Alwyn D. Rees, *Life in a Welsh Countryside;* Hermann Wein, Göttingen University, "The Categories and a Logic of Structure," *Journal of Philosophy,* 1952; Yale University Press, New Haven, Conn., *Becoming a Kwoma* by John W. M. Whiting; and *The Great Apes, a Study of Anthropoid Life* by Yerkes and Yerkes.

Contents

Final Form. Relevant Variable Systems. General Findings of the Project. Some Findings on One Tribe. Theoretical Implications. Significance of the Project.

PART II AN EMERGING HYPOTHESIS

Emphasis on Whole Emerging Events in Interrelationship. A New Conception of Causality. Passing of Traditional Concepts of Time and Space. From Rigid Boundaries to Interpenetration. A Transactional Approach. Space-Time as Integrator. Self-actualizing Activity Systems.

Mechanistic versus Organismic Models in Biology. Developments in Neurology. The Concept of Evolution Reformulated. Directiveness of Organic Activities. Organic and Inorganic Types of Systems. Developments in Ecology. Concept of the Mature or Climax Community. Relevance to Human Problems. Conclusion.

Two Types of Biotic Systems in Lau. The Advent of Man. A New Ecological Balance. An Aboriginal Community under Stress. The Lauan Pattern of Nutrition. The System of Land Use. Role of the Crop Custodian. Role of the Master Fisherman. Interisland Ceremonial Exchange. Some Checks to Overpopulation. Conclusion.

Dynamics of Community Organization. Mutual Aid: Basic Organizing Principle. Intraspecies Self-help. The Struggle-for-existence Hypothesis. The Peck-order Model. Intraspecies Competition. Parallel Findings by Psychologists. Conclusion.

Polynesia, a Natural Laboratory. Polynesian Culture. The Exploration Complex. Settlement in the New Niche. Tentative Generalizations regarding Goal-seeking Devices. Hawaii as a Case Study. Effectiveness of Goal-seeking Devices. Goal-changing Devices. Some Generalizations Emerging from the Data. Culture as a Goal-management System. Conclusion.

The Human Tendency to Symbolize. The Nature of Human Culture. Culture as a Dynamic System. Observations on Culture

Process. Symbolic Integration: More Aesthetic than Logical. Personality as Self-structured. Conclusion.

Introduction: The Objective

> Man becomes a microcosm in which the objective
> trends of the macrocosm can be mirrored and
> from whose subjective depths purpose can flow
> out to influence the trends of the macrocosm
> and, within gradually expanding limits, subject
> them to its will.
>
> *Sir Julian Huxley*

At a recent meeting of the American Anthropological Association, an ad for a Space Anthropologist headed the list of Men
Wanted. Anthropologists are not only active in every country
of the world, they are even pushing their activities into outer
space.

Thousands of research projects are under way. Hundreds
of thousands of dollars are being spent. And mountains of facts
are piling up. On the other hand, attempts to translate these
facts into general principles or laws about the human species
are lagging behind. Some stockpiling of empirical data is indispensable to achieving universally valid generalizations about
mankind as a social, culture-creating species. It is prerequisite
to the emergence of fruitful, testable, deductible hypotheses
upon which to build a mature, unified science of mankind.
But empirically based theory must keep pace with data collect-

ing, or the activities of the collectors will degenerate into mere busy work.

Faced with this confusing situation—an overwhelming aggregation of facts, and a paucity of theory firmly grounded in empirical data to explain them—some anthropologists are abandoning the once popular view that the aim of the anthropologist is to further the development of a genuine science. A number of able students are no longer striving to develop their professional discipline into a full-fledged science, such as a science of man, of culture, of human behavior, or of the community. Rather, they are content to have their respective fields classed primarily with the humanities. In view of present realities, this position is understandable, and a good case can be made in favor of it (Bidney, 1949, pp. 348–349; Evans-Pritchard, 1951; Radin, 1933; Redfield, 1953).

On the other hand, many anthropologists interpret the present situation as a transition period wherein may be detected signs of the eventual emergence of a mature, unified science of mankind. The latter believe that, in view of the difficulties involved, a period of considerable stress may be expected as the study of the human species, the most complex phenomenon in the universe, moves slowly toward maturity and unification as a science.

Scientific Maturity

But what do we mean by *science?* Do we use the term only in the restricted sense of a discipline whose basic units are quantifiable, and whose major generalizations are amenable to precise mathematical verification? Do we refer to an approach to solving problems? A good deal of misunderstanding exists among anthropologists and other students of man about the meaning of this much-used term.

By the term "science," I refer to a describable method of approach to problem solving which may be distinguished from other approaches, especially that of the humanities. For example, the scientific approach may be divided into two phases which characterize the development of every discipline which has attained the status of a mature science (Northrop, 1947). The first is the natural-history phase wherein the investigator attempts (1) to observe immediately apprehended phenomena; (2) to describe them in a general manner; (3) to compare them with similar phenomena found elsewhere; and finally, (4) to classify them according to an appropriate taxonomic scheme.

In the natural-history phase of scientific development, the investigator inspects immediately apprehended phenomena and seeks to formulate generalizations on the basis of the observed data. We call these "inductive generalizations." Since this approach yields only a general description of the phenomena under consideration, rather than an explanatory description, the investigator should not expect to make scientifically based predictions on the basis of his findings. As Whitehead (1933, pp. 147ff.) pointed out long ago, science in the natural-history phase yields general descriptions, comparisons, and inductive generalizations, not predictions. Therefore, it may not be applied to the scientifically based resolution of practical problems. I have elaborated this point elsewhere (Thompson, 1951a, pp. 117–121).

Ethnography—that is, the description, comparison, and classification of human cultures on a world-wide scale—is an example of the developing science of cultural anthropology in its natural-history phase. The only valid generalizations to be expected from ethnographic field data are inductive generalizations based on factual field findings. Attempts to treat ethnography as a mature science, whose findings may be applied systematically to practical problems, are doomed to failure. A science in the natural-history phase does not yield accurate predictions of change, nor does it yield an applied discipline. Its findings are not amenable to scientifically based application to the solution of practical problems.

Not only in ethnography, but also in other subdivisions of anthropology, much of the research currently in progress is in the natural-history phase of scientific development. This applies especially to such fields as archaeology, linguistics, primitive and comparative economics, comparative law, comparative religion, ethnobotany, ethnomusicology, etc. It should be clearly recognized, however, that descriptive research in any discipline is an indispensable forerunner to more mature scientific activity if the discipline is to reach maturity (for a different opinion, see Bierstedt, 1949). Without meticulous, natural-history research as a sound basis for hypothesis formulation, no discipline can attain maturity as a science.

The second or mature phase of development in science is that of deductively formulated theory (Northrop, 1947, Ch. 4). In the mature phase of science, a research endeavor moves out from a deductive working hypothesis whose validity the project is designed to test (Gillin, 1954, pp. 26off.). Working concepts in this stage of scientific endeavor are concepts by postulation. Their meanings are designated by the postulates of the deductive hypothesis wherein they occur (Northrop, 1947, pp. 61ff., 139). In other words, without specific reference to the way in which a proposed concept functions in some theory, it cannot be understood and evaluated for scientific purposes.

The aim of the research endeavor in this second phase is to test the validity of the working hypothesis on the basis of the available relevant facts. The upshot of the endeavor is (1) the confirmation of the initial hypothesis and the subsequent formulation of new heuristic hypotheses emerging from the research, or (2) nonconfirmation of the initial hypothesis and its reformulation in a way which promises to approach more closely a verifiable form.

Deductive Hypothesis Formulation

Scientific endeavor, of course, does not aim for absolutes, either in the form of immutable laws or permanently valid hypotheses. It aims merely for a fruitful working model, or rendition of reality, in keeping with the scientifically accepted facts available at any one historical period. Such working models of reality are temporary. They must be adjusted or redesigned as new facts accumulate.

A good deal has been written about the process of hypothesis formulation. Let us only note here that, in attempting to develop a mature science, the investigator does not merely seek a reasonably adequate working hypothesis about which to design a method of verification. Not at all. Rather, he seeks an inspired, fruitful hypothesis—a hypothesis that leads to discovery. He seeks a hypothesis that emphasizes new dynamic relationships, adequate concepts, and appropriate units of research in relation to the problem under consideration. The history of science teaches us that the seeker after maturity in any science must work industriously toward the goal. But he must also cultivate the ability to suspend judgment until the requisite evidence is at hand, to keep an open mind for unexpected relationships, and to allow new patterns of organization to emerge from the data (Larrabee, 1945, pp. 184–187).

It is probably obvious, even to the cursory student of man, that the problem of formulating a deductive hypothesis of this heuristic type regarding mankind is not amenable to the armchair approach (see Weiss, 1960). We cannot expect merely to sit and reason out the answer. The hypotheses we seek at this stage in the development of a mature, unified science of mankind are of a comprehensive, disturbing nature. They may be compared to other significant hypotheses in the history of science—Darwin's hypothesis on the formation of species; Einstein's hypothesis on the structure of the universe; Freud's hypothesis on the dynamics of the psyche, etc. These hypotheses made a difference. While building on past discoveries, they furnished a magic catalyst which suddenly precipitated the known into a fresh formulation.

New heuristic hypotheses seek the answers to new relevant questions. If we do not first ask the questions in appropriate context, we shall not seek and, perhaps in time, find the answers.

This kind of hypothesis formulation is an expression of

the creative process as it has been described by gestalt psychologists (e.g., Wertheimer, 1945). The creative process cannot be forced. Rather, discovery is the reward of long, conscious preoccupation with an area of problem—the structure of the universe, the nature of organism, the dynamics of psychic processes. It is the outcome of a dedicated concern, a strong motivation to find the answer, an interest so great that the researcher's unconscious mind becomes deeply involved in the search. Finally, in a moment when he is not consciously thinking of the subject, the answer to his problem reveals itself in a flash of insight.

Poincaré, Einstein, Pasteur, and many others have described the process, each from his own personal experience. Like the productive process in art, literature, music, or any other creative activity, deductive hypothesis formulation operates predominantly in the scientist's unconscious mind. The seeker after a new, fruitful, scientific theory cannot *make* it. He must fulfill the necessary conditions—sustained preoccupation with the area of problem, mastery of the relevant data, determination to succeed (Larrabee, 1945, pp. 178–184). In short, he must *woo* it.

A Responsibility of Anthropologists

It seems fitting that anthropology should be moving in the direction of maturity as the unified science of mankind for several reasons. One is that anthropologists, to a greater degree than other students concentrating on the study of man, seek out new, as well as historical, facts about the human species wherever they may be found, even in the most remote and inaccessible parts of the world. The approach of anthropology is global and universal. It encompasses all human phenomena without limitations of place, time, race, culture, or subject matter. In so far as their methods are sound from the natural-history point of view, anthropologists may expect to discover new knowledge about man.

Actually, anthropological field research is continually feed-

ing new information to the many disciplines centering on man
—from psychiatry, human development, and psychoanalysis,
through the life sciences, to the classical social disciplines, such
as sociology, political science, and economics, and even to the
humanities. Anthropologists pay a heavy price in blood, sweat,
and tears for this distinction, for anthropological field work
in remote, isolated regions of the world is not child's play. The
acquisition of new knowledge is their reward.

Anthropologists are in a favorable position to bridge the
gap between the biological sciences and the social sciences.
They have the information and the firsthand field experience
upon which to build a sound body of theory about mankind
on the basis of comparative empirical data. They also have
access to the body of theory which has been accumulating in
both the biological sciences and the social disciplines. Perhaps
the time is now ripe for anthropologists to construct the firm
theoretical foundations and methodology of a mature, unified
science of mankind capable of predicting group behavior with
the degree of precision needed for the solution of urgent practical problems.

Part One

The Search for Method

The mature scientist of mankind searches not for origins but for futures. That is, he searches out those aspects of the emerging future which are manifest in the present and the past. How he does this describes his method of prediction.

Chapter 1
Single-discipline Expeditions

Cultural anthropology has matured significantly during the life-time of today's senior anthropologists. In a single generation, this discipline has evolved from a natural-history phase to one which involves testing a deductive theory. We have witnessed a fundamental change in field methods, from one-man, single-discipline research to teamwork involving a dozen disciplines and a hundred or more scientists. We have observed the emergence of social anthropology, at least in the United States. And we have participated in the birth of scientifically based, applied anthropology and its proliferation into many subdivisions, such as psychiatric, medical, administrative, educational, and industrial anthropology.

These developments have proceeded so rapidly that it is difficult for practicing anthropologists, to say nothing of students, collaborators, and interested laymen, to keep up with them. Especially is it difficult to grasp the underlying direction of these new developments and their significance in regard to many urgent and unresolved problems of modern life.

The importance of these trends has been stressed, however, by a few perceptive students of organism and of man. For example, Sir Julian Huxley, discussing the ideological and moral dilemma of Western man in the light of the snowballing of undigested scientific information, writes (1957, p. 97): "There is no panacea for such a situation. But I do suggest that, if we

3

look at the position objectively, as a problem in applied anthropology, and scientifically in the light of all the relevant knowledge and methods available, we can get some way towards an
answer."

Accordingly, I shall first attempt to describe our search for
appropriate methodology in the direction of a genuine science
of mankind with predictive and clinical value.*

The first crucial step toward the development of multidiscipline, clinical anthropology was taken, as I see it, when the
anthropologist's significant unit of research in relation to his
problem—i.e., his intelligible field of study—was treated, explicitly and consistently, as though it were a system. Von
Bertalanffy (1952, p. 199) defines a system as "a complex of
elements standing in interaction." We shall consider other
meanings of the term as we proceed. But it is usually agreed
that there are general principles holding for systems, irrespective
of the nature of their component elements and irrespective of
the relationships or forces postulated between those components.
We assume that the principles valid for systems in general
eventually can be defined in mathematical language. Hence, a
new realm of science called "general systems theory" is emerging.

The Ethnographic Survey

Immediately prior to, and concomitant with, the development of a modern systems approach in cultural anthropology,
just before and during the twenties,† the cultural anthropologist, at least in the United States, tended to operate as a culture

---

* It may be impossible at this time for any single participant to do
justice to the movement as a whole. The following description is
mainly in terms of my own explorations and doubtless reflects an
idiosyncratic bias. On the other hand, it has the advantage of being
based on firsthand experience and may have a certain human interest.
† I am omitting a discussion of the unilinear evolutionary approach
in anthropology, represented especially by Lewis H. Morgan in the
United States (Lowie, -937, Ch. 6), as not immediately relevant to
the thesis.

historian in the natural-history tradition. That is, he went out as a one-man, one-discipline expedition to a natural (rather than contrived) laboratory, composed of a group of traditionally nonliterate people manifesting a primitive culture. He observed the overt behavior and the cultural products of the natives and brought back museum specimens and a general description of their culture. Then he tried to give historical depth to the unit so described.

Frequently, he surveyed a large area in this manner. Lord Hailey in *An African Survey* (1938, p. 44) wrote:*

In the early years of this century anthropologists usually followed the method of "survey work" in which the inquirer travelled over a wide area recording for each tribe the broad characteristics of physical type, social organization, and material culture. In Rivers' survey work . . . in Melanesia (1901–2) he spent a short time in each island, and sometimes questioned not more than one informant.

In this phase of development of anthropology, the anthropologist tended to define a culture descriptively as a sum total of directly observed traits. Culture was viewed mechanically as a summation of juxtaposed, elementary units. For example, Dixon (1928, p. 3) found culture to be "the sum of all [a people's] activities, customs, and beliefs." Burkitt (1929, Vol. 2, p. 237) defined it as "the sum of the activities of the people as shown by their industries and other discoverable characteristics." To Linton (1936, p. 288) it was "the sum total of ideas, conditioned emotional responses, and patterns of habitual behavior which the members of that society have acquired through instruction or imitation and which they share to a greater or less degree." Lowie stated (1937, p. 3): "By culture we understand the sum-total of what an individual acquires from his society—those beliefs, customs, artistic norms, food habits, and crafts which come to him not by his own creative activity but as a legacy from the past, conveyed by formal or informal education." The anthropologist's significant unit of research in relation

* Quoted with permission of Oxford Univer. Press.

to his problem—which was of a general descriptive-survey type —tended to be immediately apprehended units of natural phenomena, which he treated as things and called "culture traits" (see Wissler, 1923, p. 50). These units might be divided into subunits, called "trait elements." Whole cultures were conceived as aggregates of such units.

The influence of natural-history museum techniques of collecting, classifying, and displaying ethnographic and archaeological specimens is clearly reflected in ethnographic monographs produced by anthropologists at this time, especially in those monographs regarding primitive cultures no longer functioning in the traditional manner (e.g., Wissler, 1912; 1922). Anthropologists felt an urgency about "collecting" these cultures before they disappeared. As might be expected, many of the cultures collected and displayed in museums appear almost as lifeless as animals and plants collected by natural historians for museum specimens; and from subsequently published descriptions, nearly all of them suffered a loss of the vitality manifested in the indigenous setting.

According to this ethnographic survey approach, X, the unknown, equals an unspecified number of traits (embracing, e.g., the group's kinship structure, material culture, economy, religion, language, literature, etc.) added together to form an aggregate whole, namely, a culture. The ethnographer attempts to inspect and apprehend his units of investigation from a single point in historical time (frequently the so-called "ethnographic present") and from a single point in space, conceived as simply located outside the unit under observation. He seeks a general, nonpredictive description at the level of "pure" research. The products of this research may be classified as ethnography of the classic, general-survey type.

Ralph Linton's book, *The Material Culture of the Marquesas Islands* (1923), is a good example of natural-history research in cultural anthropology. Linton's report on his ethnographic field work, done as part of the Bayard-Dominick Expedition in 1920–1921, consists of a general description of each type of artifact or cultural production of the Marquesan islanders, classified into sections under headings, such as houses, canoes, stone artifacts, containers, matting, and basketry. He compiled the results of his archaeological survey in a separate volume. At the end of each section, there is a scholarly conclusion, wherein Marquesan artifacts are compared to similar ones from other subculture areas of Polynesia. No attempt is made to relate the sections of the report to one another except at the end of the monograph, where local differences in the material culture of Polynesia are discussed. Finally, a migration theory is meticulously developed on the basis of a comparative table of the distribution of cultural objects from six major Polynesian subculture areas and other data available at the time. The attempt to give historical depth to a culture in this fashion is typical of the American Historical school.

Unlike many ethnographers of the period, Linton carried to conclusion not only the descriptive phase of this natural-history project, but also the subsequent comparing and classifying phases. Thus he demonstrated his skill in applying the approach to field problems, as well as his industry.

Anthropological research in the natural-history phase is frequently misclassified and misevaluated because field investigators complete the first two steps in the standard natural-history paradigm but do not complete the last two steps. They observe and describe the unit of research, but do not attempt to compare and classify it. Still, the majority of ethnographies should be classed as natural histories.

If the natural-history approach is used by anthropologists, the findings from several *comparable* units only should be compared, of course. Such comparable units may be (1) single traits, (2) aggregates of traits, or (3) cultural wholes. The findings from the comparison should be classified according to an appropriate taxonomy of culture types, such as the popular culture-area classification scheme. This scheme was obviously borrowed from geography. It is associated especially with the work of Clark Wissler (1922; 1923).

Basically, a culture area is characterized by a distinctive trait or element content, which is apparent in the shared behavior of the members of its component societies. The classification gives equal weight to all traits or elements (Steward, 1955, p. 22).

The culture-area scheme is based on *relations of similarity*. In such a classification, as pointed out by Radcliffe-Brown (1957, pp. 21–22), the significant units of research comprising a class are treated like things—isolable and describable on the basis of their similarity to one another—such as two houses or two canoes. Relations within the class are simple relations of similarity. Each class is self-contained and there can be no relationship within or between classes except an aggregational or sum-total one, as of members comprising an aggregate. The members of such a sum may be separated and moved about within the sum without violence to them or to the class. There is no cohesion between them and no quality of integration. They are simply coordinated by similarity. It follows that no functional relationship is indicated between the members of a class, nor may one validly be postulated.

Except for purposes of trouble shooting, no attempt has been made to apply the findings from this type of research systematically to the solution of practical problems. Nor is it appropriate or even possible, in the natural-history phase of anthropology, to do so on a scientific basis. This point is discussed in Chapter 3. Indeed, users of this model frequently do not understand the problems of applied anthropology. Some tend to reject applied anthropology as subjective or unscientific (e.g., Herskovits, 1936). Others, who formerly adhered to this position, have abandoned it (Tax, 1945; 1952).

In discussing the concrete, sum-total model of culture from the historical point of view, I do not mean to imply that this model has been completely discarded. On the contrary, the way of thinking about culture stemming from this phase in the development of anthropology is implicit in a surprising amount of current anthropological literature. On the whole, however, preoccupation with the problem of developing a science of man, or of culture or society or human relations, and of comparing comparable units of research, stressed especially by Rad-

cliffe-Brown (1957) and Malinowski (1944), has led to refine-
ments of approach, field methods, and schemes of classification
(e.g., Murdock, 1945; 1954). Nevertheless, the basic natural-
history problem remains that of comparing classes of directly
observable phenomena, and pigeonholing them on the basis
of similarity. The concept of what constitutes a class may vary,
but not the method of approach.

This area of problem apparently forms one bridge from
the earlier sum-total approach in anthropology to subsequent
systems approaches, discussed in the next section.

Systems Analysis

I suggest that the main contribution of the so-called "functionalists," Bronislaw Malinowski and A. R. Radcliffe-Brown,
was not that they introduced a functionalist approach into anthropology, as is frequently assumed. As Lowie (1937, p. 230)
pointed out years ago, others, including Boas, Bachofen, and
Fustel de Coulanges, had long been concerned with the functional relations of the several elements in a given society or
culture. The main contribution of the so-called "functionalists"
to anthropology was rather that they introduced into anthropological field research the effective use of an explicit, modern
systems approach. In other words, they were the first in the
discipline to exploit systematically the idea that the basic unit
of field research in relation to the problem might fruitfully be
treated as though it were a system wherein all the parts were
functionally related to one another and to the whole. A unit
so treated might be a society, an association, or a small group;
a community, an institution, or a whole culture.

This focus tended to shift the researcher's interest, at
least initially, from historical continuities to functional relations between the several component parts of a whole unit at
a single point in historical time. However, a number of functionalists, including Malinowski (1945, Ch. 3), who in earlier
years had manifested a lack of interest in history, came in time
to appreciate the value of historical research, especially regard-

ing the study of culture change. Indeed, interest in the processes of culture change and in prediction of group behavior has led many investigators to abandon positions which are not historically oriented and to favor approaches which explicitly recognize time depth as indispensable to the frame of reference.

Malinowski's "Functionalism"

With Malinowski, the significant unit of research stressed in relation to the problem was an institution. Writes Malinowski (1944, p. 39):

The essential concept here is that of *organization*. In order to achieve any purpose, reach any end, human beings have to organize. . . . Organization implies a very definite scheme or structure, the main factors of which are universal in that they are applicable to all organized groups, which again, in their typical form, are universal throughout mankind. I propose to call such a unit of human organization by the old but not always clearly defined or consistently used term, institution.

By avoiding the aggregate-of-traits model of the American Historical school and emphasizing functional interrelationships between the *needs* and *institutions* of a tribe or community in the local setting, Malinowski clarified and sharpened the natural-history approach of the ethnographer. In other words, he translated the classic approach of the natural historian into ethnography. He concentrated on an appropriate unit of research relative to the problem of describing the culture— namely, certain regularities in the behavior of groups of individuals in a specific cultural and environmental setting; and he demonstrated how the fieldworker might observe, more efficiently, immediately apprehended phenomena regarding organization of behavior in relation to human needs and purposes in a local community. He demonstrated how the field investigator might describe what he so observed, compare his findings with comparable ones found elsewhere, and classify them appropriately.

Although Malinowski engaged in deductive speculations regarding the significance of his factual findings, he particularly stressed inductive generalizations. His theory of culture (1944) is an *ethnographer's* theory, closely related to inductive generalizations emerging directly from his field experience. It presupposes that the observer will remain outside his unit of research, which is treated as though it were simply located in space and time. To the end, Malinowski remained a behaviorist, with his point of observation outside the field unit under inspection. But he described his units of research functionally in environmental context in a way which forecast the currently emerging transactional approach. For example, he did not abstract the institutional systems he described from their environmental settings, nor did he treat them as though they represented natural isolates (see Radcliffe-Brown below).

Furthermore, Malinowski's keen interest in the development of an applied anthropology, closely related to human needs and community welfare, pointed toward the biologically based, welfare-oriented clinical anthropology which is currently emerging.

Radcliffe-Brown's "Natural Isolates"

Radcliffe-Brown, on the other hand, is considered the leading theorist of the most fashionable school of thought which uses an explicit systems approach in anthropological research. Exponents of this school, called "social anthropologists," focus on society rather than on culture. Many leading social anthropologists, both in England and in the United States, have been students of Radcliffe-Brown.

What is meant by a *systems approach* in anthropology? Radcliffe-Brown has, I believe, answered this question with his usual brilliance, by differentiating a *class* from a *system*. Prior to the introduction of a systems approach ethnographers observed, described, and compared only classes of natural phenomena, as noted above. After the introduction of a systems approach fieldworkers tended to observe, describe, and compare systems of natural phenomena.

Both class and system, according to Radcliffe-Brown (1957, pp. 21–22), exist in phenomenal reality. All classes and many systems may be directly apprehended or observed empirically by the fieldworker. On the other hand, some systems cannot be observed directly, but only inferred (Radcliffe-Brown, p. 27).

Units of research comprising a class are treated like things capable of being isolated conceptually and described on the basis of similarity. On the other hand, units of research comprising a system are treated like events or the relations between events. That is, they are isolated conceptually and described on the basis of their interconnectedness. Relations within the system are viewed as complex relations of interconnectedness. The system is seen as a genuine whole, having an inner structured unity. It is treated as though it were integrated, that is, coordinated by relations of interdependence. The component units may not be separated from the whole, or moved about, without violence being done to them and to the system. The whole manifests a functional consistency. From Radcliffe-Brown's viewpoint, its units cohere and thereby isolate the system from the rest of the universe. He states (1957, p. 20): "A natural system . . . is a conceptually isolated portion of phenomenal reality (the system separated from the rest of the universe which is then the total environment of the system), consisting of a set of entities in such relation to one another as to make a naturally cohering unity."

The art of using a systems approach, according to Radcliffe-Brown, lies in the ethnographer's ability to select and isolate conceptually those natural systems which occur in phenomenal reality. "We are able," he states (1957, p. 19), "in analyzing phenomenal reality, to isolate such a natural system from the rest of the universe. We perform a dichotomy: we have a system, and the rest of the universe becomes its environment: one cannot have the one without the other."

This, in my opinion, is the first significant methodological problem in regard to the appropriate use of a systems approach by anthropologists. The relevant question at this point would be: How much of the unit shall we consider *system* and how much shall we consider *environment?* Systematists such as Radcliffe-Brown, who focused on society, and Leslie White (1949), who focuses on culture, tend sharply to differentiate system from surround, and to treat the conceptual isolates as though their boundaries were rigid and impermeable. "This procedure presupposes that every system can be conceptually isolated from every other and from all else in the universe; it further presupposes that this conceptual isolate will have a relatively high degree of conformity with phenomenal reality" (Radcliffe-Brown, 1957, p. 23).

On the other hand, functionalists such as Malinowski and Raymond Firth, and transactionalists such as Lawrence K. Frank, Marston Bates, E. S. C. Handy, and H. Barnett, tend to extend the systems approach to include, in the intelligible field of study, the effective environment. They emphasize permeable boundaries and the interpenetration of systems.

The rigid-boundary systematists proceed to analyze a conceptually isolated system, without reference to other systems, in terms of relations within the system. These are conceived as relations of interactive interdependence. They may then compare these system units for relations of similarity whereby they may be segregated into classes of natural systems. The goal of this type of systems research seems to be to discover the essential characteristics or properties of a class or kind of natural system (Radcliffe-Brown, p. 20). According to Radcliffe-Brown (Embree, 1939, p. x), systematists of this school of thought seek universally valid sociological laws.

Following this approach, the first step in the research endeavor, for example, is to describe, compare, and classify social systems (Embree, pp. 33ff.). States Evans-Pritchard (1951, pp. 56–57):

Once the notion of system is accepted as a primary postulate . . . the object of research ceases to be ethnological classification and the elaboration of cultural categories and schemes of hypothetical development. It becomes in studies of particular societies the definition of social activities in terms of their functions within their social systems, and in comparative studies a comparison of institutions as parts of social systems or in the relation they have to the whole life of the societies in which they are found. What the modern anthropologist compares are not customs, but systems of relations.

Thus, the approach appears to be a refinement in the natural-history tradition, whereby all the social systems within a designated class presumably will have the same set of characteristics.

The second methodological problem in using the systems approach seems to be: With what types of system models are we working? What kinds of units do we set up for our system models, and what kinds of relations do we postulate between these units? Is a social system, as conceived by the social anthropologist, the same kind of system as an economic system, a legal system, a linguistic system, a neurological system, or a solar system?

To me, these are relevant questions which anthropologists, using a systems approach, need to ask themselves. Since the way each systems anthropologist answers gives direction to his investigations and even sets his goals, the problems raised cannot validly be relegated to the philosophers (for a different view, see Pitt-Rivers, 1954, p. xiv).

Actually, if an anthropologist attempts to answer this question regarding his own research and that of others, he discovers that several system models are being employed. The several types of working models currently in use, however, have not been made explicit in the literature.

Radcliffe-Brown distinguishes two classes of natural systems: mechanical systems and persistent systems. "Mechanical systems," he states (1951, p. 24), "are composed of motions and masses in relation. Their unit entities or events are positions of mass at various moments in time, and their relations, the interconnected relations between these events." He uses Galileo's system of a falling body as an example of a mechanical system. Persistent systems, on the other hand, maintain their dynamic structural continuity through a certain lapse of time;

the structure of the system is the specific set of relations between its units (Radcliffe-Brown, 1951, pp. 25–26). The social scientist, according to Radcliffe-Brown (1951, pp. 43ff.), focuses on social systems which are persistent systems of real relations of interconnectedness between individuals in space and time.

Position of Observer in Relation to Observed

According to the ideal working model for this type of systems research, the social anthropologist observes the significant unit of research, e.g., a social system, from a single point of reference outside it, according to a three-dimensional, Renaissance kind of perspective (see pp. 80–81), as in the previously cited examples. He still concentrates on a view of the unit from the outside. Thus, his approach is strictly empirical and positivistic. However, the social anthropologist usually concentrates on overt behavior, rather than on both behavior and its products, such as material culture, as in the phase described above (Warner's *Black Civilization*, 1937, constitutes an exception). He usually conceives the unknown X as a system of interpersonal behavioral interactions. Thus, the aim of the research endeavor is an exhaustive general description of the unit of research (namely, the social system) from a point of reference outside it.

Besides Radcliffe-Brown's own field work on the Andaman islanders (1922), good examples of this approach may be found in the field reports of his students: for example, Warner's Yankee City series (Warner and Lunt, 1941; 1942; Warner and Low, 1947; Warner, 1946, etc.); Evans-Pritchard's work on the Nuer (1940; 1956; etc.); and John Embree's *Suye Mura* (1939).

The working model is not essentially changed when a group of social anthropologists work together as a team in the analysis of the unit of research. According to this variation on the model, each member of the team may make observations from a different vantage point, so that descriptions of the unit of research are obtained from several points of reference. However, all the members of the team concentrate on overt behavior, and all yield an outside view of the unit. The ideal end result of this approach is a more exhaustive description of the unit under consideration than may be obtained by means of a one-man effort. The primary aim of the research, however, is still a general, not an explanatory, description of the unit.

A good illustration of the use of this team approach to investigate the organization of behavior in a modern nation is reported in Arensberg and Kimball's analysis of Irish society (Arensberg and Kimball, 1940; Arensberg, 1937). The aim of the endeavor, as stated by the authors, was to describe the unit "as observers of the minutiae of social life" (Arensberg and Kimball, 1940, p. xxvii) at a single point in time rather than in historical perspective, and to analyze the findings, compare them, and interpret them by means of inductive generalizations (Arensberg and Kimball, 1940, pp. xxviii–xxix).

Compared with an ethnographic approach, this kind of analysis shifts the emphasis from the culture and history of the community to its social behavior (Arensberg, 1937, p. 7). It assumes that the meaning of customs lies in "the social adaptation of the individual" rather than in historical continuities or environmental adaptations. Hence behavioral adaptations, rather than historical and geographic continuities, invite comparison (Arensberg, 1937, p. 4). The position envisages anthropology as a science of human relations, rather than the culture-history discipline of the cultural anthropologists.

This approach involves inductive social analysis, that is, "structural analysis through the integration of abstractions from social life" (Evans-Pritchard, 1951, p. 96). By this kind of analysis, social anthropologists aim to classify all societies, from simple to complex, so "that our understanding of each group will be greatly enhanced by our knowledge of its comparative position among the social systems of the world" (Arensberg and Kimball, 1940, p. viii). Among others, Carlton Coon has made a start toward this objective (Coon, 1948).

Such attempts should eventually yield a comparative sociology, which would include modern industrial civilizations.

Comprehensive coverage of the world at any one point in historic time seems to be the aim of the field work, and a body of universally valid inductive generalizations regarding the structure and dynamics of social systems is the ultimate goal. As a systematic discipline, comparative sociology should bridge the gap between cultural anthropology and sociology.

It is generally agreed that comparative social anthropology has made and is making a major contribution, not only to sociology, but also to anthropology. It is illuminating both the nature and the typology of human social systems. It is refining field techniques for the inductive analysis of human societies. In so far as it moves in the direction of empirical description, comparative analysis, and classification of the social systems of distinct cultural groups, social anthropology represents a refinement of the natural-history approach. To the extent that it is problem-centered, however, it may be classified appropriately as transitional from a natural-history phase to one of mature, deductive theory.

Small-Group Research

Another development of the systems approach in anthropology involves the study of small groups within a larger social whole. This development in the United States is associated with the names of Mayo, Warner, Chapple, and others, and the work they did during the twenties and thirties.

In keeping with Radcliffe-Brown's assumption regarding natural isolates, these researchers focus on a small group, such as a factory or other face-to-face unit, viewed as a system of interacting individuals. They view this small group as a naturally isolated system and do not especially concern themselves methodologically with its relation to the larger society. Characteristically, the focal unit is treated as though it were a system of the mechanical type, which may be completely divorced from the surround for purposes of analysis.

Typical of this model are its dynamics, which are frequently described as though they tended toward a condition of mechanical equilibrium or least action. If stress is applied to one part of the system, the assumption is that every other part, as well as the whole, will be affected. This type of system is usually described as tending, when thrown off balance into a condition of disequilibrium, to restore itself by reverting to the former *status quo* rather than by seeking a new equilibrium (Chapple and Coon, 1942, p. 14; Homans, 1950, p. 421). Thus many small-group researchers, while following Radcliffe-Brown in using a systems approach whereby the unit of research is treated as though it were a natural isolate, differ from him in stressing a mechanical, rather than a persistent, system model.

Another diagnostic characteristic of mechanical system models, frequently overlooked, is that the several parts are usually conceived implicitly as inert and incapable of growth, self-direction, and self-restoration. On the other hand, their several positions in the system, as well as their limited movement, are underlined. According to this approach, if a part of the whole is injured or lost, it cannot replace itself, since it does not have the capacity for self-recuperation. Nor is the system presumably capable of growing a new part, or of changing the function of other parts to compensate for the injured or lost one.

It will readily be apparent that when the parts of such a model are viewed as "interactive sets" of human relations, for example, the characteristics of a mechanical system may be projected by the investigator, perhaps unconsciously, to the human components. If this happens, the presence of essentially human qualities, such as self-directed activity, creativity, spontaneity and ingenuity, may be ignored or underplayed as irrelevant to the experiment. On the other hand, rigid, repetitive behavior is likely to be emphasized.

A patent danger of the approach is that the applied anthropologist, using this working model of a social system, will underrate the group's capacity for self-direction, including self-government. Consequently, in making recommendations for administrative action, he may stress authoritarian administrative systems as correctives. Thus, the anthropologist's preferred conceptual frame may be expected to have far-reaching consequences at the applied level in terms of his recommendations regarding administrative policy.

This point was impressed on me vividly after World War II, when the United States had just become responsible for the administration of the Pacific Trust Territory. A meeting of specialists was called by the Pacific Science Board of the National Research Council in Washington to consider the problem of natural-resources conservation of this vast, remote area, whose total land base was only 988 square miles and whose population was about 100,000.

The specialists quickly split into two camps. The majority group favored drawing up a detailed, official blueprint for resources conservation in the area, and superimposing it *in toto* on the natives. The minority group, declaring the plan impractical, favored a social-action approach, whereby the urgent need of a conservation program would be explained to leading native groups on the several islands in order to stimulate them to meet the challenge in their own way (Thompson, 1949b). The majority faction recognized certain advantages of the second alternative from the administrative point of view; but they rejected it because they considered the natives incapable of assuming responsibility for developing their own resources-conservation plan.

In terms of systems theory, it seemed as though they unconsciously perceived the natives as fixed, essentially passive, and noncreative units in a mechanical type of social system. By contrast, the minority faction perceived the field situation quite differently. They viewed each island as though it were a naturally isolated system of the organic type wherein the human component was actively interested in reinforcing natural processes which contributed to the good of the whole—men, animals, plants, and the earth and sea. This viewpoint will be discussed in the following chapters. Eventually, a compromise was worked out whereby both natives and administrators were given active roles in a local conservation program.

Human-relations Engineering

The issues at stake in the discussion of conservation in the trust territory are highlighted by a review of the development of human-relations engineering. This development is well illustrated, I believe, in the work of Eliot Chapple and his associates on small groups in industry.

Chapple and his associates (1940) stressed quantitative operational procedures and explicitly introduced the time factor as a dimension for the study of concrete, practical problems concerning "interactive sets" in small groups, such as factories, viewed as systems of human relations which might be isolated conceptually. In systems of the persistent type, it will be recalled, time was treated by Radcliffe-Brown as an integral characteristic of the unit of research. It was a built-in part of the whole system, comparable to other such systems. By contrast, time was omitted from Chapple's unit of research and reintroduced from without into the problem formulation as part of the methodology. On this theoretical base, Chapple and Coon (1942) attempted to formulate a science of human relations. They sought to develop a science wherein the variables would be viewed as the properties of human beings and the several elements of their environment, while the measures to be applied to the relations between these variables would be units of time (Chapple and Coon, 1942, p. vii).

In modern industrial anthropology, the science of human relations is applied to the solution of human-relations problems in industry, a development called "human-relations engineering." The approach has also been used to elucidate certain problems in medical and psychiatric anthropology and in administrative anthropology.

It is generally agreed that human-relations engineering has had considerable success in facilitating the improvement of human relations in small groups of limited scope over a short time span. Such groups include, for example, associations, gangs, prisons, hospitals, and business enterprises. The small group is treated as though it were a system of the mechanical type simply located in space and time, while all else, including the larger society of which the small group is a part, is regarded as environment. By treating the part as a whole, this approach fosters, with a minimum of dissonance (to use Festinger's terminology), manipulation of the part (e.g., the small group) without disturbing the structure of the whole (e.g., an association, society, or nation). Hence, many consider it ideal for research in industry, military bureaucracy, or government administration, where an immediate, short-term improvement is desired in human relations, morale, efficiency, or production at lower levels in the social hierarchy with a minimum of structural or organizational disturbance of the larger social whole. The approach obviously lends itself to perpetuation of the *status quo* (Thompson, 1951a, pp. 119ff.).

Considering the human-relations-engineering movement as a whole, we may conclude that this approach may be indicated if the immediate goal of improved human relations within a definitely bounded small group is sought without reference to the larger society. However, the model is obviously inadequate if a more inclusive, flexible, and self-corrective goal is sought, such as improved welfare and mental hygiene on a community-wide, or society-wide, basis.

In the latter circumstance, the anthropologist is faced with two alternatives. He may defer involvement, as did Radcliffe-Brown (1930, p. 269) who stated: "With the more rapid advance of the pure science itself, and with the co-operation of colonial administrations, we might even look forward to a time when the government and education of native peoples in various parts of the world would make some approach to being an art based on the application of discovered laws of anthropological science." Indeed, it is significant that, although Radcliffe-Brown initiated a movement which contributed significantly to the development of human-relations engineering in anthropology, he himself avoided involvement in regard to practical issues.

Concerning this point, Evans-Pritchard (1951, p. 22), who has done a good deal of work for the Sudanese government, remarked:

I do not believe that anthropological knowledge can be applied to any extent in the arts of administration and education among primitive peoples in any other than in this very general cultural sense—in the influence it has in shaping the attitude of the European toward native peoples. The understanding of a people's way of life generally arouses sympathy for them, and sometimes deep devotion to their service and interests. The native, as well as the European, is then benefited.

It would be naïve to assume, however, that, even though an anthropologist himself refused to become involved in applied anthropology, his findings, if valid, would not be used by others for practical purposes. Most anthropologists are aware, as Vance Packard has revealed in *The Hidden Persuaders* (1957), that the findings of anthropologists, and other students of man and society, are being very effectively used in industry and elsewhere today. We have to accept the fact that once the information is available, application cannot be avoided (see van der Haag, 1959, p. 1444).

But it would be equally naïve to assume that application means manipulation. What are the alternatives to external manipulation as an approach in applied anthropology? When faced with an assignment involving the total welfare and mental hygiene of local communities, tribes, and nations, the applied anthropologist may choose to search further for an adequate approach. Continuation of the search is discussed in subsequent chapters.

Conclusion

Our review of the search for appropriate methodology in the scientific study of mankind by means of single-discipline field work has suggested that the beginning of a mature scientific approach was achieved when the significant unit of research in relation to the problem was treated consistently and explicitly as though it were a system. This was the germinal idea which apparently led to methodological discovery.

We now note that with the introduction of an explicit modern systems approach to cultural anthropology in the natural-history phase came the beginning of a split among cultural anthropologists, especially of the American Historical school. A group emerged, the social anthropologists, who began to regard society, rather than culture, as their key operational concept. They treated social groups as their significant units of research. This movement has matured into the social anthropology of the present, with comparative sociology and the science of human relations as its main facets. The latter facet has tended to foster human-relations-engineering techniques in the solution of practical problems.

On the other hand, traditional cultural anthropology, as we shall see, has developed along quite a different path. It has continued to focus on culture and has sought out naturally isolated, local communities as its significant units of research. On the basis of these traditional roots, it appears that cultural anthropology is advancing toward a science of mankind and is developing a subsidiary discipline at the applied level, namely, clinical anthropology.

Thus, in the twenties and even before, American cultural anthropology began to split into at least two distinct schools of thought. American anthropologists today are living as it were in two theoretical worlds, neither of which has been made wholly explicit. Confusion regarding unstated premises underlying the simplest statements is frequently a source of considerable misunderstanding between followers of the two schools; the same term is sometimes used for two or more quite different referents.

For example, there are several meanings associated with the term *function*. Malinowski (1944, p. 39) used it to denote the relationship between institutions and human needs. Accordingly, "function" is defined as the satisfaction of a need by an activity in which human beings cooperate, use artifacts, and consume goods. Radcliffe-Brown (1957, pp. 85, 154ff.), on the other hand, defined "function" as "the total set of relations that a single social activity or usage or belief has to the total social system." Chapple and Coon (1942, p. 11) use the term *functional dependence* to mean the "relationship between phenomena in which a value of one variable changes uniformly with changes in another." Similarly, the words "system," "equilibrium," "institution," "integration," and many others in common use among anthropologists, are related to at least two or three distinct sets of meanings. As recent developments in method and theory are discussed in the ensuing chapters, I hope that the conceptual schemes reflected in these uses will be clarified, and that some of the confusion will be dissipated.

The breach between major trends in sociocultural anthropology has widened during the past decades. Although important at the theoretical level, the deeper significance of this split manifests itself when attempts are made systematically to apply the findings from the several schools to practical human problems. For, as has been noted, each school is developing a distinctive approach which may be used in the elucidation of practical problems. Social anthropology in its human-relations branch is developing a type of social-relations engineering, and cultural anthropology is developing a type of multidimensional community analysis and therapy.

Chapter 2
Cross-discipline Research

So far we have considered only research projects using methods from one major discipline class. By a major discipline class, I refer to a cluster of closely related disciplines, such as the social sciences, the psychological sciences, the biological sciences, and the physical sciences. We have discussed ethnography, social anthropology, and small-group research. All these are usually classed with the social sciences. A significant step toward a mature science of mankind was taken when anthropological field research involving two major discipline classes emerged. Indeed, from the present viewpoint, the bridge from the older anthropology to the new was formed by cross-discipline research which related two major discipline classes. The multidiscipline anthropology now emerging seeks to relate three or more major discipline classes.

Basic to the development of this multidiscipline anthropology are two major methodological thrusts: (1) a culture-environment spearhead, and (2) a culture-personality spearhead. The culture-environment spearhead relates sociocultural anthropology to geography, economics, and ecology; while the culture-personality spearhead relates sociocultural anthropology to psychology, psychoanalysis, and psychiatry. These two thrusts are now converging in a unified, multidiscipline methodology.

Both movements foster an extension of the investigator's frame of reference to include sets of variables hitherto ignored or treated superficially by anthropologists. Both involve a shift in the traditional position of the observer or observers, either outward or inward or both, in relation to the significant unit of research. Attempts are now being made to use multiple positions, outside and inside the unit, as simultaneous observation points. Finally, by elucidating and emphasizing facts concerning the organic nature of the human group, both movements have tended to reinforce the relationship of anthropology to the life sciences, rather than to the social sciences.

The Culture-Environment Spearhead

Initially, the culture-environment thrust grew out of systematic attempts by anthropologists and others to find empirical answers to the question: How is a given culture, viewed as a whole, related to its environment? This question was later extended to encompass the more crucial explanatory one: Why is a given culture related as it seems to be to its environment? Cross-discipline research, mainly involving ethnography and geography, or ethnography and economics, was developed experimentally in the field in an effort to answer the first or "how" question. Later, anthropologists began to use the findings of ecologists as a basis for field research in an attempt to answer the second or "why" question. This development led to the new, multidiscipline phase of cultural anthropology.

In discussing early cross-discipline research in the culture-environment sphere, we shall bypass several theorists who tried to find an answer to the "how" question in some form of extreme environmental determinism.* Anthropologists agree that extreme environmental determinists' theories have not withstood the field test (see, e.g., Goldenweiser, 1937, pp. 443–454).

The failure of field investigations to validate the position of the extreme environmentalists led anthropologists to initiate their own field projects to correct current theories and to pro-

* Examples are Griffith Taylor (1936) and Huntington (1945; 1951). Huntington's early field work reported in *The Pulse of Asia* (1907) does not fall into this category.

duce fruitful new ones. In this empirical approach they were preceded by the German anthropogeographer, F. Ratzel (1921–1922). Emphasizing a one-way effect of environment on man, Ratzel advocated a temperate environmentalism.

I do not propose to make an exhaustive survey of the many experiments along these lines which formed a bridge to the emerging multidiscipline anthropology. I merely wish to point out the relevance of research in this area to the new approach. The work of pioneers in the field of primitive economics, such as B. Malinowski (1922; 1935), Raymond Firth (1929; 1939), Richard Thurnwald (1932), and M. Herskovits (1940; 1952) is well known. In most of these field investigations the anthropologist concentrated on a particular area of problem in the so-called "economic sphere." He generally made his observations from a point outside the unit of research. He tended to view the community's culture as a unified whole functionally related to its environment, and this approach led to new insights into the relations between culture and economy.   .

In this early period no trained economist accompanied an anthropologist into the field, so far as I am aware, although several anthropologists who worked in this area of problem (including Firth and Belshaw) were trained in classical economic theory. In due course, however, professional economists and economic historians, such as Karl Polanyi (1944), began to use the new knowledge about the economies of primitive and folk communities supplied by anthropologists. Eventually, team research involving anthropologists and economists emerged. A brilliant example is the seminar collaboration between Polanyi, Arensberg, and Pearson (1957). The implications of such long-term, cross-discipline research, especially regarding culture-environment relations, have by no means been assimilated.

Some early work in primitive and comparative economics was an important forerunner of current, cross-discipline field research in anthropogeography. The latter seems to be spelling out some verifiable principles of culture-environment relations. The work of anthropologists who were trained in geography or who collaborated with geographers—for example, A. L. Kroeber (1939) who worked in association with Carl Sauer; Julian Steward (1933) ; and Daryll Forde (1934, etc.)—aided in the development of an empirical method for the field investigation of the ecologic dimension in modern multidiscipline community analysis.

According to the present view, an essential dimension needed in a theoretical frame designed to yield an explanatory description of the culture of a community, which may be used as a reliable basis for prediction of the behavior of its human members, is frequently lacking in social anthropological (and sociological) investigations. We frequently overlook the fact that in applied anthropology, as in other types of applied social research, prediction of the behavior of the group is essential to the success of the endeavor. Indeed, as I shall attempt to show, the urgent need to resolve complex community-wide problems, involving precise prediction of human behavior to the degree requisite for solution of the problem, is fostering the emergence of an ecologically based, multidiscipline anthropology.

Both social anthropologists, following Radcliffe-Brown (1957), and culturologists, following Leslie White (1949), seek to explain behavior *sui generis* entirely in sociological or cultural terms. M. Titiev (1944, pp. 97–99) carries this approach to the point of no return when he attempts to explain the behavior of Pueblo Indians during the great twenty-three-year drought of 1276–1299 (see Hack, 1942, pp. 76–77) and the concomitant breakup of the Classic Pueblo period in terms of a tendency toward social factionalism in Pueblo culture.

As emphasized by Omer Stewart (Spencer, 1954, pp. 223ff.), most ethnogeographers stressed the one-way influence of environment on man and culture rather than the mutual influence of the earth and its inhabitants upon one another, as suggested by Boas (1940, p. 646). But it was only one step from their approach to that of multidiscipline ethnoarchaeologists such as J. G. D. Clark (1936; 1951), ethnogeologists such as J. T. Hack (1942), and ethnobotanists such as George

Carter (1945; 1950). A transactional approach is employed to some extent, implicitly or explicitly, by these investigators. Each has succeeded in achieving a genuine cross-fertilization between functional ecology, such as that developed by Allee, Emerson et al. (1949), and functional anthropology as developed by Malinowski, Thurnwald, and others.

So far we have discussed two-discipline research conducted mainly by one man who was trained in two disciplines. Attempts also have been made to achieve a genuine cross-fertilization of approach, field methods, and analysis between anthropology and ecology by means of a two-member field team. An example is afforded by the meticulous field investigation of an ancient Netherlands community by the anthropologist D. Keur and the biologist J. Keur (Keur and Keur, 1955).

Finally, the work of applied ecologists (i.e., natural-resources conservationists), such as Paul Sears (1939; 1949; 1955) and Hugh Bennett (1939), has contributed to the development of theory and method in the ecological dimension of multidiscipline anthropology.

The Culture-Personality Spearhead

The culture-personality thrust in anthropology grew out of systematic attempts by anthropologists and others to answer the question: How is the individual related to his culture? These have involved several cross-discipline experiments, all concerned with relating the individual to his cultural or social matrix.

Significant investigators in this area have used anthropological theoretical approaches and field techniques, and also have borrowed approaches and/or field techniques from (1) behavioristic psychology and learning theory, (2) gestalt psychology, (3) analytic psychology, and (4) psychiatry. These developments have been subsumed under the culture-personality rubric. To illustrate the search for method, I shall consider several types of two-discipline research in this area of problem.

Early Field Research

In early culture-environment explorations and in early investigations of the relation between culture and personality, the researcher was skilled in two disciplines.

First, we find an anthropologist, who has been trained in academic psychology, going as a one-man, or perhaps a one-woman, team to study a culture-personality problem in a native community. A few of Franz Boas's students in the twenties, when Boas is reported to have become especially interested in certain psychological problems, illustrate this approach. Examples which come to mind include Margaret Mead in her early work (1928; 1930; 1935), Edward Sapir (see Mandelbaum, 1949, Part 3), and Ruth Bunzel (1929).

We now find the anthropologist attempting a problem-centered project rather than an ethnographic survey. Field problems in this early period usually involved some aspect of the following general question: In a given culture, *what* is the relationship between child-training patterns and patterns of adult behavior?

In attempting to answer this question on the basis of empirical field research, anthropologists found that the traditional sum-total concept of culture, which they had been taught, had to give way to one phrased in gestalt or configurational terms, adequate to the two-dimensional nature of the problem. Accordingly, they tended to change their working concept of culture from one involving an aggregation of juxtaposed traits to one phrased in terms of a dynamic configuration of behavior patterns, attitudes, and values.

Gestalt psychology, wherein the whole was conceived as more than the sum of its parts (Köhler, 1925; Koffka, 1924; Wertheimer, 1912; 1945), rather than ethnography of the natural-history type, supplied the model for this approach. The scientific problem tended to be viewed as one of correlating some of the culture's component patterns, namely, those dealing with overt behavior concerning child training, to the whole

administrative problems of the Kwoma, I believe that they would tend to prejudice the administrator in the direction of manipulating human relations. They would bias the layman toward the human-relations-engineering approach discussed above, since, as a rule, only external training processes of the manipulative type were emphasized.

In the Kwoma investigation, then, we find the anthropologist-observer remaining outside the unit of research. He accomplishes this rather difficult feat (1) by rejecting a theoretical approach, namely, the Freudian, which would have forced him to find a way, so to say, to get inside the unit of research— the native subjects, and (2) by seeking out and adapting to his problem a theoretical approach, namely, learning theory, which offers an explanation of overt behavior, including learning behavior, viewed from the outside. The study remained within the traditional positivistic rubric, but not without some strain.

Two Classes of Scientists

Another type of two-discipline research involves at least two classes of scientists, social anthropologists and psychologists. The collaborators investigate the designated unit of research face-to-face in field or laboratory. For example, a social anthropologist investigates the group's social system by observing its pattern of overt behavior. Meanwhile, a behavioristic psychologist studies a sample of the individual members of the group by means of psychological tests of the performance type. Both investigators, therefore, retain the traditional, positivistic frame of reference.

In this two-discipline working model, the unit of research is viewed as though it were a system of interacting individuals conceptually isolable from its context, which is viewed as environment. There is a tendency to define personality in behavioristic terms, such as "social stimulus value" (Kluckhohn and Mowrer, 1944, pp. 1–2). The unknown X represents the system of relationships between the individuals in the group, viewed as an interactive process.

The Hawthorne Experiment

The Hawthorne experiment (Roethlisberger and Dickson, 1939; Landsberger, 1958), conducted by the Harvard School of Business Administration and the Western Electric Company (1927–1939), is a brilliant example of two-discipline team research. The experiment is distinguished also by its utilization of a series of well-designed laboratory experiments. To the astonishment of the Hawthorne research team, the management, and the factory workers who constituted the experimental group, the series of experiments revealed that the output of the voluntary, sample groups at Hawthorne tended to increase, not only when working conditions were improved, but also subsequent to the withdrawal of the improvements. Apparently, almost any change in working conditions that gave the group a feeling that management was interested in its welfare tended to increase output. The experimenters were forced to conclude that other and more intangible factors, mainly in the area of interpersonal relations and morale, were crucial to the outcome of the experiment. Hence, what started as an inquiry into "the human effect of work and working conditions" turned into an investigation into the effects, on industrial production and worker morale, of changes in interpersonal relations in a factory, viewed as a social system.

A major recommendation, regarding the application of the Hawthorne research findings to the ultimate goal of increased industrial production, concerned ways to improve personal relations among the workers, their associates, and management. The experimenters suggested that an employee interviewing program be instituted. Trained interviewers were made available so that dissatisfied workers could express their complaints. According to small-group sociological theory, workers might thereby restore their "personal equilibrium." Worker complaints were later analyzed for the light they might throw on the problem of improving personal relations between workers and supervisors, toward the goal of fostering "social equilibrium" in the factory as a whole.

Throughout the Hawthorne experiment, including its applied phases, a working model of the factory as a social system of the mechanistic type was used, the observers remaining outside the unit of research. According to this model, the theoretical goal in the applied phase was to reduce stresses which tended to throw the whole system or any part of it (e.g., an individual worker) out of balance; the aim was to foster or to restore a state of equilibrium in the whole. Subsequently, the results of the experiment were applied to the Hawthorne industrial unit principally at two levels: (1) the level of the individual, by attempting to foster personal equilibrium through professional counseling services; and (2) the small-group level, by attempting to promote social equilibrium in the factory, both by changing the social structure and by re-training supervisors and others in the direction of improved interpersonal relations, both formal and informal.

The Kardiner-Linton Collaboration

In a fourth type of two-discipline research in the culture-personality sphere, we find two different classes of investigators, an anthropologist and a psychoanalyst, collaborating by means of cross-discipline seminars. A good, early example of this type of research is afforded by the experimental collaboration between Ralph Linton, anthropologist, and Abram Kardiner, psychoanalyst, reported in *The Individual and His Society* (Kardiner et al., 1939). In a case study of the Marquesans of Polynesia, Linton reports to Kardiner his own field observations and those of his anthropologist coworker, E. S. C. Handy (Kardiner et al., 1939, pp. xv–xvi), made two decades earlier. In this section of the book, Linton describes mainly the traditional social behavior and child-training practices of the Marquesans in environmental context. The field data were collected by the two anthropologist fieldworkers, mainly from a natural-history point of view. Indeed, the observations on Marquesan child training, recorded by Linton, were made on the Bayard-Dominick field survey which included not only ethnographic, but also archaeological and somatological field work. Hence, no special attention was given by either fieldworker to observing and recording native child-training practices. Actually, there were few children in this dying society at the time.

Twenty years later Kardiner, taking a neo-Freudian viewpoint based on certain assumptions of analytic psychology, attempted to reconstruct, from the incomplete ethnographic field data, the basic Marquesan institutions, which he defined as "integrational units or action systems," through which instinctual drives were consummated (see DuBois, 1944, p. 7). He also attempted to reconstruct the relationships between these institutions and to project or construct a "basic personality structure" (DuBois, 1944, pp. 9ff.) for the society.

In this type of investigation, the ethnographer makes his observations from a point outside the unit of research, while the armchair psychoanalyst necessarily has the same reference position, at secondhand. X, the unknown, equals the reconstructed group personality structure.

The Alor Study

A later development of two-discipline approach involving at least two different classes of investigators is reported in Cora DuBois's *The People of Alor* (1944). In this case, the anthropologist DuBois had studied analytic psychology and had collaborated with Kardiner in his seminar before undertaking the project. She spent eighteen months on the island of Alor in Indonesia, mainly in Atimelang village. She studied the development of the individual within the sociocultural system by means of anthropological field techniques—observation, participant observation, and interview. She also investigated the "modal personality" (DuBois, 1944, pp. 2ff.) of the group by collecting a series of autobiographies of individuals in the group and by administering to a sample a number of psychological tests, including the Rorschach Psychodiagnostic, the Porteus Maze, free drawings, and word associations.

On returning from Alor, DuBois made a psychocultural analysis of her field data. Kardiner analyzed her ethnographic findings for personality determinants. Blind analyses were made of the findings from each test by specialists, and the results of all the analyses were published in a single volume.

In this study, we find the beginning of a shift in the position of the observer which will prove highly significant in our search for appropriate methodology whereby to develop a mature science of mankind. DuBois not only observed her community from the outside, but she also attempted to study the personalities of the individuals in her sample from the inside.

However, in this excellent pioneering endeavor, we find no attempt to describe the local modal personality in explanatory fashion, except to correlate it with child-training patterns and adult institutions, behavior patterns, attitudes, and values. Rather, the question which the study asked and attempted to answer was: Assuming the validity of Freudian psychodynamics, were Alorese individuals predominantly what we might suppose them to be from our knowledge of the institutions under which they lived, the childhood conditioning they received, the values they shared, the goals for which they strove (DuBois, 1944, p. v)?

We should emphasize that an explanatory type of question was also asked by DuBois: Why is an American different from an Alorese? But a descriptive, rather than an explanatory, answer was sought. The investigator wrote (DuBois, 1944, p. 2):

That they are different is a common-sense conclusion, but explanations, from the climatic to the racial, have proved lamentably inadequate in the past. The explanations to be investigated here do not categorically deny all factors previously used to explain such differences; instead they seek the subtle processes which research in the social sciences and the psychologies has formulated and which we may use for the time being as operational concepts.

It is not generally realized that explaining the "range and the central tendencies of personality" in a particular cultural group or community, and attempting "to explain the genesis of the central tendencies" by means of common cultural pressures, illuminating though it may be, does not explain the culture-personality system as a whole and how it became the way it has been found to be, by means of empirical field operations, at any one point in time. From the present position, we are interested in exploring why the Alorese are as they are. Why do they have such child-training patterns? How did they happen to develop such patterns?

To begin to answer such questions, mainly bypassed in the Alorese study, we will probably have to appeal to some sort of historical explanation (see Morgenbesser, 1958, p. 286). It is doubtful whether psychological theories alone, much less psychoanalytic theory alone, suffice for such explanations. The explanatory descriptions we seek will probably emerge only from a multidiscipline approach, including a culture-history dimension, a sociologic dimension, an ecological and geophysical dimension, a genetic dimension, a psychic dimension, etc.

Although DuBois (1944, p. 4) admits the possibility of innate personality types, the Alor study gives us little clue of the genetic heritage of the Atimelangers, their constitutional type, or somatology, which might throw light on the above questions. Nor does the study contribute sufficient data on their culture history and prehistory to illuminate our quest. The brilliant correlation of the Alorese personality system with the sociocultural system is still generally descriptive, rather than explanatory.

Another point about the Alor investigation has relevance here. Although it was not explicitly a study in applied anthropology, the possible practical implications of the findings are mentioned several times in *The People of Alor*. For example, DuBois states (1944, p. 3): "We are very intimately concerned . . . with the adaptive processes in human beings, and until we know what these are and how they function, the manipulation of institutions qua institutions will at best remain inept, and at worst may result in the destruction of the very ends desired." And again, "Only when we have some comprehension of the link between institutions which individuals bearing those institutions may make on an emotional level, shall we begin to grasp the repercussions involved in social alterations" (DuBois, 1944, p. 5). Clearly, it is the manipulative type of alteration from without that is implied.

At this point in our search for methodology, we may profitably ask: What use might be made of the findings of the Alor study by the administrator? It seems to me that in their present form, regardless of the investigator's intentions, they might easily be used by administrators, traders, or missionaries to change native institutions in order to manipulate the group in the direction of goals superimposed from without.

Conclusion

Within the limitations of a single volume, of course, it is impossible to review all the major developments in two-discipline research in anthropology. Enough has probably been said to suggest that the theoretical split, mentioned in our discussion of one-discipline research, deepened and crystallized as two-discipline research developed.

Furthermore, since the need to understand culture and society from the inside led anthropologists to borrow ideas, methods, operations, and trained personnel from the psychological disciplines, the two major schools of thought in anthropology began to reflect recent developments in psychology, psychiatry, and psychoanalysis. As might be expected, in casting about for psychological approaches to explain field data and refine field methodology, each anthropologist tended to select the school of thought most congenial to him.*

According to a functional dichotomy of the psychological disciplines suggested by Hilgard (1948, p. 9), extreme positivists chose to affiliate with such developments in psychology as be-

* For a somewhat different interpretation of this area of problem, see Bennett 1946.

haviorism, association theory, and learning theory. Organismic-oriented anthropologists (see Chap. 6) chose their counterparts in the psychological disciplines of gestalt psychology, psychiatry, and psychoanalysis. This does not mean that anthropologists became psychologists. They merely added another dimension to their area of problem. The deeper significance of these theoretical developments in two-discipline anthropology are revealed most clearly at the applied level.

A review of the record suggests that a two-discipline approach may be successful in investigations where the significant unit of research is a face-to-face social group of limited size within a larger society. Human relations in small groups, such as factories, gangs, hospitals, associations, or clubs, have been improved through the use of this model. The Hawthorne experimenters, and other pioneer investigators of small groups, describe the dynamics of such groups in terms of human relations, by means of a modern systems approach using working models of the mechanistic type.

The basic assumptions underlying this kind of investigation stem from behavioristic psychology and sociology. These models place the observer in his traditional positivistic position outside the unit of research. The approach, when applied to practical problems in human relations, yields a method of human-relations engineering whereby the norms applied and goals sought by administrators originate outside the group itself.

Within this frame, improved social adjustment of the individual within the group may be facilitated through the psychological interview in the hands of trained interviewers. However, therapeutic interviewing of individuals obviously should be classed as personnel work or applied psychology, rather than as applied anthropology.

Thus the record suggests that, as long as the anthropologist remains outside the unit of research and observes only the immediately apprehended aspects of the unit under investigation, the project yields one of two results. It remains at the level of pure research. Or it is raised to the applied level by means of human-relations engineering tending in the direction of exotic goals (Thompson, 1950c, pp. 119–120). This generalization apparently holds whether the anthropologist uses a one-discipline or a two-discipline approach. It holds regardless of the investigator's sympathies, values, or intentions. It apparently holds whether he has investigated the unit of research by means of participant observation, interviewing techniques, psychological testing, or all three methods combined.

Success in using the small-group model discussed above apparently depends on conceptually isolating the relevant small group, viewed as a mechanical type of system, and treating everything else as environment (in Radcliffe-Brown's sense). This allows the investigators to concentrate on improving the welfare and mental hygiene of the group members, while ignoring that of the larger society whereof the small group is a component.

This type of human engineering may be expected to prove effective in improving group welfare *provided* (1) the norms and goals superimposed on the social unit from the outside by the administrator happen to be congruent with the group's basic needs and tend toward self-actualization, and (2) the exotic norms and goals are successfully implemented. Of course, the effectiveness of applied psychological methods, such as therapeutic interviewing used on individuals within the group, depends also on the knowledge and skill of the interviewers.

I suggest that the failure of two-discipline investigations to resolve certain urgent problems in applied anthropology spurred the development of a more inclusive multidiscipline approach.

Chapter 3

The Need for a More Inclusive Approach

The enigmas, whose solution seemed to elude the two-discipline methods described above, were broad-gauged, practical problems in community development. They involved questions of how to improve the welfare of whole communities and of assemblages of communities, comprising tribes, nations, and international groupings. Relevant questions in this area were: What standards shall we use for measuring social health and disease? What do we mean by a "healthy" community, from the viewpoint of mental hygiene as well as physical hygiene? What is a "sick society"? How shall we define "community well-being"?

Need for Universal Norms and Goals

In seeking answers to these questions, the anthropologist was thinking in terms of explicit cross-cultural norms, applicable anywhere in the world. He was thinking of the mental hygiene and community welfare of Navahos, Fijians, Thai, Arabs, Brazilians, and Hottentots, not merely of Western Europeans and North Americans.

He found not only that we did *not* have such explicit universally accepted norms and goals for human communities in global perspective, but that we did not even have them for ourselves. Medicine, public health, and mental hygiene had not yet succeeded in formulating universally accepted health standards for communities, although rapid strides were being made toward such a goal (Thompson, 1951b, pp. 184ff.).

During the last two or three decades, the problem of defining universally acceptable norms and goals for community health and sickness has achieved a new prominence not only in medicine, public health, and psychiatry, but also in sociology, community development, child development, city and regional planning, applied anthropology, and especially in mental hygiene, to mention only a few disciplines.

Of course, the expansion of American and United Nations interests in the development of economically underdeveloped peoples has highlighted this issue. As part of the world power struggle, technical development of nonindustrialized and partially industrialized peoples is being pushed by the United States and, on a smaller scale, by the United Nations. What is the effect of such accelerated development from a long-range, native viewpoint?

Reconsideration of Foreign Missions

Systematic studies of the effects of Point Four programs in terms of native welfare, and especially of mental hygiene, soon began to cast doubts on the usefulness of these programs from the point of view of the native. Such studies as *Human Problems in Technological Change,* edited by E. H. Spicer (1952), and *Cultural Patterns and Technical Change,* edited by Margaret Mead (1953), pointed up the delicacy of the contact situation and the extreme vulnerability of the native groups being "developed."

With the world-wide skyrocketing of population figures, doubts regarding the usefulness of medical missions also were raised. As the value of the newer missionaries—the Point Four emissaries and the public health agents—began to be questioned, the effects of the traditional missionaries, too—the spreaders of the Gospel—came under closer scrutiny. If religion, technology, social organization, art, and economy are a function of the culture system in relation to human needs and the given environmental context, as taught by some functionalists, how may the conversion—under pressure—of whole communities to new and alien systems—economic, medical, and religious— be expected to affect their social well-being and their mental health?

The Liberation of Colonial Peoples

The revolt of the colonial peoples around the world did nothing to diminish the growing public concern regarding the effectiveness, and indeed the appropriateness, of Western economic and cultural missions.

The list of colonial peoples who have recently achieved independent, or near-independent, political status is constantly growing. Among the dependencies of the United States changes in political status in the last quarter of a century have been marked. Since World War II, almost all American dependency and minority peoples have moved at least one notch up the political ladder. The Philippines have moved from commonwealth status to sovereignty (1946). Alaska (1958) and Hawaii (1959) have moved from organized territories to statehood; Guam (1950) and American Samoa (1951) from unorganized possessions to unincorporated territories and American citizenship; and Puerto Rico (1952) from unincorporated area to free commonwealth status. The Pacific Trust Territory, a United Nations strategic trusteeship, was moved from administration under the U.S. Navy Department to the Department of Interior (1951).*

Indeed, the rapid liberation of peoples in dependency political status is one of the most spectacular phenomena of our time. W. H. Kraus (1959) states:†

* Subsequently, Saipan, Tinian, and the northern Marianas were returned by Executive order to the previous status (1953 and after).
† Reprinted from *Science* by permission of the American Association for the Advancement of Science.

There is mounting evidence to support the proposition that the fundamental political issue of the 20th century will not necessarily turn out to be the cold war and all it stands for. The fundamental issue may well be found in the problem of whether the more advanced industrial societies, at present still the masters of science and technology, will succeed in associating in mutually beneficial partnership with the less developed but rapidly evolving new societies of Asia and Africa.

Trend toward Cultural Autonomy

More important than the achievement of political gains perhaps is the marked trend toward recognition of the right of all peoples to *cultural autonomy*. Within a geocultural frame, the meaning of culture, a key concept of the anthropologist and his major focus of attention, is gradually penetrating the consciousness of peoples of Western tradition, and even their formal deliberative bodies. Since the early thirties, many tribal Indians in the United States have moved from wards of the Federal government to organized tribes. And, of course, the Southern Negroes are now moving through a period in which segregation is being reduced and civil rights are being extended.

The right of native peoples to live according to their own lifeways, regardless of their political affiliations, is being recognized officially as a basic human need and human right. Indeed, it is at the core of a new theory of social justice and international accountability, which has been embodied in the United Nations Charter. According to Article 73 of the Charter, trustee nations are held accountable for the development of self-government and native welfare in their trust territories. But that is not all. Dominant powers with jurisdiction over tribes or ethnic groups in dependency status are held internationally accountable for developing self-government among these peoples and for improving their welfare (Asher et al., 1957).

Effects on Anthropology

As I see it, these new developments in social justice and international accountability figure prominently among the background factors which led directly to the development of multidiscipline team research in anthropology and its applied phase, social-action research, in the early forties. Until we began to think in terms of a native tribe's right to cultural autonomy —a tribe's right to seek its own solution to its living problem in its own way within certain limits (see Elkin, 1949, p. 228) —behavioristic applied anthropology of the human-engineering type may have seemed adequate to our colonial welfare problems abroad, as well as to our industrial problems at home.

In the colonial situation, a professional social anthropologist, or an administrator trained in social anthropology, was assigned to the administrative staff of the colony. This official then functioned as an expert in native affairs; he helped to implement regulations devised by the dominant power to further its interests or its idea of native interests. The government anthropologist also acted as a trouble shooter when native behavior conflicted with colonial regulations or in any significant way failed to measure up to official expectations.

Trouble Shooting

The government anthropologist was frequently asked to suggest methods of dealing with the messianic, nativistic, or cargo cults, which tend to arise spontaneously among native peoples in contact with Western civilization. At a point when the native peoples are depressed by the loss of their traditional lifeway and confused by innovations, a leader emerges who promises to overthrow the new and restore the old. Usually magical methods are recommended, but occasionally outright revolt is sanctioned, as for example among the Kikuyu of Kenya. A cult is organized and spreads so quickly that the colonial administrators and white settlers feel threatened. At this point, the government anthropologist may be called in to report on the nature of the disturbance. He is expected to spot the leaders, study the native belief system, and suggest methods for dealing with the disturbance, viewed as a cultural phenomenon. This is called "trouble shooting."

It is difficult for the layman, without experience in the field of dependency administration, to realize what a difference anthropologists as staff members or consultants can make in government practices toward their native wards and dependents. In-service training of administrators in anthropology also helps significantly (Hall, 1959).

I think of a device used by the naval administration in Guam, and elsewhere in American possessions under naval rule, before this was changed to administration by civilians under the Interior Department in 1950. When the Guamanians persisted in objecting to naval rule as an infringement of their rights as human beings and as civilian subjects of the United States, naval officers who governed the colony were ordered to divest themselves of their military uniforms and wear civilian attire while attending to their native civil government functions. In this way, it was reasoned, the natives' objections to military rule would be met!

The trouble-shooting applied anthropologist engaged by the naval government to aid in administration, on the other hand, might have suggested changing the government structure so that capable, experienced natives would be trained to move up the ladder, and eventually, if they proved competent, to occupy top positions (Thompson, 1947a, pp. 299ff.). For a case study of trouble shooting by an anthropologist on the staff of the United States Trust Territory, see Barnett (1956, pp. 158–170).

It should be noted that the trouble-shooting applied anthropologist may fulfill his customary functions by using the anthropologist's traditional field techniques of observing and interviewing from a point outside the unit of research. He may still view the native tribe or community as though it were a system of the mechanistic type which, with proper procedures, is amenable to manipulation from without, according to a preconceived plan and to mechanisms of implementation devised by a dominant administering group.

When, on the other hand, we changed our attitude toward native groups—when we began to think of them as ongoing communities of human beings with universal human rights, including the right to cultural autonomy within the limitations of geocultural necessity—we began to see that trouble shooting and human-relations engineering techniques were inadequate. Behavioristic applied anthropology failed to answer the new questions which arose with the new attitude toward native peoples and dependency administration.

Implementing the New Concept

Looking back across the years, I realize that implementing the new concept of cultural autonomy in terms of action programs necessitated a shift in the frame of reference of the administrator from outside the native community to inside it. Whether the administrator was a member of the alien group or the native group, his frame of reference had to become a native frame if he were to be successful in implementing the new concept (Thompson, 1959, pp. 132–133).

But how could the administrator develop a native frame of reference? For help in this area, he turned to the applied anthropologist. In attempting to solve these new problems, the pioneer collaboration between the British administrator, A. M. Hutt, and the Canadian anthropologist, G. Gordon Brown (Brown and Hutt, 1935), illustrates the emergence of this new type of applied anthropology.

The applied anthropologist, like the administrator, had to shift his point of observation from outside the unit of research to inside it. Indeed, in the event, he actually developed multiple observation points inside and outside the unit, above and below it, one might say. But all this happened gradually as new theories and methods emerged in response to urgent need.

In other words, the movement toward maturity in the science of mankind has necessitated an extension of our perspective of Homo sapiens as a species, *both inward and outward.* We have discovered slowly that in order to approach an understanding of human groups with long-range predictive value, we need somehow to get inside the group, as well as outside it, to view it from above and below and all round, both at long range and at close range. In other words, we need to *extend* our view by developing *depth.*

Need to Solve the Problem

This development parallels a discovery made at the end of the nineteenth century about the human psyche. The discovery of the unconscious and the emergence of depth psychology grew out of the need for deeper and more telling knowledge about the human individual.

In both cases—in the study of the human group and of the human individual—discovery was the reward of intense effort motivated by deeply felt need. The researchers felt they *had* to achieve a genuine understanding of the community under investigation with predictive validity appropriate to the problem. Why?

Freud, Jung, and many other explorers of the individual unconscious were physicians. They were motivated by the urgent need to relieve human suffering and improve health. Similarly, many of the explorations of the group unconscious were motivated by the need to improve human welfare and to relieve human suffering on a community scale.

I emphasize this point because I believe that success in this difficult area of discovery is contingent upon deep interest in, and even dedication to, the need to solve a problem. This interest must transcend the immediate self-interest of the investigator, such as the desire to enhance personal status, to win fame, or to secure economic gain (see Mayer, 1958, p. 125; Collier, 1945, pp. 300–301). The difficulties involved are so great that only with a high degree of disinterested motivation can the investigator, under propitious circumstances and with a modicum of good luck, hope to overcome them.

This point reinforces a discovery made by perception psychologists, namely, that we attain and retain a habitually complex, holistic approach to the solution of problems only when we are compelled to do so—only when life offers no alternative at a less complex level of perception.

Gardner Murphy (1947, p. 342) recognizes three stages of perception: the blur stage, the differentiation stage, and the integration stage. All three stages, he believes, are manifest in a person, whether child or adult, whenever he confronts a novel situation. But it is characteristic of the dynamics of perception that all perceptual responses are maintained as long as they *work* well. They are shaken down and reorganized on a mature level only when absolutely necessary to permit a functional structure. A person, whether child or adult, moves to the third level or integrative perception stage only when life's demands admit no escape (see also Cantril, 1950, p. 44). According to the present thesis, the complex, holistic approach to the solution of problems is an essential prerequisite to designing, and carrying through to a successful outcome, multidiscipline team research and its correlate at the applied level, welfare-oriented, social-action research.

To achieve the perspective needed to predict group behavior on a long-range, community-wide scale, with the degree of accuracy required to solve the problem, it was necessary to do more than *add* disciplines to the methodology and workers of the research team. We have noted that cross-discipline research of the behavioristic type did not yield a satisfactory answer to the methods problem. The field investigator retained his traditional point of reference outside the unit of research. Nor did cross-discipline research involving behavioristic social science and depth psychology solve the problem of methodology. It is true that for successful solution of the problem in the latter type of research, the researcher had to shift his position inward. The result was a considerable gain in depth. Still that was apparently not enough. For an explanatory understanding of the behavior of the human members of the community, a millennium-long time perspective on culture change was indicated, that is, an extension of perspective outward to encompass geophysical, ecological, and historical factors.

This point, and several others concerning the development of method in multidiscipline community analysis, are well illustrated by the Indian Education, Personality, and Administration project discussed in the next chapter.

Chapter 4

Multidiscipline Community Analysis*

The Indian Education, Personality, and Administration project was a broad-gauged policy project in multidiscipline applied anthropology. It grew out of a felt need on the part of top administrators in the United States Indian Service to evaluate and improve the government's long-range Indian policy and program. The official policy toward Indians was changed in the early thirties. From attempting to convert the Indians into white men as rapidly as possible, the aim became that of helping the tribes to organize and rehabilitate themselves and to improve their lands and natural resources. After a decade had passed, it was generally agreed that progress toward the new goal had been made in many areas of Indian administration, such as soil and moisture conservation, improved herds and crops, and economic growth. But officials felt that there was still a long way to go toward genuine rehabilitation of the Indians, both as tribal groups and as individuals.

At this time a good deal was known about the natural resources of the Indians, their economic status, general health, and schooling. But very little was known about their human

* Information presented in this chapter is taken mainly from the following sources: Joseph, Spicer, and Chesky, 1949; Kluckhohn and Leighton, 1946; Leighton and Adair, Ms.; Leighton and Kluckhohn, 1947; Macgregor, 1946; Thompson and Joseph, 1944; Thompson, 1950b; 1951b.

resources. What were they really like as personalities, and what was happening to their personalities under the impact of modern industrial civilization? Administrators thought that if, through scientific research, discoveries could be made regarding the psychological impact of recent changes on the several Indian tribes, it might be possible to define more precisely the real needs and resources of the Indians. On the basis of such findings, they might help the Indians to make a practical and functional adjustment in the modern world.

With these questions in mind, Indian Commissioner John Collier in 1941 launched a long-range, multidiscipline research project to be carried out, under Interior Department contract, by the University of Chicago's Committee on Human Development. The Indian Education Research Committee of the University of Chicago, headed by W. Lloyd Warner, was in charge of the scientific work. A Special Indian Bureau Committee, with the Indian Commissioner as chairman, facilitated its administration. The writer was appointed project coordinator.

Search for Methodology Adequate to the Problem

The research committee was confronted with a complex problem for whose solution no adequate methodology had yet been developed by any scientific discipline. At the time, only the working models of single-discipline projects and cross-discipline projects of the behavioristic type, mentioned above, were available. Not even the results of cross-discipline research of the depth-psychology type (e.g., DuBois) had as yet appeared. There was no working model of requisite scope and depth to guide a policy project in applied anthropology of the magnitude of the IEPA.

To meet the challenge, the research committee, with the advice of a roster of distinguished consultants (see Thompson, 1951b, p. 199), set about to develop its own methodology. It is significant that the group of committee members and consultants represented several schools of thought. It included social anthropologists, cultural anthropologists, and psychologists who represented the behavioristic-learning-theory approach, as well as the gestalt-psychiatric-psychoanalytical approach.

The research committee designed the project in two sequential phases: a pure-research phase and an applied phase. For the first or pure-research phase, the two-discipline system of the mechanistic type described above became the basis of the working model. The scientific problem of this phase was formulated operationally in terms of two-level community analysis; it aimed to collect and correlate the data from field investigations which would proceed simultaneously on two fronts: the social anthropological and the psychological.

In developing the research design, not one but three significant units of research were found relevant to the solution of the IEPA problem: (1) the local community which served as the basic unit; (2) the tribe or group of communities, to give outward depth; and (3) the individual members of the local community, to give inward depth.

Sampling Procedures

To implement the field investigations of these three units of research, four sets of samples were selected for intensive study. These were as follows:

1. A sample of six selected tribes (Dakota Sioux, Hopi, Navaho, Papago, Zuni, and Zia) out of the total of some 250 tribes under Federal supervision was selected on the basis of (a) their representation of Indian Service problems; (b) their representation of different types of Indian cultures and authority systems; (c) the adequacy of the available descriptions of their social systems, to facilitate the task of gathering socio-anthropological field data; (d) their accessibility for field work and project supervision; and (e) their administration by a staff sympathetic to the project (Thompson, 1951b, p. 13).

2. A representative sample of two or more communities within each tribe was selected on the basis of evidence of greater and less degree of stress from influences from the sur-

rounding industrial civilization. Two tribes, i.e., Zuni and Zia, comprised only one community each. The number of communities in the sample totaled thirteen.

3. A random sample of individual children, aged six to eighteen years, within each local community was selected. The number of individuals in the sample totaled 1,000. These were selected randomly from the community school censuses, but subsequently corrected to give a balanced view by sex and age-grade, and then each sample was checked by staff statisticians. The original plan was designed to test a random sample of individuals by age-grade from early childhood to old age, but this had to be abandoned when the pilot study demonstrated its impracticability under reservation conditions during World War II, when the field work was done.

4. A sample of five or six special cases within each sample of individuals was selected from among those most fully described from the sociopsychological viewpoint in order to give concreteness to the statistical findings. The number of special cases in the sample totaled sixty-four.

Thus, the samples represented four concentric sets of data: (1) a sample of six tribes within the 250 tribes of the United States as a whole; (2) a sample of thirteen communities within the six selected tribes; (3) a sample of 1,000 children within the thirteen selected communities; and (4) a sample of five or six special cases from each community within the sample of 1,000 children, totaling sixty-four special cases.

To facilitate the psychological investigation of the sample of 1,000 individuals, a battery of relatively culture-free psychological tests was assembled by the research committee and the coordinator, with the advice of the consultants. The battery included instruments from several schools of thought: (1) performance tests of the behavioristic school (Grace Arthur Point Performance Scale with eight subdivisions); (2) guided interview tests of the Piaget school (Moral Ideology, Emotional Response, and Immanent Justice); and (3) depth-psychology tests of the psychiatric-psychoanalytical schools (Rorschach, Thematic Apperception, Goodenough Draw-a-Man, free drawings, etc.).

To expedite the medical examinations on the sample, a standard examination form was prepared by the project staff physicians.

To facilitate the investigation of the thirteen communities, field guides were prepared by the coordinator, with the help of the research committee and the consultants (Thompson, 1942a; 1942b).

The field work was divided into two kinds of operations: (1) operations, such as performance-type testing, which lay volunteers, after training at the seminar, could carry out under supervision, and (2) operations, such as depth-psychology testing, medical examinations, and community studies, which had to be implemented by professionally trained personnel, such as anthropologists, psychiatrists, psychologists, and physicians.

The operations in the tentative research design, including the test battery and field guides, were then tested in a three-month pilot study on the Papago Reservation, supervised by the coordinator, and the research design was adapted accordingly.

Next, volunteer fieldworkers were solicited from the sample communities. Teachers, school principals, nurses, physicians, range managers, extension agents, several agency superintendents, and Indian residents from each selected community responded to the call. Then the volunteers and the professional staff members were trained together in field operations and procedures at a three weeks' Field Workers Training Seminar, held at Santa Fe in June, 1942.

Field Work

Immediately after the training seminar, the fieldworkers began to collect data in their respective communities. The entire staff totaled seventy-five, and included anthropologists, psychiatrists, psychologists, physicians, linguists, volunteer fieldworkers from the selected communities mentioned above, and even the Indian Commissioner himself at times.

The random samples of individual children in each of the thirteen community samples were worked out on the basis of the school censuses, adjusted by sex and age-grade and checked by the coordinator and the project statistician. As the psychological and medical testing progressed, the staff decided to add another operation, namely, the collection of life histories and autobiographies of the children in the sample.

Early in the field phase of the research program, the staff decided to omit the Zia tribe in New Mexico as a research unit of the project because of the adverse reaction of the Zia people to the psychological testing program. Thus, a total of twelve communities in five tribes were studied.

Processing the Field Data

As soon as the field data from one tribe—the Hopi—were available, the processing and analysis phase of the project commenced. This took place in September, 1942, at the University of Chicago's Committee on Human Development, under the direction of the research committee. Specialized personnel, such as statisticians and test analysts, were added to the staff at this point to facilitate the work.

Since no design of analysis for such extensive, multidiscipline field findings was available at the time, the staff worked out its own design by experimentation. This involved several steps, which were repeated for each tribe in the sample. The first step was one of processing the raw field data from each of the several tests and operations, according to standard procedures, and testing the results for statistical significance. The second step involved describing a tribal personality, with variations within each component community in the tribe, for each tribe in the sample. The main method used was that of blind analysis of all data collected and processed on each special case in a tribal sample of special cases, and a discussion of the special case in a series of closed, multidiscipline staff seminars. A total of sixty-four such seminars were held during the fall and winter of 1942–1943 at the University of Chicago.

In analyzing the processed field data, some staff members favored using a behavioristic-learning-theory approach, while others favored using a gestalt-psychiatric-psychoanalytical approach. The former favored a model of the mechanistic type, while the latter preferred one of the organismic type. Indeed, a development occurred at the analysis stage of the IEPA project which reminds us of the Kwoma project dilemma, described in Chapter 2. In both investigations some of the participating anthropologists, having initiated depth studies in the direction of an inward penetration of the units of research, withdrew, while the field findings were in process of analysis, to the traditional positivist's perspective outside the unit. They chose to interpret their data from a traditional behavioristic viewpoint, rather than develop a new approach adequate to the changing position of the observer. In the IEPA project this dilemma was eventually overcome, and an approach combining both schools of thought emerged. It used a model of the organismic type and emphasized multiple-observer positions and depth perspectives, described below.

Research Design, Final Form

The design of the IEPA project, as it eventually developed, retained the traditional position of some of the investigators (e.g., the social anthropologists and behavioristic psychologists) outside the units of research (tribes, communities, individuals), but it shifted the position of some of the investigators (e.g., psychiatrists, physicians, ecologists, cultural anthropologists) from outside to inside, above, below, and beyond the traditional positions in relation to the several units of research. This shift contributed depth to the findings by illuminating several dimensions of community life not previously encompassed in a single working model; it illuminated the psychic dimension, the somatic dimension, the ecology-geophysics dimension, the culture-history dimension, as well as the behavioral and the sociological dimensions.

After three years of field work, data processing, analysis, and follow-up field work, the second or applied phase of the IEPA project (1944–1947) began, sponsored by the Society for Applied Anthropology. The practical assignment of the IEPA project was reformulated into a scientific problem which could be resolved by scientific methods. The initial society-personality formulation of the research problem sought a correlation between the sociocultural data and the psychological data, collected from a positivistic viewpoint. The second and final formulation focused on Indian personality needs and trends in relation to the available resources, both natural and human, within the sociocultural context of each community. The frame of reference of the project was thus brought into focus with that of the government administrators.

The final formulation assumed that, while the ecological community in geophysical context should set the frame of reference of scientists and administrators whose aim is to improve community welfare, the biosocial personality needs and trends of the members of a community, under changing pressures from without and within, should focus the investigation. Thus, the relevant problem was found not to be contained in the question: How can the tribe's or the individual's standard of living be raised? Rather, it was more extensive and involved the question: How can the health, mental hygiene, total resources, and group welfare of the whole community, viewed as a supersystem of the organic type, be nurtured and conserved within the limitations and pressures of its total environment?

The IEPA problem, therefore, gradually developed into that of defining the geophysical, biological, and psychocultural resources and needs of the communities under investigation viewed as supersystems, and of the human individuals within them viewed as developing personalities-in-community context, and of suggesting how the Indian Service might increase its effectiveness, through a long-range policy and program, by helping to conserve those resources, meet those needs, and nurture those personalities.

Relevant Variable Systems

When the scientific problem of the IEPA project was rephrased as noted above, the number of variables assumed to be relevant to its solution was increased. It will be recalled that, as the problem was initially phrased, only two variable sets were assumed to be relevant to its solution. These were the social system and the personality system of each tribal unit. The systems of variables eventually found relevant to the solution of the Indian community-welfare problem were grouped as follows: (1) the ecologic system (the pattern of transactions between the community and its natural environment); (2) the sociologic system (the transacting human organisms which comprise the community, viewed as a society or social structure); (3) the symbolic system (the communal symbolic system, including language, ceremonials, arts and crafts, mythology, folklore, etc.); (4) the psychic system (the community viewed as a group of transacting personalities in process of formation and self-realization); (5) the somatic system (the community viewed as a system of transacting somatic units); (6) the core value system (the community's system of largely implicit, emotionally tinged beliefs and attitudes regarding the nature of the world, of man, of animals and plants, the relationships between them, and the sources and dynamics of power within that system).

Constructing a multidiscipline model adequate to the IEPA problem in applied anthropology, therefore, underlined the importance of selecting variables relevant to its solution.

General Findings of the Project

The IEPA field findings, tested for statistical significance where relevant and supplemented by data from the available literature, were analyzed in ecological and geophysical context and presented in six tribal monographs: *The Hopi Way* (Thompson and Joseph, 1944), *Warriors without Weapons* (Macgregor, 1946), *The Navaho* (Kluckhohn and Leighton, 1946), *Children of the People* (Leighton and Kluckhohn, 1947), *The Desert People* (Joseph, Spicer, and Chesky, 1949), and *People of the Middle Place* (Leighton and Adair, Ms.). Several detailed monographs and papers, presenting the methods used, sampling procedures, and findings regarding the several psychological tests used were also published (Havighurst et al., 1944; 1946; 1955; Henry, 1947; 1956; Thompson, 1948a). And finally, the findings from the tribal monographs were compared, and their implications for government officials were formulated in *Culture in Crisis* (Thompson, 1950b) and *Personality and Government* (Thompson, 1951b).

The published results of the IEPA project present, in comparable form, a multilevel, explanatory description of each of the sample twelve supercommunities under stress in five Indian tribes. They also formulate concisely some generalizations and recommendations regarding Indian administration problems in the United States. They do not attempt a systematic, comprehensive study of Indian administration as a whole. Rather, they outline and illustrate a consistent orientation and method of approach whereby the long-range policy and program of the Indian Service may move systematically in the direction of improved Indian welfare and mental hygiene.

This point may be clarified by a brief presentation of the findings from one tribe in the sample, namely, the Papago Indians of Arizona.* It should be emphasized, however, that the following description and analysis refer to the culture, personality, and administrative problems of the Papago tribe twenty years ago when the project was carried out.

* The following section is taken mainly from Joseph, Spicer, and Chesky, 1949; Thompson, 1951b, Ch. 5; Underhill, 1939; Mss. a, b, c, 1946.

Some Findings on One Tribe

The Papagos are a very ancient group of Indians who inhabit the Lower Sonoran Desert of the American Southwest and Mexico. The American Papagos own a Federal reservation area of almost three million acres in southern Arizona. At the time of the IEPA field investigation, the tribe numbered about 7,000 persons, practically all of whom were classed as Papagos of full blood. All these Indians spoke the Papago language, which belongs to the Piman branch of the Uto-Aztecan stock. Less than 40 per cent spoke any English, and less than 20 per cent could read and write.

Apparently the Papagos have always lived in or near their present habitat (Haury, 1950). The region has limited resources, long droughts, and sparse rainfall (5 to 18 inches annually), which falls in cloudbursts during the early summer. Through a combination of circumstances, the Papagos have been less disturbed by alien cultural influences—both Spanish and American—than most Indian groups in the United States, and contacts with the white man have been relatively peaceful.

After the tribe acquired agriculture about five thousand years ago, the Papagos developed a dual economy and lifeway which was highly functional. During the hot summer months, a community lived in its traditional village, located in one of the many valleys which bisect the area. The people cultivated corn, squash, and beans in adjacent fields by ingenious dry and flood-water farming methods. When the limited annual water supply in the valleys had dried up and the crops had been harvested, the Papago village communities would move to hunting camps near springs in the mountains for the winter. Here they lived by hunting and collecting wild edible plants.

According to the project findings, the Papagos not only practiced a dual economy, but they also had two views of the world and a double set of attitudes toward what they believed to be their sources of personal and supernatural power. Underhill (1946, pp. 16–17) notes:

Contact with the supernaturals was achieved by two methods that differ so much that they amount to separate religious systems. On the one hand was a calendric round of ceremonies, conducted by a priestly hierarchy and bringing blessing to the whole community. It was a system of group control, in which the average man made no individual approach to the supernatural and received no individual power. . . . The blessing he received was the general one of well-being for his village. Opposed to this was the . . . concept of the guardian spirit, opening the power quest to everyone. Formerly a Papago expected no success in life unless he had met some spirit tutelary who had given him a song for use in time of need.

Traditional Papago village organization and family structure revealed a similar polarity. On the one hand, the individual —especially the male, but to a certain extent also the female— was given wide scope to pursue his own activities, musings, and vision quests with little discipline of instinctual urges. On the other hand, problems of group import were met and solved by devices involving group participation and responsibility. For example, each village traditionally had a village council, composed of all the adult males (Underhill, 1939, p. 78). This group met nightly under the leadership of a village chief. It considered village problems as they arose and reached practical decisions by a process of achieving unanimity. Thus the Papagos were able to tap the human resources and wisdom of the whole group.

The project findings revealed that Papago child-training usages fostered in individuals growing up in the tribe the formation of a kind of dual personality structure, which functioned as a normal, healthy mechanism of adjustment to the dual life situation. The Papago personality was characterized by a unique adjustive feature which allowed the normal individual to live now in one reality, now in the other, without profound disturbance, ambivalence, or confusion. In this, he was aided by a strong tendency to evade commitments whenever possible and to avoid clear categorization of concepts.

To sum up, the project analysis showed that Papago traditional culture and tribal personality represented a highly functional, balanced, and self-regulatory development of great time depth, inner coherence, and durability. The dual way of life, with its corresponding dual system of beliefs and attitudes, apparently influenced the development of an emotional and social climate in both village and family life. A balanced adjustment between the needs of the group and those of the individual had been institutionalized.

The question which concerned Indian Service administrators, teachers, nurses, etc., on the Papago Reservation was: What was happening to Papago culture and personality under the stress of pressures from the surrounding American civilization?

The ancient Papago lifeway was not significantly affected by pressures from alien influences until the twentieth century. The establishment of the main Papago Reservation and the digging of deep wells to supply year-round water to the valley villages precipitated a number of changes.

Improved water supply, followed by the development of permanent villages, was accompanied by other factors which in their aggregate engendered far-reaching alterations in the Papago subsistence problem. Paramount among these was the disappearance of wild game and the deterioration of the resources base through increasing aridity and critical soil erosion, related to overgrazing by range stock.

The process of change was accelerated in the 1930s when large expenditures were made on the reservation by the Federal government under the Civilian Conservation Corps-Indian Division (CCC-ID). Thus, until very recently, the Papagos retained their ancient lifeway virtually intact, although many relatively superficial changes occurred in technology and social organization. Faced with these difficulties, many Papago families began regularly to engage in seasonal wagework off the reservation during the winter months. They retained permanent homes in their valley villages, where they spent the remainder of the year farming and herding.

Papago men still meet in village councils but meetings are less frequent and regular (Joseph et al., 1949, p. 63):

Here all the village problems are discussed: lands are assigned for farm use; stock-owners air their problems, and the doings of the Agency are talked over. Everyone has his say if it takes all night. . . . Nowadays, there is not always unanimity for the simple reason that there is not time. A government proposal may have to be accepted or rejected and white men call for prompt action.

In time a new dual life pattern developed among the Papagos. By reinforcing the rhythmic balance of traditional culture and personality systems, the new pattern apparently met, to a certain extent, both deep-rooted sociopsychological needs and immediate economic needs. Of the tribes studied in the early forties, the Papago, with the least adequate natural resources in relation to population size, had the highest average annual income per family.

In this context, the staff began to understand why, despite a rapidly deteriorating land base (62 per cent overstocked in 1941), comparatively poor natural resources, poor health, widespread illiteracy, and a low per capita Federal appropriation, the Papago tribe was relatively well off—psychologically, socially, and economically—compared with the other tribes studied; indeed, it probably compared favorably with most Indian groups in the United States. The project findings suggested, however, that the security of most Papagos and their integral adjustment to changing conditions depended in no small part on their having retained their roots in cooperative family and village life in the traditional homeland, while ingeniously dovetailing their economy with that of the outside world. The maintenance and development of these traditional physical, social, and psychological ties counterbalanced the wagework cycle; they were of vital importance to Papago well-being, providing a pivot around which the individual might make his own idiosyncratic adjustment to modern conditions.

The project results indicated that the new dual orientation might well serve as a focus for administrative planning.

This focus suggested a two-sided program for improving Papago welfare and mental hygiene. On the one hand, it underlined the need to improve reservation conditions. On the other, it highlighted the need to face, and so far as possible solve, the specific educational, employment, and welfare problems of the Papago wageworker. The psychological findings led the staff to expect that influences toward culture change which reinforced the sociocentric facet, rather than the egocentric facet, of the Papago personality system would be most therapeutic in advancing the Papagos' creative adjustment in the modern world.

Theoretical Implications

Thus, the IEPA findings suggest that each tribe has not only its own definite and describable socioculture-environment system, including its deep-rooted and extremely persistent attitude and belief pattern; but that it also has a characteristic communal personality system, including typical patterns of social-psychological reaction to pressures toward culture change. Each community within the tribe manifests a variation on the tribal model. The tribe's socioculture-environment system and its personality system are functionally and symbolically interdependent, as a result of centuries-long tribal experience, conditioned by many factors including those of a historical and geographical nature. Thus, these tribal configurations are by no means fortuitous aggregations forming a patchwork of technological traits, behavior patterns, and miscellaneous themes, as is often assumed. On the contrary, they are functional wholes operating through the medium of ecological, sociological, and psychological process.

The key relationships between these interdependent systems of variables are not conspicuous and easily recognized; rather they are hidden and intangible. Hence their discovery requires multidimensional depth analysis and structural insight (see Dobbs, 1947, p. 8). For example, the personality system, eluding casual observation, emerges as a key unit in an attempt to understand the structure of the community supersystem through depth analysis. Moreover, the transactional relations between the several variable systems emerge only when the range and depth of relevant variables are extended sufficiently to reveal the community's basic attitude and belief pattern.

It appears that the community's pattern of basic attitudes and beliefs (i.e., its core value system) functions as the key integrating mechanism between the several interdependent systems of variables relevant to the solution of the supersystem's welfare and mental hygiene problem (see Lewis, 1951, p. 422; Lantis, 1959, pp. 40–41 for similar findings). Indeed, this discovery reveals why the welfare problem cannot be solved merely by seeking a correlation between social structure and group personality structure. These two systems of variables are interdependent, not overtly and directly, but indirectly and covertly through a common set of basic values and through a communal symbolic system.

Pursuing this line of inquiry, the investigators discovered that the personality system of variables is related also to the ecologic system, not directly, but indirectly through the core value system and through the somatic system. On the other hand, the somatic system and the personality system are interrelated both directly as aspects of the psychosomatic system as a whole, and indirectly through the core value and symbolic systems. Similarly, the ecologic system and the sociologic system are related directly through the community system as a whole and indirectly through their reflection of a common set of core values.

According to the project findings, of the six systems of variables, the ecologic, somatic, sociologic, and symbolic may be described partially, at least, by investigating the community supersystem; this can be done by studying overt behavior through observation, interviews, etc., from a point of reference outside the unit. The communal personality and the core value system, however, are revealed only through depth analysis and structural insight. In other words, these aspects of the supersystem yield to analysis by shifting the position of the observer inward, by means of the newer gestalt and depth-psychology techniques. According to the findings, the personality system and the core values function as covert connecting links between the other four systems. Therefore, multidiscipline depth analysis and structural insight are necessary to understand the dynamics of the community supersystem with the degree of precision needed for reliable predictions regarding the key factors which contribute to its total welfare.

These community studies suggest, moreover, that every pressure toward change in the behavior of a local community may be viewed, in its simplest form, as a relationship between two juxtaposed configurations of relevant variable supersystems. The first is indigenous, local, and under stress; the other is intrusive, exotic, and generating stress. Also, in an aggressive pressure-toward-change situation, key contacts are limited and occur mainly between the two juxtaposed psychosomatic and symbolic systems.

Our view of the solution of the supercommunity-welfare problem will depend on how we pose the problem and on the variables we select as relevant to solution. The task of selecting proper and sufficient variables may be comparatively simple for laboratory problems wherein certain variables can be artificially isolated for investigation and others kept constant. It assumes critical proportions, however, in a clinical, multiscience depth inquiry, such as that of the IEPA, which seeks to describe and compare the dynamic structures of a sample of communities in spatio-temporal context, in order that reliable predictions may be made. In this intricate and subtle inquiry into live, ongoing units, the problem of variable selection involves not only the discovery of new significant variables, but also the discovery of new relationships between interdependent systems of variables. Not until the correct formulation is achieved, and the relevant variables discovered and related correctly, may the solution emerge.

The findings also suggest that the personality system of a community or tribe, along with the ecological and sociocultural systems, are fundamentals. These systems are the foundations of community organization. Hence government policy, if it is to prove beneficial from the long-range community-welfare point of view, and if it is to be economical and efficient, must build in relation to them.

In attempting to build on these systems, the government administrator is greatly aided by the new social-action research approach. Social-action research is distinguished by the following characteristics (Thompson, 1950a): (1) A group, grappling with an urgent practical problem, solicits the help of a social scientist. (2) The scientist and the user-volunteers participate in a cooperative effort to solve the practical problem. (3) In this joint effort, the scientist functions in two roles, as a scientist-technician and as a group leader. He endeavors to draw out and foster the talents and leadership qualities of the members of the group and to minimize his own roles, except as catalyst of the potentialities of the group. In his role as integrative leader, the scientist trains and supervises the work of the user-participants.

Thus by using his professional tools, the scientist-technician helps to create a favorable climate wherein the members of the community may solve their problems by means of their own culture-personality systems in relevant environmental context.

Significance of the Project

If validated by further research, the final formulation of the IEPA project, with its focus on the health and maturity of personality in full communal context, gives promise of universal significance; it will have contributed a fruitful approach and scientific method whereby any community anywhere in the world may begin to move in the direction of improved welfare and sanity. The project also suggests that by means of systematic procedures a community may test its progress toward, or regression from, a scientifically based ideal goal.

Like all genuine solutions to scientific problems, however, the results of this project should be viewed as hypotheses whose validity must stand or fall on the basis of further systematic testing in the field. The original design of the IEPA project included plans for such testing by means of field research. Although these plans were not utilized, for political reasons, they may be implemented at any time. Meanwhile, the results of the project have been studied in the field and described by a disinterested observer (Kelly, 1954, pp. 712–714). A systematic appraisal of the results, however, has not yet been attempted.

Probably the point of greatest moment regarding the IEPA project is that through it an old problem has been posed in a new and heuristic way. This has necessitated the development of new working hypotheses and concepts, marking an advance toward a unified science of mankind. In view of the commitments and activities of the United States and the United Nations regarding the development of underdeveloped nations, the practical implications of this scientific advance should be significant, not only for the tribes studied and the Indians of the hemisphere, but for all peoples interested in genuinely improving human welfare.

The major task of the remainder of this volume will be to sketch out some new theories and concepts emerging from this development in multidiscipline team research. We have noted that implicit in every scientific hypothesis is a core of fundamental assumptions which are usually unstated, but which exercise a controlling influence on the research endeavor at both the conceptual and the behavioral levels. These assumptions yield a model of reality which represents the faith of the scientist as a scientist. Of course, the ultimate nature of reality is forever beyond our grasp. It is a philosophical question that plays no part in the goals and designs of scientific endeavor. But a scientist's working model of reality is of key importance in fundamental scientific research; it is important not only at the theoretical level, but in the design and execution of the field or experimental phase of research, and in the interpretation of the findings at all levels, including their application to practical problems.

Hence, we shall start with a consideration of a number of basic assumptions implicit in some of the findings of modern science, since they appear relevant to the development of a model of reality which may be fruitful for an emerging unified science of mankind.

It should be emphasized that, in attempting to formulate certain aspects of the question, we seek only a working model of reality useful for present, multidiscipline field research purposes in the sciences of man. I am aware, of course, that several seemingly conflicting reality models are reflected in the scientific work of our time. But discrepancies in the several models currently emerging from modern physics, mathematics, and biology are, in my judgment, irrelevant for our particular purposes. Major trends implicit in modern scientific research, which prove heuristic for a unified science of mankind, are what signify from the viewpoint of the new anthropology.

Part Two

An Emerging Hypothesis

And now, in our time, there has been unloosed a cataclysm which has swept away space, time and matter, hitherto regarded as the firmest pillars of natural science, but only to make place for a view of things of wider scope, and entailing a deeper vision.

Hermann Weyl

Chapter 5
Perspectives on Reality

A fundamental change appears to be taking place in the thinking, attitudes, and values of peoples of Western European tradition. This change is so far-reaching that it might more appropriately be called a conceptual metamorphosis. It seems
largely responsible for the schizoid gap deeply hidden in our
present cultural life (Snow, 1959).

Certain disciplines—such as nuclear physics, the non-
Euclidean geometries, modern architecture, abstract painting
and sculpture, general semantics, developmental psychology,
perception psychology, psychiatry, and psychoanalysis—express
the modern direction of conceptual development to a considerable degree. By contrast, other disciplines—such as classical
physics and chemistry, classical sociology and political science,
behavioristic psychology, classical economics, documentary history, and law—illustrate, in varying degrees, a cultural lag.
Still others—like cultural and social anthropology, comparative
sociology, comparative economics, social psychology, city and
regional planning, much of biology, including ecology, psychosomatic medicine, and nutrition—are in a transition period
from old ways of thinking to new. This process of change toward new working hypotheses, more in keeping with the findings of modern science, generates much discussion, even a certain amount of name calling.

The controversy over Frank Lloyd Wright's Guggenheim Museum in New York, for example, illustrates the strong feeling which marks this transition period in architecture. The new museum has been mocked and ridiculed as not art, not beautiful, and not good. Nevertheless, Wright's work is steadily gaining adherents.

The current trend involves not merely a change in our traditional ideologies, moralities, social and personal values, aesthetic tastes, and so forth—whether one accepts or rejects a Picasso, T. S. Eliot, Ravel, Freud, or Joyce. It involves a change in our view of the very nature of reality, as was noted long ago by Whitehead. Indeed, the transformation actually expresses a change in our underlying, and usually unexpressed, assumptions regarding the nature of the universe, the nature of man, the relations between man and nature, and the whole field of interpersonal relations, including relations between the sexes and between social classes, minority groups, castes, and races. It even affects our basic attitudes toward animals, plants, the earth, the sun, and the natural elements, and how we conceptualize their roles in the cosmic scheme. We are moving in the direction of new (to us) preferences in relationship patterns. We are exploring unfamiliar ways of organizing ourselves, our ideas, and our values.

We have already noted some of the far-reaching practical effects of this ideological metamorphosis in the passing of the colonial epoch; changing relationships between governors and governed; the emergence of new concepts of international justice with increasing emphasis on cultural autonomy; and the world-wide attention to problems of mental health, individual fulfillment, and community well-being. Many other examples will occur to the thoughtful reader.

What are some characteristics of the emerging views of reality toward which Westerners seem to be moving, although at a halting, confused, and uncertain pace? And what significance have they for the development of a mature science of mankind?

The new views of reality, implicit in the revelations of the modern physical and biological sciences, are merely glimpsed now and then in their entirety by a few advanced explorers, who find them difficult to explain in simple words. This may be because our habitual common-sense words convey images, perception patterns, concepts, and attitudes which reflect traditional models now becoming outmoded. Perhaps, however, we can grasp some of the major trends and express them by whatever means are available—by using new terms if necessary or redefining old ones, and especially by contrasting salient features of new reality models with more familiar ones.

Emphasis on Whole Emerging Events in Interrelationship

First, we note that the new views of reality tend to be holistic. They perceive sensory phenomena impinging on consciousness as wholes rather than as large or small details, discrete and unrelated to one another. They emphasize relatedness. They perceive the wholes as composed of parts interrelated one to another, rather than as vague or simple or global wholes. In Murphy's (1947, p. 343) terminology, they represent the third or mature level of perception. Conversely, the new views do not tend to see wholes as dualistic; e.g., mind and body, matter and spirit, nature and man, good and evil, etc. Rather, they reflect wholes which tend to be complex, multivalued, and unified.

Second, these emerging views of reality emphasize dynamic, rather than static, phenomena. Component parts are conceived as systems of activity. Significant units are viewed as though they were events or occasions or happenings in flux. Focal problems become the changing relationships between these changing units.

It seems to me that one simple way to measure the progress of a discipline in the direction of the modern value orientations is to apply the following test: Are events the significant units being featured by the discipline? That is, are events being stressed or isolated as intelligible fields of study? Or, on the other hand, are things so featured? If the former, the appropriate relationship between events takes the form of a dynamic gestalt or system; if the latter, a static sum total or aggregation.

Things, of course, usually have a place in the new schemes, but not the primary place. Indeed, the models of the universe heuristically depicting reality for our time (and remember that ultimate reality is beyond our grasp as scientists) are definitely not categorical, sum-total models; rather they are put together so that every event grows out of past events and is the forerunner of future events, not in a linear sequence (see Lee, 1950) but in a multidimensional, self-activating process.

A New Conception of Causality

Accordingly, each emerging event is perceived as containing within itself all its past and the seeds of its future (Whitehead, 1926, pp. 106ff.). Each event is viewed as though it were a whole which is not only more than, but quite different from, the sum of its parts. A sum-total, statistical aggregate view has become irrelevant regarding the changing internal organization of such units.

In short, the new working models of reality express a new conception of causality (Bohr, 1950; Bridgman, 1928, pp. 80ff.), if we may still refer to their functionalism by that outmoded term. And they move us toward dynamic, multidimensional views of history (Dorner, 1949, p. 19). No longer do we tend to conceive an event as acted on externally by agents or forces extraneous to it. "Cause," according to the new views, is inherent in the organization of the total field. It is explained in this way by the neurologist, E. G. Coghill (Herrick, 1949, p. 221):

My objection to the dogma of a causal agent is directed against the notion of something extrinsic to the situation acting upon it. "Cause" is our name for the inter-connections among natural processes in their contingent relations. B as a pattern of events does not occur unless A is present in the situation, and, conversely, if A is present, B always accompanies it or follows it. This observed contingency has given rise to the idea of causal necessity, which is a logical artifact. The important point is that cause is inherent in the organization of the total situation. It is not imposed upon it from the outside by some *deus ex machina*.

It is typical of the new approaches that they do not strive to superimpose on the kaleidoscope of sensed or perceived reality a single rigid or absolute model. Rather they seek to discover diverse emerging patterns of organization in nature (Bridgman, 1928, p. 3). As suggested by Neils Bohr (1933; see also Whorf, 1956, p. 58), they even explore the possibility of discovering several possible ways of looking at the universe, ways which may be complementary, equally valid, and simultaneously entertained.

Thus, the new views tend to be organizational views, seeking new patterns of relatedness and "complementarity" in the universe; they look with disfavor on the projection of sumtotal and linear arrangements of parts or units which, for the sake of analysis, are recognized as major subdivisions of reality directly experienced in consciousness. Rather, the new views favor, as basic units, organizational patterns less familiar to everyday Western thought, speech, and attitudes.

It is especially noteworthy that these presently favored organization patterns are characteristically conceived as actively self-changing and self-actualizing. The universe tends to be perceived implicitly by modern explorers as a process of constant self-formation, re-formation, and transformation; the integrating factor in this activity pattern is multidimensional space-time.

Passing of Traditional Concepts of Time and Space

According to these new views, ultimately there may be no rigid three-part division of time into past, present, and future. Past merges with present and with future in a single duration, or becoming-later, which reflects the experience of time in human consciousness (Bergson, 1911; Whorf, 1956, p. 140; 1941, pp. 80–81).

The psychologically experienced duration of time may be treated fruitfully in many ways appropriate to the new views. Indeed, we now recognize that time has been, and is, conceived and treated variously by the several culturally diverse peoples of the world. Such variations are expressed specifically in the grammars, especially the verb forms, of thousands of languages recorded and analyzed by anthropologists who specialize in linguistics. The concept of a three-part division of time, familiar to us, is not, as is frequently assumed (see, e.g., F. Kluckhohn, 1950, p. 378), a universal formulation. Rather it is a device that peoples of Western European tradition have found convenient and culturally compatible in treating the experience of duration in consciousness, which is time in its human psychological dimension. As Whorf (1941, pp. 78–79) has brilliantly pointed out, in keeping with our mental set, we Westerners slice up the experienced duration of time into objectified, discrete units—a minute, an hour, a day, a year—and proceed to act as though our construct were a physical entity, like a thing, that we may treat quantitatively. Indeed, we build a whole system of mathematics on this analogy and then experience great difficulty when the universe fails to conform to our construct (Bridgman, 1928).

The new world views, on the other hand, usually have a place not only for the psychological experience of time as a duration, but also for the symbolic time of the dream world and mythology, and for the absolute time and absolute space of our Western common-sense, three-dimensional universe. Most modern science, of course, explicitly recognizes the relativity of time and space concepts. According to the new working models of reality, the several ethnocentric concepts of time and space become parochial, each to its own frame of reference, against the background of the multidimensional space-time continuum, the newly postulated absolute.

For example, in the world of painting, according to this

frame, three-dimensional (Renaissance) perspective—whereby the observer views the painting (from a fixed, static point outside it) as a fixed static object in absolute space and absolute time—falls into place historically as a dated culture trait, discovered in Europe about 1400 (Giedion, 1949, p. 31). It ceases to be a valid criterion whereby non-Western styles of art may be judged inferior or underdeveloped, as compared to fifteenth-to nineteenth-century Western styles (Dorner, 1949, p. 25). By the same token, the absence of lineal perspective in modern painting is illuminated, and we begin to understand the significance of certain recent trends in the treatment of space in Euro-American painting, sculpture, and architecture (Laporte, 1948). The release of Western man from outmoded and culturally dated stylistic devices in painting and sculpture has, as in other fields of endeavor, set the stage for increasing appreciation of forms and styles which characterize cultures quite different from, and historically unrelated to, his own (Fry, 1924, pp. 88–104). It has helped to emancipate him from extreme, dead-end ethnocentrism. This emancipation tends toward further development of his appreciation of the culturally unfamiliar (Shapiro, 1957).

Growth along these lines has tended to emphasize the importance of the position of the observer, or knower, in relation to the observed, perceived, or known (see Dewey and Bentley, 1949). It has opened up whole vistas of ethnocentricity which heretofore were virtually closed to systematic exploration. We simply had never thought of asking the relevant questions in relevant context. And by this I do not refer to superficial culture traits, such as the wealth of technological innovations developing out of the needs and drives of our industrial civilization. I refer rather to certain implicit assumptions regarding the form and organization of the world, assumptions which are so firmly implanted in the subsoil of our classic tradition that they are accepted without question.

From Rigid Boundaries to Interpenetration

One such assumption is our tendency to categorize aspects of the external world in terms of a contents-and-container model. Certain aspects of the phenomenal world, such as liquids, may be conceived appropriately as confinable quantitatively within a physical receptacle, shaped by its form and size as potter's clay is by a mold. A cup of coffee, a glass of water, a bottle of beer—these are ways of expressing aspects of the external, sensory world which seem to us in keeping with perceived reality and with sensory experience, even though the mode of expression frequently emphasizes the container, whereas the contents are the real issue (Whorf, 1941, pp. 79–80).

However, English speakers and other Western Europeans have taken the contents-and-container paradigm and made it into a habitual way of slicing and whittling experience to the extent that we now impose this model on phenomena where it is strikingly inappropriate. To view the mind or the personality, for example, as a receptacle filled with contents, conveyed by phrases such as "the contents of the mind," or to conceive a culture as a container filled with an aggregate of traits (Wissler, 1923, Ch. 4), are farfetched and deceptive extensions of this linguistic device. Such uses of the model are not only inappropriate. They reflect a sum-total, physical view of the phenomena under discussion, which tends not merely to impede understanding but, still more serious, to obscure their dynamic nature as postulated by most modern scientists. They impute to the phenomena a pseudo concreteness, rigidity, and permanence.

One model which seems appropriate to the emerging views of the universe as revealed by modern science, but difficult to grasp and hold firmly, might be called the *transactional view of reality* (see Dewey and Bentley, 1949). The difficulty stems partly, I believe, from the magnetic attraction that the contents-and-container stereotype has for us. The latter model implies definite boundaries, familiar and measurable shapes, impermeable surfaces, and also I believe, a type of perspective whereby one tends to view the phenomena under consideration only from without. We call this "positivism."

When, for instance, we talk about a cup of coffee we tend to sense the object as it looks from the outside—perhaps a large china cup brimming with fragrant, dark-brown liquid. We do not see the cup from within, either by visualizing its inside surface or by imaginatively plumbing its depth. By this phrasing, we do not emphasize the degree of strength or weakness of the brew, the dregs at the bottom of the cup, or the pattern painted on the inside of the porcelain. We do not emphasize the caffeine or essence of the drink. The object under consideration is definitely bounded and shaped, and our attention is safely concentrated on those aspects of it which we can observe and encompass easily and superficially from without—its exterior form and quantitative contents. Even the aroma, as pointed out by Barnett (1953, p. 412), although wafted to our senses, has for us the same rigid homogeneity within itself.

A Transactional Approach

As might be expected, we are frequently at a loss when confronted with a transactional approach to reality, wherein theoretically the observer is expected to observe simultaneously outside and inside, above and below, and all around the phenomenon under scrutiny. Accordingly, boundaries may not appropriately be conceived as rigid and impermeable, but the relation of whole and parts tends to be characterized by interpenetrability. Even the unit itself is not thought of as simply located in space, in Whitehead's apt phrase, but rather as an event moving in its own direction and at its own pace in the multidimensional space-time manifold.

Much though we try to reeducate our ingrained conceptions of structure—much though we attempt to change our perception and thought habits—we find ourselves constantly reverting to the familiar models of common-sense reality, so deeply imbedded in our patterns of consciousness and grammar that we have difficulty in expressing ourselves in other terms. This approach may be illuminated for some readers by considering an analogous development in the evolution of modern painting, namely, cubism. Giedion (1949, pp. 357, 358) wrote:

> The cubists did not seek to reproduce the appearance of objects from one vantage point; they went round them, tried to lay hold of their internal constitution. They sought to extend the scale of feeling, just as contemporary science extends its descriptions to cover new levels of material phenomena. . . . The cubists dissect the object, try to lay hold of its inner composition. They seek to extend the scale of optical vision as contemporary science extends the law of matter. Therefore contemporary spatial approach has to get away from the single point of reference.

The transactional approach to reality challenges practically all our cherished ways of thinking about the world, but particularly the social scientist's tendency to simplify human relations so that they may be treated quantitatively, as relationships between pairs of correlates or things or persons. Only by a great effort do we accept the empirical fact that the human being transacts in space-time with his entire effective physical and organic environment simultaneously. He does not merely interact interpersonally with this individual and then that one. He inhales oxygen through his respiratory organs and his pores and he exhales carbon dioxide. He takes in food and drink and excretes waste products. The male impregnates the female who conceives, gestates, gives birth, and nurses—all basically transactional, rather than interactional, processes.

Indeed, all major body processes are indisputably transactional; the apparent boundaries of the body and its integral parts are permeable and characterized by interpenetrability. Lawrence K. Frank (1951, p. 37) says:

> We exist in the geographical environment, moving about in space-time, as we carry on our continual intercourse with nature, through breathing, drinking, eating, absorbing light, heat and other forms of radiant energy, eliminating through breathing,

urination and defecation, through the skin and by radiation of heat, as the geographical environment flows in and out of us, as it does in all other organisms.

According to the newer approaches, the human body may no longer be viewed appropriately as a rigidly bounded unity inside its own skin, reacting to, or interacting with, definitely bounded units of the environment. Rather, it may be viewed appropriately as a dynamic organic event in transactional relationship with the effective,* changing environment, throughout its developmental cycle from conception and birth to death, and even, of course, after death.

As Dewey and Bentley (1949, p. 272) acutely observe: " 'Environment' is not something around and about human activities in an external sense; it is their *medium,* or *milieu,* in the sense in which a *medium* is *inter* mediate in the execution or carrying out of human activities, as well as being the channel *through* which they move and the vehicle *by* which they go on."

Why this exaggerated concern about clear-cut boundaries? Perhaps we fear justifiably that if we abandon the obvious traditional boundaries to the units which we habitually recognize as adding up to our real world, it will fall apart. We shall find ourselves suspended without visible support; and with nothing to hang to, we shall find our security lost. By seeking to penetrate below the surface appearance of phenomena viewed as self-changing processual events, and by rejecting the notion of rigid, enduring boundaries in favor of flexible, changing, and permeable ones, the newer approaches to reality shift emphasis from visible outlines to hidden, inner dynamic structures and their fields of action.

* According to Allee et al. (1949, p. 1), "those parts of the total environment that are evidently of direct importance to the organism are regarded as constituting the *effective environment.*"

Space-time as Integrator

Actually, in the newer models of reality, the concept of "space-time" functions as the crucial integrator. There is no need to hold the parts of reality together by rigid boundaries and frames. It cannot be too strongly emphasized that, from the newer viewpoints, the multidimensional space-time manifold is an integral component of every universal equation. Space-time is conceived not merely as a background phenomenon like the notion of "environment" in common-sense thinking. It is, for example, not viewed as a stage on which cosmic events take place at various levels from macrocosmic to microcosmic. No. Space-time, as conceived in the present operational approach, is the universal constant, permeating all reality.

Space-time, so to speak, is inside and outside, in front, behind, above, below, at the nadir, at the center, and at the zenith of events in all dimensions of the newer realities. Paradoxically, space-time may be thought of as spaceless and timeless in common-sense terms. It is indivisible; it cannot appropriately be split, decomposed, or separated into two or more essential parts. It is the basic presupposition without which the present working model falls apart. It is the integrator par excellence.

I believe it is impossible to comprehend the present working concept of space-time without a transactional approach to reality. Just as the concept of interaction as habitually used in common-sense parlance presupposes an action-reaction, pendulumlike movement in absolute space and absolute time, so the present concept of space-time requires that of transacting, interpenetrating process as its complement (see Chap. 6).

In developmental biology, for example, full comprehension of the working concepts of organic growth and development requires the postulation of that of space-time as their complement (see Herrick, 1949). Growth considered as a self-activating, irreversible, transforming process requires the concept of the space-time manifold as integral to all organic events.

Similarly in the new anthropology, as here presented at least, space-time is hypothesized as an irreducible constant component of every organism-environment event—immanent, neutral, primordial. Space-time replaces matter in the old as "irreducible" and "stubborn."

Self-actualizing Activity Systems

In sum, we may say that many of the newer working models of reality, including the present one, project a certain meaning on what Max Weber (Shils and Finch, 1949, p. 81) refers to as "the meaningless infinity of world process." Accordingly, they view reality, for purposes of scientific research, as characterized by a process of interpenetrating, self-transforming activity systems in multidimensional space-time. Two types of activity systems seem to be especially stressed. Both are conceived as self-changing and self-actualizing. The first type may be described as systems of turbulence. These may be characterized by the constant ebb and flow of great whirls that look like large eddies emerging out of small ones, which are in turn formed by still smaller ones.

For present purposes, I favor the view of the physicist Gamow (1952, p. 30; see also p. 28; Dorner, 1949, p. 229) who states:

Turbulence and gravity must be considered cosponsors of the evolutionary development of the universe. . . . From the cosmic point of view we must consider turbulent motion the natural thing and laminar flow a special case. We should accept turbulence among the large-scale masses of the universe as the natural condition in the same way as, at the microscopic level, we accept as natural the irregular thermal motion of molecules.

For example, the vast ocean-current systems of the earth "which flow through the oceans like rivers" (Carson, 1955, p. 24) represent an interpenetrative pattern of turbulence of planetary scope. Similarly, the galaxies of the heavens express an interpenetrative pattern of turbulence of cosmic scope.

Thus paradoxically, patterns of turbulence, perceived in appropriate perspective, are patterns of a certain kind of order.

It is not generally realized to what extent the pattern of turbulence in nature—a pattern of so-called "statistical disorder"—has yielded to statistical treatment. Osborne Reynolds established the basic laws of turbulent flow, especially the fact that the critical velocity at which turbulence sets in varies in direct proportion to the viscosity of the liquid and in inverse proportion to the diameter of the container (Gamow, 1952, p. 26).

This order, i.e., turbulent order, is here viewed operationally as a primary condition of the universe. Just as ocean currents, though generally imperceptible to the eye of the landlubber, probably more than any other single process are conceived as creators of the marine climate of the earth (Carson, 1955, p. 24), so other systems of turbulence are conceptualized as primary activity processes of the universe. Indeed, according to this approach, every system of "statistical order," if viewed in sufficiently broad perspective, will be found to be a part (fluctuating and temporary though it may be) of a larger, more inclusive system of turbulence.

The second type of activity system, stressed in many of the newer models, is characterized by so-called "statistical order," that is, by a tendency toward symmetry, self-regulation, and self-perpetuation. The latter category of systems—those of statistical order—include two basic types: (1) closed systems of the inorganic type which, when thrown out of order, tend to revert to the *status quo* by basically reversible and circular-type processes; and (2) open systems of the organic type which, when thrown out of order, tend to re-create the whole by re-creating the damaged part through major processes, predominantly irreversible and spiral, but also through reversible and circular-type processes.

According to the working model of reality presently favored for research purposes in the emerging science of mankind, universal process is treated as though it were characterized by a tendency toward self-organization of systems of statistical order out of systems of turbulence. Axiomatic to the model is the supposition that, because of the nature of universal process, systems of statistical order tend constantly to interpenetrate one another. If the stress accompanying interpenetration of such systems reaches a point beyond the self-recuperative potential of any one system, that system dissipates into turbulence. Hence, no statistical-order type of system can be maintained indefinitely. Constant change in the postulated space-time manifold is here attributed, for research purposes in the science of mankind, to the above described, interpenetrative processes.

Chapter 6

Life as Self-transcending Process

> *All* problems of life ultimately are biological
> ones, and the facts with which the student of
> organisms deals should be explored not for them-
> selves alone but for the suggestions they may
> offer for the more complex phenomena of life.
>
> *Edmund Sinnott*

Not only the physical and social sciences, but also the life sciences are in a state of profound change. Pioneers in biology have only recently moved from the natural-history phase to the mature phase of scientific inquiry. In the life sciences, as in the social sciences, we find scientific development hampered by anachronistic modes of thought. Hence a good deal of controversy characterizes the present transition period in biology.

It is my impression that in the life sciences, as elsewhere, the relation of this transition period to the current shift in working models of reality is not generally understood. A better grasp of the nature of the change presently occurring in the biological sciences, and its relation to the newer world views, would do much to clarify current issues and to liberate students of biology for more fruitful research.

Mechanistic versus Organismic Models in Biology

Most research biologists are still operating on the premises of a strictly common-sense view of reality. They live in a world of absolute space *and* time. As noted by Moulyn:*

The biologist in the restricted sense deals with the organism in so far as it is a causal unity which exists in a three-dimensional space and in one-dimensional, objective time. He dissects the organism into organ systems, organs and cells, and he shows the causal relations that exist between them and also between the organism and its environment. Examples of such organ systems are: the skeleton, circulatory system, nervous system, endocrine glands, liver. The skeleton enables the body to withstand the pull of gravity and it enables muscles to move joints; our bones and joints are one set of conditions which make erect stance and locomotion possible. However, there is no need to go beyond a causal description and to say that it is the purpose of the skeleton to make erect stance and locomotion possible.

To biologists of this persuasion, it seems, the organism is assumed implicitly to be equal to the sum of its component parts, and its behavior is believed to be explainable in terms of a general description of those parts.

Although mechanistic biology is probably still the standard of our day, a new biology which may be called *functional* or *organismic* is rapidly gaining ground (von Bertalanffy, 1952, p. 9). The new biology stems mainly from empirical research in living laboratories, as contrasted to those that have been contrived. These living laboratories include isolated biotic communities, ecological associations, and the clinics or life situations of the resources conservationists, fish and wildlife specialists, extension agents, range managers, foresters, veterinarians, public health officers, social workers, physicians, and psychotherapists.

In direct contrast to the sum-total, morphological approach referred to above with its built-in assumption of linear causality

* From A. C. Moulyn. *Structure, Function and Purpose.* 1957. p. 166. Reprinted by permission of the publishers, The Liberal Arts Press, Inc., New York.

as a universal principle, the new biology tends to center interest in *life action* as the primary process in the organic world. The significant units of research are usually conceived as life-action events viewed as whole systems and the unknowns tend to be formulated in terms of the relationships between such units.

Developments in Neurology

Some of the most fruitful research with this focus was done by the neurologist, George Ellett Coghill. A meticulously empirical scientist, Coghill succeeded in reducing his laboratory findings to brilliant formulations which clearly reflect a newer working model of reality. In this, he was assisted by his friend, the neurologist C. Judson Herrick who, after Coghill's untimely death, edited and published his papers and conversations (Herrick, 1949).

Focusing on action, behavior, and expressive experience of organisms viewed as life-action events in space-time, rather than on alleged passively receptive experience in space and time, Coghill concluded that "all experience is an expression of vital activity and the end toward which this activity is directed shapes the course of the experience" (Herrick, 1949, p. 86). This fits in with the later conclusion of G. H. Parker (1919) that muscle is the original and most ancient constituent of the neuromuscular system, and that motility is the key factor in the differentiation of the nervous system. Coghill also emphasized, as did Gesell at a later date, the primacy of motor expression in the embryogenesis of human behavior and of human mentation. Movement, Gesell said (1945, p. 197) is primary in the development of the individual.

Thus, Coghill emphasized "changes in the internal structure of the body concomitant with the different modes of expression and stressed the part played by forces generated within the body in the determination of patterns of behavior in accordance with the structural arrangements present. Expression in behavior was set out as the key factor in both racial and individual development" (Herrick, 1949, p. 86).

According to this view, "In the beginning is the act" is fundamental to life science. The act is here conceived as self-generating within the organism and forerunner to the development of bodily form (skeletal structure), the development of expressive behavior, of mentation (concept formation), and of values. A not-to-be-forgotten corollary would be, "The whole organism acts." Cause is not superimposed from without, but may be thought of as inherent in the functional organization (i.e., the interrelationship between components) of life-action systems.

Actually this approach presupposes space-time, rather than space and time, as the necessary component in living-action systems, including behavior and mentation patterns, although this fact is frequently, indeed usually, overlooked. Coghill, however, astutely noted that in the development of the individual's sensing processes an integrated space-time approach is antecedent to perceptual (common-sense) space and time. He conceived space-time as a component of every life-action system. He stated (Herrick, 1949, pp. 208–209):

What we observe is that operationally in behavior integrated space-time is antecedent to individuated space and time as we recognize these perceptually. . . . Movement is in integrated space-time, and it is so sensed in our first conscious experience of it. The spatial and temporal components are individuated mentally. . . . This analysis is handed down to us in our cultural tradition, and the individuation of space and time is effected so early in psychogenesis that in naïve experience they seem to be separate elements and are commonly so described. It is only at a higher level of abstraction that a clear-cut concept of space-time was formulated. Now, once we grasp this concept, it is perfectly clear that integrated space-time is antecedent to perceptual space and time. In other words, it is a real component of the action system of every organism. The description of the organismic individual in terms of space and time is incomplete. There must be added to this an account of those activities which can be described only in terms of integrated space-time. This gives us the complete picture of the psycho-organismic individual.

It is interesting to note that Jean Piaget's experiments (1957) have quite independently substantiated Coghill's suppositions regarding our first conscious experience of space-time. This statement of the problem of life not only shifts the researcher's focus from parts to whole living-action systems, but it extends the researcher's frame of reference to encompass transacting systems in space-time as an indispensable component of his significant units of research. Now it becomes apparent that within this perspective, controversies regarding teleology lose their meaning. Extreme deterministic positions, such as economic determinism, social or cultural determinism, and psychological determinism, are thereby outmoded as reflecting partial views of a partial statement of problem. The only valid determinism, if it can appropriately be so termed, becomes the "determinism" of life action.* But since both its origins and its goals are conceived as *inherent* in the life process itself, and as a function of the total life-action situation in space-time, references to teleological processes become irrelevant, while purpose and trend, conceived as biologically based, become the focus of attention and problem formulation.

The Concept of Evolution Reformulated

Reawakened interest in the concept of evolution, reformulated to encompass new knowledge and to fit a currently workable model of reality, is another sign of this focus in functional biology. Evolution has recently been redefined as "a self-maintaining, self-transforming, and self-transcending process, directional in time and therefore irreversible, which in its course generates ever fresh novelty, greater variety, more complex organization, higher levels of awareness, and increasingly conscious mental activity" (Huxley, 1955, p. 3). Neoevolutionists have extended their hypotheses to encompass not only biologi-

---

* Regarding two so-called "schools of thought" on organic life—the mechanistic and the teleologic—Nicolai Hartmann (1953, p. 41) remarked, "On both sides the fact is overlooked that the organism has its own peculiar form of determination. And that is the . . . determinism of a formative process by a system of dispositions."

cal facts and concepts, but also physical and psychic ones. Indeed they have revamped the evolutionary hypothesis as the primary process in the universe. Sir Julian Huxley (1955, p. 3) states:

In the last few decades, it has become clear that the whole of phenomenal reality is a single process, which properly may be called evolution. . . . Though the process of evolution is unitary, embracing the entire universe both in space and time, it is divisible into three very distinct sectors or phases, each with its own mechanism of self-transformation, its own characteristic tempo of change, and its own type of products. The earliest and also the largest is the inorganic or cosmological sector; the much restricted organic or biological sector arose as a later phase of the inorganic; and a still further restricted human or psycho-serial phase arose much later from the organic.

It should be noted that many of the neoevolutionists, in revamping a nineteenth-century hypothesis which was rooted in common-sense notions of space and time, have not succeeded in freeing themselves wholly from the nineteenth-century frame, which tends to center their position at a transition point between old and new reality views. While projecting an evolving processual principle as basic in the universe, many still do not grasp the meaning for science (especially for applied science) of the newly postulated life-action "determinism" which encompasses both origin and trends of life-action systems in a single space-time frame. Their frame tends to remain one of linear space and time. Thus, while recording the facts accurately, their interpretations are frequently limited, from the viewpoint of the present thesis, which considers the evolutionary process one of the primary processes of the universe.*

* It is interesting, however, that neoevolutionists are beginning to notice (Huxley, 1942, p. 574), and even to acknowledge a scientific basis for, some telepathy phenomena and other extrasensory activities of mind (Sinnott, 1955, p. 112). Thus biologists of the modern functional school have been quicker to take cognizance of certain startling findings of modern parapsychological research (Rhine, 1953; Rhine and Pratt, 1940; 1957) than most social scientists, to whom such recognition would necessitate a major revamping of basic theoretical assumptions.

Exceptions are the outstanding contributions of Edmund Sinnott, von Bertalanffy, Ralph Lillie, E. S. Russell, Alfred Emerson, and other ranking biologists and life scientists, whose work expresses an organismic approach. As defined by von Bertalanffy (1952, pp. 18ff.), leading principles of an organismic conception may be summarized as follows: "*The conception of the system as a whole* as opposed to the *analytical* and *summative* points of view; the *dynamic conception* as opposed to the *static* and *machine-theoretical* conceptions; the consideration of the organism as a *primary activity* as opposed to the conception of its *primary reactivity*."

Some organismic biologists tend to be apologetic about their position, which they classify in the realm of metaphysics or metabiology (e.g., Sinnott, 1955). So classified, it may be ignored as irrelevant by classical biologists whose frame is a common-sense, space and time one.

Directiveness of Organic Activities

One major contribution of the organismic movement in biology to an emerging science of mankind is the clarification by certain exponents of the problem of life-action system goals and norms. "Goal seeking and directiveness in organism," writes Sinnott (1955, p. 102), "should be recognized as a basic fact and life's most characteristic quality. About it center the great problems of biology and philosophy."

Certain neoevolutionists have made us acutely aware that according to their positions, organic systems have a built-in direction of development. This they find to be inherent in the nature of organisms. Accordingly, healthy change in an organic system is characterized by growth and development. Organismic biologists accept this and postulate clearly in addition that this built-in developmental process of all living stuff is self-directed toward certain biological goals.

Directiveness, they assume, is a primordial property of protoplasm. "From *Amoeba* to *Homo sapiens*," writes Sinnott

(1955, p. 100), "in all the complex systems it builds, protoplasm is a goal-seeker, and unless we take this carefully into account we shall find ourselves committing the error of treating organisms as far too simple things, and thus miss the vital core of what they are."

A living system as differentiated from a nonliving one, according to this approach, is self-directed toward completion of its particular life cycle. The life experiences of each individual of the species vary according to the interplay of inner tendencies with outer stresses but all without exception are energized from within to seek self-actualization according to the life-cycle pattern of the species. Russell explains (1945, p. 8):

> We should think . . . of the living organism, not merely as a unitary or holistic system, but as a unified complex of activities that are directive for the completion of its life-cycle. They are also constructive or creative, for the organism does actually build up by its own powers, and in this sense create, its own elaborate structure in development and in the preparations for reproduction. There is in the life-cycle, which *is* the organism, no passive lapse into a static equilibrium, as in an inorganic system, but an active movement towards creation, maintenance and reproduction of a highly complex and specific functional organization.

Organic and Inorganic Types of Systems

In stressing the directiveness of organic activities toward biological goals, the organismic biologists also clarify another crucial point in understanding the nature of systems. That is, they describe with appropriate precision essential differences between organic types of systems and inorganic types of systems. From the present viewpoint, it would be difficult to overemphasize the importance of this distinction for the development of a mature science of mankind since, as we have already had occasion to note, social scientists frequently describe sociocultural systems as though they were inorganic in type (Thompson, 1951a, p. 124). In other words, inorganic system models are frequently used by sociologists, social anthropologists, and other social scientists in the analysis of human group behavior.

Organismic biologists differentiate between the two types of systems as follows. Both inorganic and organic systems tend to move toward a natural end state. In inorganic systems this end state is a stable one of static equilibrium or least action. On the other hand, in life-action systems the end state is a goal of directive activities of development and is a highly complex unstable organization capable of being attained and maintained only by ceaseless activity of an elaborate and coordinated kind (Russell, 1945, p. 7). Hence, it is a homeostatic type of balance or equilibrium. In other words, equilibrium in inorganic systems refers to an end state reached by a reversible process of closure and is characterized by a stable condition of least action. Conversely, equilibrium or homeostasis in organic systems refers to an end state of irreversible, directive, developmental activities which is highly complex, unstable, and self-regulatory.

This means that, according to organismic theory, biological-type goals and the norms representing the steps toward their actualization (i.e., their expression in structure and behavior), are *by their nature* open, flexible, complex, coordinated, self-adjustive, and self-restorative in counterdistinction to inorganic end states which are closed, rigid, static, and brittle. The crucial significance of this distinction in the practice of applied ecology (natural-resources conservation) and clinical anthropology (human-resources conservation) will be discussed in due course.

Let us emphasize here, however, the relationship between the dynamics of organic systems, as described above, and their innate tendency to grow and evolve in space-time. It is only the organic that manifests this growth pattern. Sherrington (1941, p. 157) writes that organic evolution is "a corollary to organic growth; inorganic does not grow and does not exhibit organic evolution." A relevant question for an emerging science of mankind based on organismic biology is: Does this growth and evolutionary tendency manifest itself in sociocultural systems? And if so, how? This is a key question suggested by the present approach.

Developments in Ecology

Turning now to another subdivision of biology, namely, ecology, we find evidence of a transitional situation similar to that discussed above.

Ecology is usually defined as that branch of biology which treats the relationships of organic species to one another and to the inorganic environment. But a point to be emphasized in the present context is that ecology treats of biotic communities, i.e., arrangements or assemblages or organizations of organic species in a specific habitat (see Allee et al., 1949, p. 1). In ecology, we find for the first time an attempt by biologists to describe, and analyze systematically, groups of organic species interacting and/or transacting with one another in specific geophysical areas. Since, according to the present approach, the community is considered to be the elemental social unit, discoveries and theories of ecologists regarding community organization have a special relevance.

Classical ecologists have made great progress in describing systematically what occurs in a biotic community, according to a Renaissance type of perspective. But because they tend to conceive the community as simply located in absolute space and changing through absolute time, they still may come out with a general description of an ecological aggregation and its succession through time to a climax. The aggregation is conceived as a web of niches (Bates, 1952, p. 207) or statuses (Elton, 1935, p. 63), each of which is occupied by a species. The species are related by means of food chains which form a web of life. By processes of accommodation, competition, and symbiosis, a state of equilibrium is reached wherein one species is usually conceived as dominant. When disturbed, this mechanical type of equilibrium tends to revert to the *status quo*, unless an external agency, such as climate or substratum, changes. Paul B. Sears (1949, p. 240) states:

The mature community tends finally to a type of organization approximating a steady state in terms of thermodynamics. The dominant organisms tend to reproduce themselves instead of being replaced by other species, and so it is with the subordinate organisms. In the absence of definite change in the physical environment —climate or sub-stratum—this climax condition tends to maintain itself. Even evolutionary forces, the introduction of aggressive new forms of life, while altering the composition, have little essential effect upon the pattern of organization.

Besides the advent of the human species, natural changes in climate or in substratum* precipitate a condition of disequilibrium, which becomes a basis for a new ecological process toward a climax arrangement appropriate to the new environment.

Within this mechanistic frame, references to directiveness or goals in regard to the biotic community are frequently classified as "teleological" and "unscientific." In other words, such references are viewed as signifying the notion of a causal agency introduced into the situation from without.

This kind of thinking persists in ecology, according to the literature, despite the fact that a highly successful applied or clinical ecology, namely, natural-resources conservation (especially soil and moisture conservation), has developed, mainly in the United States, during the past few decades and has spread rapidly to many parts of the world. Sustained-yield forestry, a forerunner to the soil-conservation movement in the United States, developed much earlier in Europe. It is not generally realized that the success of modern resources-conservation measures depends on the scientist's identifying the norms and goals of transactional ecological process inherent in the ecological community itself and identifying man-made purposes with these inherent norms and goals (Thompson, 1951a, pp. 126–127).

Within this frame the applied ecologist uses his knowledge and skills to aid, reinforce, and utilize natural community-development processes to carry out specific man-made aims,

---

* Such changes include volcanic activity, uplift and subsidence of the earth's crust, erosion, deposition, etc. (Sears, 1955, p. 34).

such as arresting soil erosion on a range, promoting sustained yield in a forest, or developing a watershed. He is successful to the extent that he accurately defines and reinforces natural processes and biological goals.

The successful applied ecologist—whether soil and moisture conservationist, forester, range manager, or fish and wildlife warden—has learned well the lessons nature has to teach. He has mastered, in his particular province of organic life, the fact that all nature is transactionally interdependent, and living species tend to form communities which organize themselves into patterns in relation to a particular habitat. The component species of the community, in the process of pursuing their biological goals, seek out, by a process of trial and error—by limitation and elimination—and tend to perpetuate a mutually self-sustaining and self-helping arrangement, which approaches an optimum for the community within the particular habitat. In this community self-organization process, certain species may be eliminated, and others may move themselves out of the life web. Elton (1935, p. 21) remarks, "The important idea to grasp is that plants react on their surroundings and in many cases drive themselves out." Animal species behave in similar fashion.

Concept of the Mature or Climax Community

Still more crucial, perhaps, in understanding community dynamics is the fact that each species tends to explore the principles of community living inherent in natural community process to the extent that they are applicable and, so to say, makes its peace within the limits of the order or laws of nature inherent in the dynamics of natural communities. The end result of the process is what ecologists call a *mature* or *climax community*, a stabilized homeostatic type of organization representing an optimal arrangement of flora, fauna, microorganisms, etc., on a mature topography covered by a mature soil profile within a given climate (Sears, 1939, p. 100). Hawley (1950, p. 54) writes:

The final result of growth, as applied to the community, is termed *climax*. . . . The climax is reached when a complement of species appears which, through its control of climate, its ability to avoid unfavorable reactions on the habitat, can withstand indefinitely attempted invasion by foreign species. . . . A given combination of organisms permits a most efficient utilization of the resources in a given habitat, and research has shown that this type of organization always tends to be produced in the area.

Before the emergence of modern ecology, naturalists started with the supposition that "a given area is stocked with animals to its fullest capacity, and that a keen competition for the sheer means of existence is consequently going on between all the inhabitants—each animal being compelled to fight against all its congeners in order to get its daily food" (Kropotkin, 1902, p. 54). They came out with the concept of the struggle for existence. Now we start with the facts as observed in the field by zoologists, botanists, etc., and come out with the modern ecologist's concept of the natural biotic community. The earlier assumption, stemming from Darwinism, was one of unorganized competition of an aggregate of unrelated species or individuals occupying a given geographic area.

This idea has been superseded, on the basis of biological field research, by the assumption that, as the several species of plants, animals, and microorganisms arrive and establish themselves in an area—e.g., an isolated island—they organize themselves into a biotic community system. Thereafter, each species in the community usually tends to promote the welfare of the whole system in relation to the geophysical base; each species plays an active part in the fulfillment of the ultimate goals of species perpetuation, maintenance, and self-actualization. When such a balanced, functional arrangement is achieved it tends to persist and, if thrown off balance, to reestablish a similar model. This is called a mature or climax community. If individuals representing a new species arrive on the island and seek a niche without success, the species they represent cannot establish itself as part of the island's biotic system. Therefore they perish. The climax system contains within itself not only mechanisms for perpetuation of its component species, but also devices whereby their population growth, and that of new species, tends to be checked within the limits of the effective resources base.

Relevance to Human Problems

Ecologists have long pointed out the relevance of their findings and generalizations on natural communities to problems dealt with by the students of human communities. Elton (1935, p. 190) states that "we are now in a position to see that animals live lives which are socially in many ways comparable with the community-life of mankind, and if these resemblances be only considered as analogies, there yet remains the important fact that animal communities are very complicated and subject to regular rules."

The significance to man of natural community self-regulation is also stressed by Marston Bates (1950, p. 251):

We have, particularly in the last few centuries, escaped from the controls that maintain balance and proportion in a biotic community. We have run wild like a weed escaped on a new continent. We have retained the birth rate that we acquired during our Pleistocene evolution through savagery, and at the same time radically altered the nature and the incidence of the factors causing death. The result is a density of population that exceeds all reason, all possibility of support, and the end is still not in sight. This is, beyond question, the biggest problem that faces man. . . . It is a problem in which the naturalist must cooperate in finding a solution.

Although their specific points of view and suggestions may differ, most ecologists agree in stressing the orderliness of natural community process and the importance of its built-in controls and limitations to the understanding of the behavior of organisms, including man. Alfred Emerson (1954, pp. 78ff.) even suggests some applications of biological principles to man's ethical problems.

Conclusion

On the basis of the evidence, may we not conclude that the assumption of an immanent unity in the universe, basic to some of the new models of reality (Einstein and Infeld, 1942, p. 313), is infiltrating the biological sciences and is drawing all life phenomena into the cosmic scheme? Organic process may now be viewed appropriately as a subclass of universal, cosmic, self-changing process, and all organic species, including Homo sapiens, are gradually being incorporated into the over-all picture of the universe.

We have noted that the new biology focuses on life action as a basic process of organisms, and life-action events or systems are viewed as its basic research units or intelligible fields of study. Significant problems in the new life sciences center on relationships within and between life-action events or systems.

From what has gone before, it seems that the crucial missing ingredient in the classical ecologist's frame, from a modern viewpoint, is the space-time concept as the inherently integrating component. As soon as the ecological community is conceived as an evolving, life-action, processual event or system in space-time, its origins and direction of development come into focus as part of, and inherent in, the life process itself. Positions or niches in the organization of the community may be viewed as changing points in a relatively persistent pattern of transacting relationships in space-time, the whole life-action system comprising not only an evolving biotic component, but also a changing geophysical one. These may, or may not, assume a hierarchic order, with one or more species becoming dominant. For example, in a tropical rain forest, according to Bates (1952, p. 209), one may not say categorically that any one species is dominant over the rest. On the other hand, in many temperate-zone communities, the arrangement is usually such that one species appears to be dominant.

At this point, the notion of teleology becomes irrelevant to an explanatory description of the natural community as an ongoing life-action process or event—self-activating, self-restoring, self-maintaining, and self-preserving—and moving in the direction of inherent biological goals. What matters to scientific endeavor is that a working model has been proved heuristic and of immense practical importance in explaining crucial life-action events.

Thus, we may postulate streams of interpenetrating life-action events, transacting with one another and with their inorganic components, in a universal process of self-transformation. Space-time, not space *and* time, becomes the hypothetical primordial reality, the constant factor in this interplay of action events.

As Alexander Dorner (1949, p. 229) suggests:

Life . . . is nothing but one tremendous act of ceaseless self-transformation. Life is not united statically but energetically, namely by the continuous process of interpenetrative transformation of all its energies resulting in an open growth never closed by any tombstone of immutability. Life never repeats itself. It has an overwhelming directing force revealed by evolutionary history. The urge of growth is the real force in our present life. Our new rationality is no longer one of Being but of Becoming.

In attempting to integrate the findings of modern physics and biology into a single unified theory, L. L. Whyte (1949, p. 13) writes:

Every system tends to perfect its own inner symmetry, but as a component of more extensive systems it tends also to develop its symmetry in relation to its neighbors, and so to conform to the general state of the universe. But the universe is in a condition of finite asymmetry, instability, and disturbance, and every local system therefore partakes of the general state of disturbance. Every isolable system tends toward its symmetrical state, but no system remains isolable indefinitely. Nature is a disturbed system of systems, and there is never anywhere a final end to process.

Chapter 7

An Island Community in Fiji*

What actually happens when the new species seeking to colonize in an isolated ecological community is Homo sapiens, the human species? Does an entirely new kind of community system develop with the advent of man, as is apparently assumed by many social scientists (e.g., Kroeber, 1917, pp. 208ff.; 1939; Redfield, 1955, Ch. 2; Steward, 1955, Ch. 2)? Or, if the new species succeeds in establishing itself, does it do so as one component in a total web of life, according to the basic principles of natural ecological system building?

To test the latter question, stated in the form of a hypothesis, I attempted some years ago to analyze, within the frame of functional ecology, the field findings obtained by a geologist, a botanist, a naturalist, and an anthropologist on an isolated community in Fiji. This experiment anticipated by a decade the suggestion of Alexander Spoehr, Director of the Bishop Museum in Honolulu, regarding a strategy for anthropological exploration in the Pacific.

"What is called for . . ." Spoehr (1957, p. 182) stated

* The following case study is taken from my article, Relations of Men, Animals, and Plants in an Island Community (Fiji). *Amer. Anthropologist*, 1949, 49:544–556. Reprinted here with permission from *Amer. Anthropologist*. It is based on material presented in Thompson (1938; 1940a; 1940b). For a critique of the method of historical reconstruction used, see Weltfish (1960). Unless otherwise specified, conditions and social practices are described as of 1933–1934.

"is a well-defined approach stemming from what is not a well-defined field—human ecology. Yet because the principal objects of study are tangible life forms clearly related to man, an ecological point of view is essential to progress in the understanding of culture history in the Pacific." Kenneth Emory (1953), a veteran specialist in Oceanic ethnology, recently expressed a similar view.

The field projects basic to the present analysis were unrelated, although all except one (that of the naturalist) were carried out simultaneously. So far as I am aware, none of the four investigators collected his data within a systematic ecological frame. Their approaches tended toward the natural-history type. Edwin H. Bryan, Jr., naturalist, made a comprehensive survey of the Lau Islands in 1924. Albert C. Smith, botanist, collected plants there in 1934. In the same year Harry S. Ladd, geologist, gathered material to reconstruct the geological history of the area. In 1933–1934, I made an ethnographic survey of southern Lau, and also investigated culture-history and culture-contact problems.

It should be noted that the available data are limited, particularly regarding certain aspects of the problem relevant to botany and zoology, but I believe they are adequate for the needs of the present experiment, which is designed to be suggestive rather than definitive.

Two Types of Biotic Systems in Lau

The community selected as the significant unit of research is located at the southern end of the Lau or Eastern Archipelago of Fiji, a north-south arc of 100 small islands, 30 of which are inhabited. It is on the border between the Polynesian and the Melanesian culture areas. The unit of research consists of an isolated group of six inhabited islands and their uninhabited satellites.* Three inhabited islands, Fulanga, Ongea, and

* The uninhabited satellites are Karoni, Tavunasithi, Wangava, Marambo, Yangasa Levu, Navutu-i-loma, Navutu-i-ra, Yuvutha, and Ongea Ndriki.

Namuka, as well as all the uninhabited ones, are composed of elevated limestone. The other inhabited islands, Mothe, Komo, and Kambara, are formed, either wholly or in part, of volcanic rocks.

While no two of these islands are exactly alike in structure or mode of origin, the volcanic islands (e.g., Mothe) have eroded to rounded, reed-covered hills and gentle slopes or low, rocky promontories. They exhibit miniature drainage systems which originate at high points near the central interior and form small streams with dendritic patterns. Their valleys are lined with relatively deep, rich soil which supports a variety of vegetation, including yams (*Dioscorea*) and other garden crops. Bryan (Ms.) states:

> The dominant plant over much of the volcanic islands is a plume grass, *Eulalia japonica*, called *ngasau* by the natives. There are also several species of wiry ferns, including the "staghorn"; a low scrub, made up of about a half a dozen widespread species of shrubs and stunted trees; and scattered *Pandanus* and *Casuarina*. The dominant littoral species are: *ndilo* (*Calophyllum inophyllum*), *vutu* (*Barringtonia speciosa*), *evu* (*Tournefortia argentea*), *evuevu* (*Hernandia peltata*), *nawanawa* (*Cordia subcordata*), *tatangngia* (*Acacia lauriflora*), *vevendu* (*Scaevola koenigii*), *tavola* (*Terminalia littoralis*), *ndrala* (*Erythrina indica*), etc. Besides these there are the usual *Pandanus,* numerous vines and groves of coconut palms.

The limestone islands (e.g., Fulanga) are characterized by forested low plateaus, which tend to erode into basins whose sharp-crested rims drop steeply to the sea. They have no valleys or streams; the rain seeps underground and reaches the sea by an intricate system of subterranean caverns. Except in Namuka, where the soil is relatively deep, only a thin layer of rather poor topsoil occurs in pockets in the interior basins. The soil supports a distinctive flora. Useful hardwoods, such as the greenheart of India (*Intsia bijuga*), *mbau* (*Pittosprum brackenridgei*), and *makota* (*Dysoxylum richii*), as well as other jungle plants which are absent or scarce on the volcanics, flourish on the limestone islands. However, yams do not grow well in this type of soil. Apparently these islands supported no plants suitable for horticulture by native methods before manioc and sweet potato (*Ipomoea batatas*) were imported into Lau in post-European times. According to Bryan (Ms.):

> All the limestone islands . . . support one type of forest. It is made up throughout the group of the same fifty or so species of trees and tall shrubs, with an undergrowth of *Piper* (*wangawa*), bird's-eye pepper (*rokete*), ferns, herbs and several vines. The luxuriance alone depends upon the size and elevation of the island. There is an interesting, rapid and progressive increase in the number of species and the height of growth, from the nearly bare rocks, such as Latei Viti and Bacon Island with but two or three species of prostrate herbs, to the splendid forests of Kambara, Mango, etc. First to appear after the herbs and vines are low, stunted trees of such widespread species as *Hernandia peltata, Tournefortia argentea,* and a *Ficus* with orange fruit commonly eaten by pigeons. A few of the small islands have native palms in considerable numbers. *Pandanus* and *Casuarina* appear early in the scale.

In sum, good garden land and food tend to be limited on the limestone islands but plentiful on the volcanics, while forest products are scarce on the latter but abundant on the former. Thus, the resources of the two geological types complement each other. Together, the fifteen islands form a naturally balanced supercommunity, which is a potentially self-sufficient native trade area.

The foundations of this ecological arrangement extend far back into the geological history of the region. On the basis of paleogeological evidence, Ladd and Hoffmeister (1945; Ladd, 1934) infer that organic life in the form of coral polyps developed there as early as the Lower Miocene period (before the Lau group had emerged above sea level), and it played a major part in forming the several islands and in laying the foundations for their present biotics. As soon as an islet emerged above sea level and natural erosion processes began to develop topsoil, we assume that the basic species of its life web began to gain a foothold. Limestone biotics assembled on the limestone islands and volcanic biotics on the volcanic islands.

Though we lack the necessary facts to describe these two types of biotics in detail, geologists suggest that their development in Lau has been fostered and limited by several factors (Ladd and Hoffmeister, 1945; Bryan, 1948; Thompson, 1940a; 1940b). Rocks are of two types only: impervious-volcanic and soluble-limestone structures. Most of the islands are small, isolated, and closely surrounded by open sea at least 100 fathoms deep. They are separated from the main Fiji group to the northwest by some 200 miles and from Tonga to the southeast by some 400 miles. Located mainly between 17 and 19 degrees* South Latitude and in the vicinity of 179 degrees West Longitude, the Lau group has a tropical climate; the mean annual temperature is estimated at about 73 degrees Fahrenheit, and the humidity range from about 70 to 90 per cent. The islands lie in the belt of the southeast trade winds which prevail during the cool, dry season from April to November. These conditions are reflected in reef and island contours and in the distributions of various types of rock. During the remainder of the year—the warm, wet season—the southwest monsoon blows intermittently, especially from January to March when hurricanes may be expected. Practically all the annual precipitation, which averages about 80 inches, falls during the wet season, much of it in the form of torrential downpours which erode basins and caverns in the limestone islands, and valleys in the volcanics.

The basic ecological balances of each island developed in the absence of large land animals, including man. According to Bryan (Ms.):

Except for birds and insects there is a poverty of native animal life in Lau. The only mammal noted was the rat. About a dozen species of water birds and over 28 species of land birds were encountered throughout the group. Two species of land snakes and one banded water snake were caught. Lizards of various species

* Vatoa and Ono-i-Lau lie farther to the south, and accordingly have a slightly cooler climate.

were abundant. The largest was the green *vokai*. Various sizes of geckos and skinks were more abundant. Land crabs, including the large "coconut" crab and hermit crabs, were present in quantity.

The Advent of Man

Long before the first human beings arrived in Lau* the delicately balanced biotics of southern Lau presumably had matured. The advent of man meant much more to these islands than the arrival of a new ocean-borne or air-borne species would mean. It meant the intrusion of a whole complex of exotic species of fauna and flora carried by man during his migration by canoe eastward into the Pacific. Culture-history evidence in southern Lau (Thompson, 1938) suggests that these newcomers included domestic animals, such as the pig, the dog, and the fowl, and food plants, such as yam, breadfruit, and banana. The aborigines of Lau, furthermore, brought tools of stone and shell, such as adzes, gouges, awls, and pounders whereby they could alter somewhat the face of the islands. They possessed certain skills such as fire making, stone cutting, house building, basketry, mat plaiting, and horticulture. They sailed in seaworthy canoes, and were thus able to travel between the islands and connect heretofore disparate ecological arrangements.

Not much is known of these first human inhabitants of Lau, but on the basis of internal cultural evidence and of archaeological and linguistic data (Thompson, 1938; 1940b; 1947b; Capell and Lester, 1941–1942), we may infer they came from the west and settled in the bush on the larger islands. In time, each clan group formed a small clan hamlet. On the limestone islands the aborigines apparently subsisted chiefly on jungle fruits, fresh green leaves, jungle fowl, and fish, while on the volcanics this basic diet was supplemented with garden produce such as yams.

* We do not yet have exact dates for the settlement of Lau, but the available evidence suggests that Fiji was settled by 1000 to 500 B.C.

112 AN EMERGING HYPOTHESIS

A New Ecological Balance

After the first human beings arrived, a new ecological arrangement seems gradually to have emerged; recently introduced species of flora and fauna, including Homo sapiens, were incorporated into the community supersystem. The reconstructed culture of the first human inhabitants of Lau indicates that, on the basis of attitudes and behavior patterns which they brought with them, the aborigines developed a way of life which tended to integrate the human group with the other species of the natural community in environmental context and which symbolically explained, validated, and supported the culture.

In time, the ancestral migration from the west was forgotten. The aborigines came to believe that they had originated locally in some natural phenomenon such as a tree or an animal and they believed in a local abode of the dead. The inhabitants of each island regarded a species of bird and a species of fish as sacred to the island group. They made offerings at sacred places, such as caves, trees, or stones, to their deity, apparently a great, pervasive, spiritual force believed to be the source of all *mana* (impersonal superhuman power).

What effect the aborigines had on their immediate environment we do not know. It has been suggested, however, that gardening on the volcanic islands has been responsible to some degree for the degeneration of their flora to rank grasslands and other low growth. In the limestone localities, on the other hand, where cultivation is limited, the dense, scrubby forest, with its tangled underbrush and pitted terrain, tends to discourage man's interference with nature's balances (Bryan, 1948).

An Aboriginal Community under Stress

The next major event in the culture history of southern Lau seems to have been the conquest of the aborigines more than fourteen generations ago according to the natives' method of reckoning time, by a small band of warriors reputed to have come from northwest Viti Levu in west Fiji. The conquerors differed markedly from the aborigines in skills, interests, attitudes, and values. They were a raiding, fishing people who preferred to sail and to gather their food from the sea rather than till the soil. Marrying aboriginal women who were dowered with parcels of land, they settled on the more fertile islands and founded new clans. Each new clan claimed three organic species sacred to it, namely, a tree, a fish and a bird. The newcomers, moreover, were fascinated by their genealogies and by the idea of rank based on male primogeniture. Their own clans formed an upper or noble class above the clans of the aborigines. They required that their first-born males be regarded as sacred chiefs and be rendered tribute by the people in the form of first fruits. By means of hereditary priests in small temples, they developed a system of worshipping their warrior forefathers, and thus introduced ancestor worship into Lau.

The aborigines and their descendants, however, kept most of the land, their own traditional food-producing patterns, and the basic ecological system whereby they related themselves to the natural environment. They also kept the nature religion and many traditional attitudes and values which sanctioned that system.

In time, manioc and sweet potato, exotic food plants which could be grown to a limited extent on the limestone islands, found their way into Lau, a factor which contributed to population growth. On its natural ecological base, the isolated community supersystem of southern Lau gradually developed a new balance. Although Tongan and European influences have induced certain changes in recent years—warfare has ceased and most Lauan native religious practices have been discontinued because of Christian missionary influences—this basic community supersystem still persists in southern Lau, according to the field findings.

Space limitations do not permit a complete description of the Lauan socioculture system in an ecological frame, even to the extent that data are available (see Hocart, 1929; Thompson, 1940b). It will suffice for our purposes, however, to note certain

aspects of the native productive and distributive system in ecological context.

The Lauan Pattern of Nutrition

The food problem looms large in this island community.
Many interrelated factors are responsible for this problem: the
frequency of drought and destructive hurricanes; the scarcity
and poor quality of garden land on the limestone islands; the
difficulty of preserving and storing food under native conditions;
the fact that most of the manioc (staple of the limestones since
its introduction) produced is poisonous until it has been tedi-
ously processed; etc.

Under such circumstances, we might expect the diet of the
Lauans to be deficient both in quantity and in nutritive balance.
So far as I am aware, no systematic studies of the native diet
have yet been made. We may note, however, that a satisfactory
meal, from the native point of view, must consist of two parts:
steamed "true food" (called *kana ntchina*), that is, a staple such
as yam, breadfruit, sweet potato, manioc, or Tahitian chestnut
(*Inocarpus edulis*); and a boiled relish (called *mboro*) made of
fresh green leaves, fish, and coconut cream, seasoned with bird's-
eye pepper. Pigs and sea turtle are regarded as feast foods. This
diet is rather well balanced; the true food provides the bulk
of carbohydrates, some proteins, fats, minerals, and vitamins,
while the relish furnishes proteins of superior quality and fat,
from ripe coconut cream, as well as certain indispensable
vitamins and minerals found in fresh green leaves and red
peppers. Furthermore, although food does not drop off the
trees and rot on the ground (as it does on some Pacific islands),
the Lauan diet appears, under native conditions, to be relatively
adequate in quantity for the needs of the population, except
in time of hurricane or drought. It is relevant to note that
this nutrition pattern requires little or no fresh water, and this
is an important factor in a community where fresh water is
exceedingly scarce.

The traditional diet of the Lauans is rooted in a complicated and ingenious system of attitudes, habits, and institutions. This system functions to develop and reinforce the basic natural resources of the area according to the needs of the population; it also serves to relate human groups to the supercommunity. To gain some insight into this system, let us begin with the daily menu.

The Lauans eat their one main meal at about sundown, and the major activities of both sexes are directed toward procuring and preparing the food for this meal. The men and boys of each household are responsible for the daily supply of true food for their group. They either raise this food in the household's garden land or collect it from the bush. They carefully prepare the daily harvest, scrape and depoison the manioc, etc., wrap the food in leaves, place each package in the earth-oven pit on stones which have been heated, cover the whole with leaves and earth, and allow the food to steam for at least an hour.

The women and girls of the household are responsible for the relish. They go to considerable trouble to find fresh green leaves daily—either edible leaves from the bush or sweet potato leaves from the garden. They also fish with nets in the lagoon or collect shellfish on the reef, and they clean the catch on the beach. Then at the kitchen huts, they pick the leaves from the stems, grate and strain the flesh of ripe coconuts to make coconut cream, and boil the mixture in pots with the fish and bird's-eye pepper for at least an hour over a wood fire.

When both portions of the meal—the men's true food and the women's relish—are finally ready, they are combined and divided into shares, one for each member of the household according to rank, age, and sex. Thus, the two essentials of the daily meal are always procured and prepared separately by the two sexes. Indeed, no woman is allowed near the earth oven, which is strictly a male domain and is located some distance from the kitchen hut. This complementary and balanced sex division of the rather time-consuming labor of meal getting functions effectively toward ensuring that the daily diet will be reasonably adequate, varied, and sufficient in quantity to fulfill the needs of the household group, without overburdening either sex or any one individual or age group. The method of sharing the feast results in a rather systematic and equitable distribution of food.

The System of Land Use

Now it should be noted that, for the self-maintenance of the Lauan diet pattern, each household must have access to three types of resources: garden land, bush, and fishing grounds. With this point in mind, let us glance at the system of land use in southern Lau (for details, see Thompson, 1940a; 1940b).

After the British took over the Fiji Islands in 1874 and peace was established between native factions, the clan hamlets of Lau moved out of the bush and settled in coastal villages on the windward * shores of the islands. Each clan hamlet occupied a section of the village but kept its proprietary clan rights in land. Volcanic islands, like Mothe, continued to be divided into pie-shaped sections, bounded by the natural ridges which separate the fertile valleys, and each local clan retained the use of the garden lands, uplands, and fishing grounds of the section wherein its hamlet had formerly been located. On limestone islands, such as Fulanga, where there is no valley and ridge conformation, land sections were not pie-shaped; but a similar principle of land division nonetheless prevailed. Formerly, the bush and fishing grounds in the vicinity of each site occupied by a clan hamlet belonged to the hamlet, along with its jungle fruits, garden lands, and other resources. Each household within a clan hamlet had the use of a piece of the hamlet's garden lands and all the households of the hamlet had access to the hamlet's bush and fishing grounds. After the establishment of coastal villages, the bush and fishing grounds belonging to the clans of a village were used in common by the whole village group, but the ancient division of garden lands by clans and households persisted.

* Except Tokalau and Lomatchi, which are located on Kambara's leeward shore near the anchorage.

Furthermore, certain clans or villages retained their traditional claims to one or more of the small, uninhabited limestone islands in the vicinity. For example, Naivotavota clan of Nggalinggali village on Kambara claims the island of Wangava; its members supplement the crops they raise on their meager garden lands on Kambara with those they raise on Wangava, and they also use Wangava's rather extensive forest and lake products. Undu village on Kambara claims ownership of Marambo island and uses its resources. Indeed, all the uninhabited islands of the supercommunity are claimed and used to supplement the resources of owning groups.

Thus the land-use system of southern Lau is closely related to the basic ecological arrangement of the area. It functions to ensure a balanced distribution of the several types of island resources among the local groups of each island and to render accessible to each household the means of obtaining a balanced daily diet.

Role of the Crop Custodian

The traditional diet is further safeguarded by an ingenious and self-regulating system of cooperative production and distribution, which encompasses all the local groups in the supercommunity. On each inhabited island a hereditary officer, called the *vaka vanua,* is custodian of the jungle fruits and garden crops. The traditional role of the crop custodian was to guard the island's food supply and, as each major food crop (whether cultivated or wild) matured, to place a tabu on it. When the custodian considered a crop under tabu to have ripened sufficiently, he removed the tabu and arranged for the village and clan groups to collect a tribute of first fruits for the chief. The first fruits were then placed on the village ceremonial ground (*rara*) and divided by the crop custodian into two portions, one for the island chief and one for the people. The chief's portion was presented ceremonially by the custodian or by another officer of the aboriginal class called the *takala.* The portion of the first fruits reserved for the people was divided by still another officer, called the headman of the ceremonial ground (*tui rara*),* a hereditary title in an aboriginal clan. It was the responsibility of this official to divide the food so that each clan received a fair share. When crops were abundant, part of the first fruits were set aside to be fermented and stored against time of scarcity. After the first-fruits ceremony the people of the island were free to gather the remainder of the crop, each household group from its own lands.

In this island community where food was none too plentiful and famine a constant threat, the crop custodian obviously functioned, in total context, to conserve and augment the food supply of each island by preventing the crops from being consumed before they had attained their full size and maturity and, let us note, their highest nutritive value. The custodian institution thus provided a public-health and resources-conservation measure of considerable significance; it tended to guard against famine, to obtain the optimum size and food value of the crops, to ensure a more equitable distribution of the limited food resources of the community as a whole, to build up community health through more adequate nutrition, and to accumulate a surplus in times of plenty for use in times of scarcity. Note that, on each island, only the major food crops were placed under tabu. These differed from island to island and from season to season, depending on local conditions as judged by crop custodians; thus the custodian institution had considerable flexibility.

When the British system of indirect rule was established in Lau, however, the office of crop custodian was not incorporated into the administrative setup. Indeed, its very existence was probably unknown to Europeans. The Lauans soon became confused: Which chief should receive the offering of first fruits —the traditional island chief whose office had not been recognized officially in the new administration, or the local village chief, newly created by British regulation? By the 1930s the crop custodian, although continuing to function in a limited

* On Fulanga the *tui rara's* functions were performed by the *tui naro,* an aboriginal clan title.

way on all the inhabited islands of the community (except Namuka where the crops abundantly cover the needs of the population), had lost considerable authority and prestige. The number of fruit and garden crops placed under tabu had decreased in number, and at least part of each crop was consumed before it fully matured, especially on the limestone islands. Food was rarely stored against time of famine, and in general the crops were smaller and less nutritious.

Role of the Master Fisherman

As part of the Lauan production-distribution system, each inhabited island also had a master fisherman (called *ndau ni nggoli*), who was charged with responsibility for the island's fishing grounds, communal fishing expeditions, and turtle hunts. The master fisherman was always a member of a clan of the noble class, except on islands where that class was absent. The *ndau ni nggoli* controlled the fish lore and fishing techniques of the island. His function was to study the tides and currents, the weather, the lunar cycle, the seasons, the habits of edible species of marine life in relation to the local fishing grounds, and the presence of noxious plants rendering edible species poisonous. Men and women, singly or in groups of two or three, caught fish offshore by means of nets, lines, and spears for their daily household needs without special permission from the master fisherman. But they observed his regulation of the fishing grounds, and no large, organized fishing expeditions occurred without his sanction. Indeed, the master fisherman himself organized and led all communal turtle hunts and most large fishing parties. Women's communal fishing was led by the master fisherman's wife or daughter.

The institution of the master fisherman tended to increase the total catch by protecting the local fishing grounds from overfishing and undue disturbance, and by taking advantage of the various group-fishing techniques in relation to the weather, the seasons, and the habits of various edible species. In a community where fishing provided the major protein ingredient in the daily diet and an indispensable part of every feast, this institution obviously operated as a public health measure of prime importance in creating and maintaining a balanced relation between the human group and its marine food supply. The ecological significance of the role of the master fisherman is clarified by the fact that, although his authority has not been reinforced by the British and consequently he has lost status, unofficially he still operates to a limited extent on every inhabited island in the community. As a result of his lowered status, however, the fishing grounds of the several islands tend to be more disturbed, there are fewer organized fishing expeditions, and the catches tend to be smaller than they used to be.

Interisland Ceremonial Exchange

Another institution which functions as part of the total production and distribution system of Lau is the intervillage ceremonial exchange of property (solevu). This involves a complicated pattern of competitive exchange of goods between two related but rival villages, focused in a four-day ceremony and based on the first-fruits rite. Food from the volcanic islands is exchanged for craft goods, such as mats, barkcloth, wooden bowls, and canoes, from the limestone islands. There is also some nonceremonial barter of goods between related individuals from the two villages, and this gives a high degree of flexibility to the arrangement. The solevu also provides an occasion for the exchange of feasts, dances, and songs between the two rival groups and for intervillage games and sports.

The institution of the solevu functions to provide a pleasant interlude in the routine of hard work, necessary for group survival and self-actualization in southern Lau. It also provides an efficient and self-regulatory device which stimulates the production of food and craft articles, and extends each island's system of distribution to include a supercommunity, whose complementary resources form a natural trade area. We have noted that the institutions of the crop custodian and the

master fisherman, in environmental context, functioned traditionally to increase the size and nutritive value of the local
food supply, and operated toward its more equitable distribution. We now note that competitive ceremonial exchanges between villages on different islands provides an integrating link
in the production-distribution system, which unites the various
islands of the supercommunity into a balanced, interdependent
supersystem, whereby sectional limitations in natural resources
are transformed into assets, and each group, regardless of its
natural endowments, may fulfill its needs for a balanced nutrition pattern.

Some years ago the British officials outlawed large *solevus*
in Fiji. Rumor reports that they thought such a prohibition
would prevent waste of needed native energy and natural resources. Doubtless, in other parts of the Crown Colony where
food was more plentiful, there was a wastage of resources in
connection with the ceremonial exchanges. The effect of the
regulation in southern Lau, however, was not to abolish the
solevu, but rather to reduce the number of exchanges held.
This, in turn, tended to reduce the output of the main craft
goods, especially mats and barkcloth.

According to the local division of labor, the women make
mats and barkcloth, tend the babies, care for the houses, and,
as noted above, procure and prepare part of the daily food.
The men, besides fulfilling their food-producing and cooking
functions, hunt and fish with spears, care for the feast pigs,
build and sail seagoing canoes, trade between the islands, and
produce wooden bowls and sennit. This nice balance of labor
between the sexes in Lauan traditional society has been disturbed of late. With the diminution in the production of
women's crafts, related to the government's prohibition of the
solevu, the women are left with a considerable amount of time
on their hands. The men, on the other hand, tend to labor
more than ever, trying to compensate for the diminished food
supply. But since local garden lands are insufficient in quantity
and quality to meet the needs of the population on most islands,
food is scarcer than ever, regardless of the amount of energy

expended on gardening by native methods. We note also that although the supply of hardwoods, found only on the limestone islands, is limited, there seems to be little danger that the forests will be depleted by the small amount of timber cut for canoes and craft goods. Thus, instead of operating to prevent wastage of energy and resources, the official prohibition of the *solevu* actually tends to upset the nicely adjusted system of food production and distribution and the balanced sex division of labor in the Lauan supercommunity. It reduces the productivity of the women, increases the work of the men, and engenders a food shortage on several islands.

The entire production-distribution system described above, it should be noted, is basically accommodative and co-operative. It is effected with a minimum of coercion, since rewards in the form of prestige go automatically to the group (and incidentally also to the individual) who willingly gives or contributes most to the whole. Stinginess means loss of prestige. Within the system, however, rivalry between groups functions as a creative stimulus toward increased production of high-quality products and more equitable distribution of these within the supercommunity as a whole. Apparently competition operates as an indispensable ingredient contributing to the self-maintenance and self-regulation of the system. Moreover, institutionalized, competitive gift giving by groups prevents the development of an economic monopoly, which might otherwise emerge in an area where the distribution of local resources is limited and spotty, and where rank is highly developed. Not even the chiefs may keep their tribute. Rather, to prevent losing face, they must redistribute it to their followers. Thus, traditionally, the system operated against the accumulation of wealth in the hands of any one group or individual, and it ensured that the natural resources of the area would remain available to the whole supercommunity for immediate use, according to need.

Some Checks to Overpopulation

Finally, we note one more point which is vital to an understanding of the Lauan production-distribution supersystem. Despite its elegant adjustment to the natural setting and its basically self-perpetuating rhythm, this supersystem could not operate effectively unless it was counterbalanced by an effective sociopsychological device which tended to limit the size of the population in relation to the natural resources available through indigenous technology. Analyzing Lauan culture from this viewpoint, we find a complementary set of institutions which actually tend to function toward such an end.

For example, after the birth of a child the father moves out of the family dwelling and sleeps in the men's house of his clan. He is not allowed to have intercourse with his wife until the baby is weaned, a period of from nine months to two years. The efficacy of this custom is suggested by the fact that, by actual count of every individual in the supercommunity, siblings in southern Lau are almost without exception at least eighteen months apart. Thus, the institution of the men's house, correlated with certain tabus, functions as an effective mechanism for birth spacing and population control and as a means of protecting maternal and infant health.

Ritual continence was formerly practiced in Lau on many occasions. Several methods of abortion were used, mainly by unmarried mothers. In Fulanga, old people who had outlived their usefulness, according to native standards, were formerly abandoned on a small island in the lagoon. Where chieftainship was highly developed, those who broke tabus concerning the nobility were clubbed to death. Raiding between rival villages, in the course of which men, women, and children were killed, was not infrequent in the area, and those who were captured, regardless of age or sex, were likely to be consumed by the victors.

These are some Lauan practices which, together with accidents, hurricanes, disease, and a rate of infant and maternal mortality which was doubtless rather high, tended to limit the size of the population in relation to the available natural resources. Although in historic times Fijian population totals were greatly reduced, especially by the ravages of diseases introduced by the white man, the low point was reached around 1911. Thereafter, the trend has been slowly upward. The population of southern Lau gained 155 per 1,000 between 1921 and 1935 (for details, see Thompson, 1940a, p. 137). In 1933, the population of the supercommunity under discussion was about 1,500.

Conclusion

On the basis of these findings, certain significant generalizations may now be formulated.

We noted that in our isolated island supercommunity a unique and balanced biotic system developed over a very long period of time, in the absence of any large land animals. The advent of man, which occurred relatively late in the biotic developmental sequence, meant not only the intrusion of Homo sapiens and the first large land animal; other species of fauna and flora, and certain artifacts and skills, were also brought by man as part of his cultural equipment. More important perhaps, the event augmented the fundamental ecological processes, already operating in the area, with human cultural processes. In a relatively short time there emerged, on the basis of the fundamental island biotics, a new community supersystem which involved plants, animals, and human groups in a mutually interdependent and balanced web of life. Whereas previously each island had formed an independent natural community, the new ecocultural arrangement, including man, extended over several islands and tended to relate a number of heretofore disparate communities.

Certain ecologically significant institutions which developed in this island supercommunity have been analyzed, namely, various aspects of the production-distribution system in relation to population controls. The system's foundation in the self-selected, balanced daily diet of the household group was noted. The findings suggest that, although certain of the activities of the human community may be harmful to the whole arrangement, it has tended to organize and integrate its habits of feeling, thought, and behavior systematically with the world of nature in such a way as to play a basically positive, emotionally satisfying, and logical role in the multidimensional process of attaining, and maintaining, a healthy balanced supersystem.

The findings also suggest that the major economic institutions of the Lauan social system are basically accommodative and cooperative, with competitive attitudes and arrangements serving as an essential dynamic in the development of a high standard of production and a high degree of creativity toward the healthy self-maintenance of the supersystem.

We have noted that, according to ecological theory, isolated natural communities tend in time, by processes of mutual aid and symbiosis, accommodation and competition, to develop a homeostatic, ecological organization wherein the various species of flora and fauna attain a mutually advantageous arrangement in transaction with the geophysical environment. Ordinarily, we think of the process mainly in terms of plants and animals, on one hand, and geological structure, climate, soil, water supply, and other features of the physical environment, on the other. However, analysis, in a broad, multidiscipline frame, of the available data from this remote, relatively isolated supercommunity (where geological and ecological processes have proceeded for millenniums relatively undisturbed and where, until recently, cultural processes have operated for centuries with little interference from without) suggests that all life is involved in a self-regulating web of relationships. Human groups are involved as well as the lower animals and plants. Seen as a whole, it appears that the natural supercommunity includes the total organic population—plants, animals, and human beings—in a complex transactive relationship.

The analysis indicates, however, that the structure and dynamics of this supersystem emerge only if processes whose time span is relatively long are taken into account. But such long-phase processes have tended to escape the attention of social scientists studying man for many reasons, including the limitations of certain fashionable frames of reference; a predilection for observing only short-phase processes; the propensity to concentrate on one dimension of the nature or culture process, and even on one limited aspect of that one dimension; and the tradition of working independently rather than as part of a multidiscipline, cooperative team.

The data suggest further that, once a functional, balanced, ecocultural supersystem becomes firmly established and built into the symbol system, the attitudes, and the habits of the human community, the supersystem tends to endure as long as the human group is not wiped out or removed from its natural setting. The data also suggest that such a supersystem is the living core of relationships which the human community, consciously or unconsciously, tries in multiple ways to perpetuate.

Thus, an understanding of this core relationship pattern may be expected to throw light on the problem of so-called "cultural resistance"; that is, a community's acceptance or rejection of certain external patterns of belief, thought, and behavior. For example, in Lau the natives have tended, regardless of the penalties involved, to reject foreign patterns of feeling, thought, and behavior which interfere with, or break down, their basic ecocultural structures. It would seem that, to the extent the Lauans have been unsuccessful in their resistance to harmful interference with their basic communal life processes, the intentional or forced introduction of nonfunctional patterns, or the prohibition of functional ones, has tended to throw the community's supersystem off balance. This has operated directly against the well-being of its components, including the human group. The implications that these findings have for the problem of prediction of group behavior are manifold.

Finally, the findings point up the practical significance of a multidiscipline, ecocultural approach in clinical anthropology.

They suggest that understanding a community's long-term supersystem, in environmental context, is basic to the formulation of adequate norms or standards for the advancement of community welfare and for the development of community-oriented government administration (see Thompson, 1949c). Accordingly, the significant problem regarding the improvement of community welfare and the conservation of community resources does not emerge simply as a series of questions: How may human health and social institutions be improved? How may topsoil be saved? Or watersheds and forest land protected? Or organic species preserved from extinction? Despite the importance of each of these aspects, the significant problem in community development emerges as that of using and adapting local beliefs, attitudes, habits, and institutions, supplemented where necessary by appropriate new ones, to the end that human groups themselves, through natural ecocultural processes, may foster the development and maintenance of a balanced, healthy supercommunity, including plants and animals, as well as human beings, in environmental setting.

Chapter 8

The Key to Community Organization

The case study of Lau, an isolated, ongoing island community, based on systematic field work by investigators from several disciplines, suggests that our generally accepted principles of community organization are in need of revision. As empirical evidence on the basis of meticulous field work accumulates, perceptive students of the community are tending to agree with H. Godwin (see Clark, 1952, p. 9) who states: "There is no break in kind between the relationships of the great eco-systems of plant and animal communities, and those which include fewer or more human beings. . . . Since . . . the human agents remain animal in nature, sustain themselves within communities, and subsist on biological materials, they are no less part of the eco-system than were their ancestors."

Dynamics of Community Organization

As might be expected, there is evidence of a timely trend among biologists toward reconsideration of the dynamics of community organization. Marston Bates (1950, p. 108) states:

We have got into the habit of looking at the organic world as a mass of struggling, competing organisms, each trying to best the other for its place in the sun. But this competition, this "struggle," is a superficial thing, superimposed on an essential mutual dependence. The basic theme in nature is cooperation rather than competition—a cooperation that has become so all-pervasive, so completely integrated, that it is difficult to untwine and follow out the separate strands.

The same authority, as noted in Chapter 6, has pointed out the absence of ecological dominance in tropical biotic communities. This point takes on special significance when we bear in mind that a tropical climate seems to have been the normal climate during most of geological time (Axelrod, 1959, p. 203). Even in communities where the human species is present, man may not be dominant, as for example, among the forest Indians of Brazil (Bates, 1952, pp. 209–210), or among the cave-dwelling hunters of the Upper Paleolithic period. Obviously, dominance may no longer be accepted as a *universal* principle of natural community organization. Rather the presence of dominance among species in a community may be regarded appropriately as evidence of the existence of special conditions. The relevant question for scientific investigation along these lines becomes: Under what special conditions (degree and kind of stress) does ecological dominance develop in natural biotic communities and also in human communities?

A similar trend toward reconsideration of the dynamics of community organization may be observed among anthropologists. Note that the number who take their cue from biology, especially functional and applied ecology, is still quite limited. When this is done, as in the present position however, several working concepts emerge which may prove fruitful to students of both lower animal communities and human communities. The concept of homeostasis, which has been discussed and illustrated, is one. It is not generally realized that the physiologist Walter B. Cannon (1932, p. 24), who first defined the concept, was also, I believe, the first to suggest its possible usefulness as a conceptual tool for the study of human societies (Cannon, 1932, pp. 287–306).

Mutual Aid, Basic Organizing Principle

The concept of cooperation or mutual aid as the basic organizing principle of the isolated, ongoing ecological community seems to be another working concept that the field anthropologist is in a unique position to clarify and sharpen as a basic principle of community organization.

The principle of cooperation or mutual aid is frequently called the "reciprocity principle." But obviously, we are referring not so much to a reciprocal process as to a correlative process. The term *reciprocity* refers technically to the exchange of identical values, while the term *correlativity* refers to the exchange of equivalent but not identical values. This distinction may seem to be an unimportant one, especially to peoples of Western common-sense tradition, but it is crucial to the emergence of a fruitful working hypothesis of community organization.

The ecocultural supercommunity, according to the present viewpoint, takes a central position as the key unit of research in a unified science of mankind. It is the smallest unit of observation wherein all factor sets relevant to most of man's basic social problems are present. Precise terminology in field ecology and field anthropology will not only facilitate accurate, on-the-spot observing and reporting, but also lay the groundwork for more effective interdisciplinary cooperation and more heuristic hypothesis formulation.

Let us take time now to discuss some points about the principle of correlativity which seem to be relevant to our understanding of the structure of community organization.

Intraspecies Self-help

The principle of species self-help within the order of nature apparently has been known to Homo sapiens and applied to the problems of group living throughout most of man's history; it is also applicable to most other species of the animal kingdom (Allee et al., 1949, pp. 397ff.). As biologists have frequently observed, cooperation and mutual self-help appear to be the rule *within* the species (for a different view, see Darwin, 1859, pp. 6off.), whereas competition and the "struggle for existence," when it occurs, are most marked *between* species.

Even when marked combat occurs between individuals within a species, it rarely is carried to the point of lethality or mortality, according to Alfred Emerson (see *Proceedings,* 1954, p. 233). He cites the case of the male rhinoceros beetle's use of his horns: "The only function of the horns . . . seems to be in male combat over the female. . . . The horns are used to tip over the [opponent] . . . so that he lands on his back and cannot turn over readily. [The device] . . . functions very well to eliminate the competitive male in terms of mating with the female, but it does not kill [him]. . . ."

On the other hand, competition and combat between species are often deadly. Warfare among ants is between species, not within a species, for example. The parasitic cuckoo nestling, by means of adaptive devices such as a hollow back and aggressive behavior, shoves itself under the foster parent of another species and pushes its rival, the foster sibling, out of the nest and thus actually kills him. Emerson (see *Proceedings,* 1954, p. 234) explains these evolutionary developments as follows:

The competition between species, the drastic elimination of the competitor, is very often to species' advantage in survival, while the drastic elimination within the species, where they also have cooperative relationships in terms of group systems, is not to the advantage of the organism. There seems to be an evolution of dominant behavior and physiological and mechanical pattern involved in this competitive system.

Evidently there is no conspicuous prototype in nature for man's propensity toward intraspecies combat. According to Turney-High (1949, p. 244), "Many people think that the universal state of all persons below literate levels has been one of war. This hardly squares with the facts." War does not appear in any systematic or large-scale fashion among hunting peoples. It appeared only after man had begun to cultivate the land and settle permanently on it (Montagu, 1941, p. 351). Indeed, the evidence suggests that organized warfare is but a recent development in man's long history, resulting from the activities of men under stress living in highly civilized groups.

On the other hand, the presence of a principle of group correlativity and self-help in primitive communities has been observed by most field anthropologists. We have already noted a manifestation of it in the Lau Islands (Chap. 7). Malinowski's field experience in Melanesia led him to posit reciprocity and mutuality as basic principles of human society (Hogbin, 1934, pp. xxxiiiff.). Montagu (1952) has come to similar conclusions (see also Lowie, 1935, p. 15).

That modern Western man has lost sight of this mutual self-help principle, which seems to be a basic ingredient of the folk wisdom of the ages, should not blind us to its presence elsewhere in the contemporary world and throughout the history of the race. There are signs that, with the aid of science, the principle may reemerge in the form of a new universal ethic, sponsored by the community of nations in the world-wide struggle with the complex problems of our time. Growing acceptance of the principle of cultural autonomy and its incorporation into codes of international justice, noted in Chapter 3, may be one of these signs.

The Struggle-for-existence Hypothesis

It will be recalled that Darwin recognized the cooperative principle as basic to organic life. He analyzed the "struggle for existence" merely as one factor in interspecies adjustment and evolution. But he (1871, pp. 471ff.) also felt that the struggle might be explained by the principle of cooperation. It was his followers who emphasized the struggle or competitive principle, almost to the exclusion of the cooperative principle. On the other hand, Kropotkin (1902) led the effort to point up the importance of the cooperative principle as a primary factor in social life and evolution.

Nevertheless, many biologists, ecologists, sociologists, and anthropologists with a mechanistic approach have stressed the competitive aspects of group adjustment in biotic communities. For example, Julian Steward (1955, p. 32) states: "Underlying biological ecology is a relentless and raw struggle for existence both within and between species—a competition which is ultimately determined by the genetic potentials for adaptation and survival in particular biotic-environmental situations. Biological cooperation, such as in many forms of symbiosis, is strictly auxiliary to survival of the species."

Interpretations of ecological organization patterns, similar to that described above, have been used by many social scientists to interpret human behavior. For example, an interpretation of the organization pattern of fowl, the so-called "peck order" of chickens, has been applied frequently to human society.

The Peck-order Model

T. Echjelderup-Ebbe, a Norwegian psychologist, first formulated the peck order among chickens. He observed that, in any flock, one hen usually dominated the others. She could peck any other hen without being pecked back. Second in the order came a hen which pecked all but the top hen, and the rest were arranged in a descending hierarchy. It ended with an unfortunate hen which was pecked by all and could peck none. Cocks do not normally peck hens. They have their own peck order. Hence a breeding flock usually has two such hierarchies, one for the females and one for the males.

So far as I am aware, most experiments regarding the social order of chickens have been conducted in chicken yards or coops under conditions more or less like a laboratory. There is some question whether the peck order exists, exactly as defined by laboratory experimentalists, in natural biotic communities unless they are under a certain degree of stress. My own observations* of flocks of fowl living on small farms where they are completely free to move about, rather than in the artificial confines of a pen or barnyard, suggest that the organizational pattern of each flock or community of fowl follows a definite

* The following observations were made on a farm at Cherokee, North Carolina, over a period of three months in the summer of 1950 and on a farm at Whittier, North Carolina, over a similar period in the summer of 1951.

social order, within self-imposed geographic boundaries, wherein the strongest cock takes responsibility for the entire group. By means of a well-defined set of activity patterns, including sound signals, he warns the whole community of approaching danger, seeks out safe roosting places, sees that the immature birds, as well as the hens, go safely to roost at twilight, helps brooding females to find desirable nesting places, and prevents cocks belonging to neighboring flocks from trespassing on the territory he recognizes as his own domain. I do not doubt that, when necessary, the leader maintains order in his community by means of pecking all and sundry. He certainly establishes and maintains by this means his sex rights to the hens, and he defends his patriarchal role against encroachment by maturing cockerels as long as possible. But he does not monopolize the hens by keeping the cockerels from them. Rather, it is between cockerels that the fiercest struggles occur, and these are mainly over sex rights to the maturing pullets. Such conflicts are characterized not merely by pecking, but also and mainly by clawing, as seen in a cockfight.

It is hardly appropriate to call such a communal organization a peck order, even though pecking doubtless establishes some of the hierarchies within it, as within the mature hen suborder and within the rooster-cockerel suborder. It is, I submit, predominantly a functional organization wherein the leadership pattern operates in the direction of the maintenance, self-preservation, reproduction, and long-run self-actualization of the community of fowl within a definitely bounded territory, across the generations.

On the other hand, a sort of peck order apparently does tend to emerge in a flock of fowl confined in close artificial communities, such as barnyards, chicken coops, and commercial hatcheries, where the balance of nature, including the ratio between the sexes and the age groups, is disturbed. Such conditions, it should be noted, are similar to those in a concentration camp, which also tends to produce stress types of order usually absent in communities which are not under such extreme pressures. A great deal of work has been done since

World War II on the sociology of concentration camps and prisons (see, e.g., Bettelheim, 1943). These findings may well be studied for the leads they suggest concerning the emergence of so-called "peck orders" among human beings under certain types and degrees of stress (see A. H. Leighton, 1945, pp. 328ff., for example).

According to the present thesis, peck-order types of social organization, if found to be characteristic of a human group or community, might appropriately be considered evidence of a high degree of stress. They would be interpreted as symptomatic of overstrain, a reaction to emergency conditions, and if set in such a postulated frame of reference, I believe that their investigation and explanatory description would be facilitated.

The hypothetical existence of a peck order among chickens and of an analogous trend toward dominance in human society, however, has been used to document a whole school of sociological thought. This is a good example of what is judged here to be the fallacious interpretation and use of biological data by social scientists. Obviously, if chickens are to be studied for purposes of generalizing on their behavior patterns, they should be investigated within the flock as a whole in natural habitat conditions, and not merely under the stress of rigidly bounded laboratories simulating highly commercialized conditions which upset the normal sex ratio and other factors.

This point has, of course, been made in other contexts by many investigators of animal behavior. For example, Yerkes and Yerkes (1929, p. 112) state: "Captivity may well transform the attitude, physical condition, and activities of a subject, especially by reason of malnutrition, disease, social deprivation, timidity, dependence on human care, and imitation of human acts."

I have dwelt on the peck-order and dominance hypothesis in order to highlight the significance of the patterns or models of sociocultural process which social scientists entertain in relation to their research operations and the generalizations they are likely to come up with. If a researcher is looking for a peck order, he will very likely find one, especially if he confines his observations to contrived, unnatural laboratories. What matters from the present viewpoint is not merely the observed facts, important though they are, but as Max Weber (Shils and Finch, 1949, p. 81) suggested, the researcher's *frame of reference* whereby he relates the observed facts and gives them meaning.

In this connection, a false analogy is especially regrettable in the interests of scientific accuracy. But actually, such an analogy is not merely regrettable but downright vicious as soon as an attempt is made to apply the research findings to the solution of practical social problems. For example, belief in the universality of a peck-order trend in human groups may be used to reinforce authoritarian rule among dependency or colonial peoples.

Intraspecies Competition

Our analysis of the peck-order hypothesis in an appropriate frame in which whole communities of fowl in natural settings were observed (and not merely small groups, such as hens, cocks, and cockerels, without reference to the over-all community organization) suggests that when the appropriate unit of research—namely, the community supersystem—is selected, observed as a unit, and analyzed, it is characterized by correlativity as the basic self-organizing principle in the direction of the self-actualization of the group through generations. Within this mutuality system, rivalry between subsystems seems to function as a necessary ingredient to establish and maintain a healthy degree of tension.

In the investigation of an island community in Fiji, it will be recalled, a similar conclusion was reached. When the appropriate unit of research in relation to the problem was selected and observed as a whole unit—namely, fifteen islands which formed a relatively independent native trade area—it appeared that correlativity functioned as the basic organizing principle of the community's ecocultural supersystem. Intrasystem competition, on the other hand, added zest to life and an appropriate degree of tension to the life-action process. Similar situations have been found in other societies. For instance, according to Mead (1937, p. 460), "The Maori strove to outdo one another in bird snaring and were honored publicly for their success, but the cooperative distribution of the catch was not affected; the rivalry served only to create higher productivity. The Dakota vied with one another for prestige, but the very terms in which they vied were a general giveaway to all and sundry."

In many island communities, particularly those of Oceania including Lau, anthropologists have found that the population traditionally organizes itself into two sides or moieties which compete against each other for social prestige. This competitive situation exists within an over-all system of correlativity and mutual aid whereby the local natural resources, including human resources, tend to be organized into a balanced, self-perpetuating supersystem, oriented toward long-run resources conservation and group self-perpetuation within the limits of the effective environment. As part of this conservation supersystem may be found cultural mechanisms which, taken as a whole, function in a way to limit the size of the population within a certain range suited to resources as related to native technology.

Our world of today may be viewed as an island type of community, gradually shrinking in size because of improved communication and transportation, the spread of industrialism, etc. The tendency, mentioned above, for the population of an island to line up in two rival groups seems now to be manifesting itself on a global scale. But, far from containing themselves within an over-all correlativity system, these two power groups are contained each within its own mutual-aid system, so that we are witnessing the phenomenon of two competing mutual-aid systems on a world-wide scale. Can anthropology teach us any lessons relevant to the present world situation?

In her study of cooperation and competition among primitive peoples, Mead (1937, p. 463) found that in general the "richest" peoples were organized in a basically cooperative manner. It should be added that she considered the more adequate food supply of these cooperative societies to be an end result of their form of social organization, rather than a factor determining their greater cooperativeness.

Parallel Findings by Psychologists

It may be relevant to note that the findings of ecologists and anthropologists regarding the primacy of the correlativity principle in the development of order in the community are paralleled in a rather striking way by the findings of depth psychologists and psychiatrists regarding the development of personality organization in the individual. Over and over again we read of the individual's need for a positive emotional environment, for warmth, affection, and love from birth to death and even from the moment of conception (see, e.g., Menninger, 1942). Indeed, as we are all aware, positive affect is so crucial to the child that without it, even with the best of physical care, an orphan may sicken and die.

But the need for positive affect is not a one-way process. Just as the infant needs the mother's loving care, so does the mother need the infant's need of, and response to, mothering. The relationship is a correlative one, an exchange of equivalent but not identical values.

According to findings of the culture-personality school of anthropologists, as well as those of child-development specialists, if this correlative relationship is reinforced by the institutions, symbolic systems, attitudes, and values of the community's culture, a positive basis exists for the development of a balanced, healthy personality by the child. On the other hand, if this relationship is not reinforced culturally, as, e.g., in Alor (DuBois, 1944) and the Marquesas Islands (Kardiner, 1939), we get the seeds of personality impoverishment in the individual and a tendency toward retardation of the maturation process.

Similarly in mating and marriage, according to the personality-development theory, male needs female in a positive way, and vice versa. In the long run, the success of the mating relationship depends on a correlatively structured arrangement whereby each sex may reinforce the other in a mutually satisfying manner in the pursuit of mutual, biologically based goals. When the structures of the culture reinforce this type of arrangement between the mated or married pair within the ecocultural supersystem as a whole, a basis exists for balanced, healthy personality maturation by both sexes through mutual self-actualization and fulfillment.

On the other hand, if the culture does not create a favorable environment for a healthy, mutually fulfilling relationship between the sexes, and indeed if it does not successfully steer each sex toward its culturally defined role and functions, we find a large number of individuals failing to attain full maturity in their respective adult sex roles. It took modern psychoanalytic psychology and psychiatry to make clear to modern man that his sex is his second most important attribute; his species, Homo sapiens, is the first. It is a commentary on the alienation of modern human beings from their biological roots that such a truism would not be part of the innate equipment of every individual. But failure to accept one's sex in this fundamental way, with all its biological, social, and cultural implications, is one of the widespread difficulties of modern man and modern woman which leads directly to neurosis (for a different view, see La Pierre, 1959).

It is the genius of modern psychotherapy that its practitioners have, by trial and error clinical experience, discovered the therapeutic role which an environment, positively structured emotionally, plays in the human individual's self-development, self-organization, and self-integration of his own personality. Stated in terms of the therapeutic situation in modern Western civilization, where the developing individual is frequently almost overwhelmed by threats against his need for inner integrity, we may say that "under certain conditions, involving primarily complete absence of any threat to the self-structure, experiences which are inconsistent with it may be perceived, and examined, and the structure of self revised to assimilate and include such experiences" (Rogers, 1951, p. 517).

Conclusion

Cooperation and mutual aid in the form of correlativity are postulated in the present thesis as basic to the emergence of homeostatic balance in the ecocultural supercommunity. From this point of view, rivalry, expressed with or without open combat, is viewed as a secondary principle. Both correlativity and rivalry are postulated as ingredients necessary to the attainment of community homeostasis. The means of such attainment are discussed in Chapter 10.

It should now be clear that this working hypothesis is very different from, but comparable to, the peck-order and dominance hypothesis discussed above. Both hypotheses attempt to explain sociocultural process: the one, by a process of competitive jockeying for power attributed to animal origins and prototypes; the other, by postulating an innate directive and correlativity tendency in organic group life manifest at the level of community organization, both in natural biotic communities where the human species is absent and in communities where the species is present.

From the present viewpoint, competition is postulated as one of several principles usually operating in the community organization process, but not necessarily the dominant one. In climax communities the chief function of competition seems to be to foster a healthy tonicity in the group and to maintain high group morale. As suggested by the Lau Island case, without a healthy rivalry between certain traditional groups, life would indeed be dull in many isolated communities. Competition, it seems, has a very important, indeed an indispensable, function in community life. Only when it becomes the dominant principle does it tend to exercise a fundamentally disorganizing function, rather than one that is organizing and integrating from the viewpoint of long-range, balanced community development.

Chapter 9

Polynesian Goal-management Systems*

One advantage to the working model of the supercommunity presented in Chapter 8 is that it not only sanctions, but also facilitates, the investigation of cultural goals and the means whereby they may be implemented. It guides the investigator of cultural phenomena toward a concern with ends as well as means. Indeed, within this frame, community organization may be investigated fruitfully as though it were not only a system, but a goal-management system.

Polynesia, a Natural Laboratory

Casting about for a laboratory to illuminate the point, I have selected Polynesia, especially certain isolated, native Polynesian supercommunities. Polynesia refers to the culture area

---

* In this chapter, an attempt is made to apply Jurgen Ruesch's outline, indicating matters relevant to systems of relationship (Grinker, 1956, p. 303), and to community supersystems. Ruesch presented his outline at the fourth Unity Seminar of the Michael Reese Hospital's Psychosomatic and Psychiatric Research and Training Center (*Proceedings*, 1953, pp. 3-5). This chapter is a modification of a paper, "Goal-seeking and Goal-changing Devices in Polynesian Culture," which I presented at the sixth Unity Seminar (*Proceedings*, 1954, pp. 197-255). Use of the term "goal-management system" in this context was suggested by Dr. Berton H. Kaplan.

of "many islands" in the Pacific Ocean Basin, mainly east of the submerged continental shelf. It forms a triangle, whose points are marked by Hawaii to the north, Easter Island to the east, and New Zealand to the south. The Lau Islands lie on the western margin of the area.

Polynesia encompasses a large ocean mass, 5,000 miles from north to south and 4,000 miles from west to east (Buck, 1945, p. 5). The island groups are generally widely separated from one another and from continental areas. For example, Hawaii, one of the most isolated archipelagos in the world, is some 900 nautical miles from the nearest islands to the south, about 2,060 nautical miles from the Society Islands whence probably came the first settlers, some 2,000 miles from the mainland to the east with no intervening land, and about 4,000 miles from the Philippines and from Japan to the west and northwest with the Micronesian islands in between.

With the exception of marginal southern areas, such as New Zealand which is cool and temperate, Polynesia has a tropical maritime climate. The several districts within an island, the several islands, and the many archipelagos, however, differ considerably regarding (1) local soil types (whether volcanic, coral, or raised coral limestone); (2) climate and exposure to the cooling trade winds; (3) coral-reef construction and lagoon formation; (4) natural resources related to the above; and (5) degree of geographic isolation.

Ecologists postulate that, before the coming of the first human inhabitants, there had developed through millenniums in each island, and indeed in each island group, a unique homeostatic type of biotic system. In these prehistoric biotic systems a large percentage of the species of flora and fauna were endemic, that is, unique to the specific locale and found nowhere else. The biotic systems of many of the islands have been well described by zoologists, botanists, and other natural historians. In Hawaii, for example, about 92 per cent of 1,897 species and varieties of native plants were endemic (this figure excludes those plants which arrived through the agency of man); 80 to 90 per cent of the 110 species of native birds, and

95 per cent of the 3,800 species of native insects were endemic (Bryan, 1960). These systems were so delicately balanced that the introduction of even one alien species might engender immense damage.

Polynesian Culture

It is generally agreed that Polynesia was one of the last large areas of the world to be settled by man. The first settlers were Polynesians, generally believed to have stemmed from Indonesia and southeast Asia (Bryan, pp. 11ff.). At the time of their rediscovery by Europeans, most Polynesian archipelagos sufficiently fertile to maintain human group life were populated.

Each island group had its own version of a basic Polynesian culture (Buck, 1945, pp. 13ff.). This was distinguished by certain preferred patterns of organization: for example, the tendency to relate people to one another and to the world of nature in terms of a genealogical model. Indeed, the Polynesians tended to categorize and systematize the flux of perceived sensory images genealogically. This tendency is illustrated in the well-known Polynesian pattern of relating blood-kin lineages with emphasis on the first-born of the first-born, wherein the *mana* (i.e., impersonal supernatural or superhuman power) of the kin group was believed to concentrate. The Hawaiian Kumulipo chant (Beckwith, 1951) well expresses how genealogical relationships tended to be extended outward to include all aspects of the known world believed to be important to the lifeway. The tendency to deify chiefly ancestors was part of this pattern.

Apparently related to the above was the tendency to divide natural resources into two categories—products of the land and products of the sea—and to slice up each island so that the basic social units of the settlers would have access to the several types of resources from each category. A sky-earth dichotomy was usually also present in their thinking: the male personified the principles of light, generation, sacredness, and power—Polynesian characteristics of the sky; the female represented the principles of darkness, the material, the profane, and the contaminating—Polynesian characteristics of the earth (Buck, 1939, p. 48).

It appears that the Polynesian concepts of *mana* and *tabu* tended to tie together social system and world view; the tabu of the sacred (i.e., *mana*-full) was the core of the Polynesian law or morality system, and the "most sacred" in many Polynesian cultures was conceived as the first-born of the first-born as vehicle of lineage power. This feedback tie-up between social system and world view tended to be further elaborated by the characteristically Polynesian concept of a hierarchical pantheon of superhuman beings—creation and generational deities, departmental gods, and guardian spirits of families and individuals (Buck, 1939, pp. 7ff.).

The Exploration Complex

Now, the question arises: How were these far-flung islands discovered and settled by a Stone Age people lacking metals, the wheel, and the compass—a people who had only wooden sailing canoes for transportation? An inquiry into the operations of discovery and settlement starts our quest for clear examples of goal-management cultural devices in isolated and definitely bounded communities. We search first for cultural mechanisms which may be viewed as goal-seeking devices (Grinker, 1956, p. 303).

According to reconstructions by Buck (1938), aboriginal exploration of Polynesia was accomplished by island hopping. There were two main types of settlement groups: planned and accidental. If the settlement group was bent on exploration for new lands, owing perhaps to population pressure in the homeland, to quarrels over women, or to irksome demands for chiefly tribute, preparations were systematic. A fleet was made up of several large double canoes, with pandanus-mat sails and deep paddles. A double canoe measured some 60 to 80 feet long and carried from 60 to 100 persons. Each canoe was stocked with the necessities for a long voyage, such as drinking coconuts (the green, immature fruit), cooked taro or preserved breadfruit, and the dried fruit of the pandanus. Fishing gear for deep-sea fishing en route and for use in the new land, seed plants, animals, such as pigs, dogs, and domestic fowl, and various kinds of implements were also taken. Each canoe carried a skipper or chief (who probably was a family head but not the first-born son of his generation, since the first-born, as highest in rank, would probably remain in the homeland) and the chief's household (which consisted of near relatives and retainers, including women, children, and various experts in technological and esoteric lore).

On the other hand, if the settlement group was a fishing expedition blown off its course, or a refugee group suddenly forced from its homelands by invaders, it would not have been so well equipped. Easter Island may have been settled in this accidental way. Apparently it was populated from the Marquesas (see Freeman, 1951, p. 51) where intervalley and interisland warfare, which forced the losers into exile, was common (Handy, 1923, pp. 123ff.).

The Polynesian navigators had expert knowledge of the stars by parallels of latitude. They were familiar with ocean currents, and especially with winds, waves, cloud formations, and seasonal variations. Judging from historic practices in the Tuamotus where this type of sailing was still in vogue twenty-five years ago, the explorers looked for land-nesting birds. They may even have been guided by the routes of migratory birds, such as the golden plover and the bristle-thighed curlew, which fly seasonally between Alaska, Hawaii, Tahiti, and other islands of Polynesia (Gatty, 1958, pp. 41ff.). They also watched the nostrils of their cargo pigs, which quivered in the direction of land as it was approached. Thus, in terms of present perspectives, the whole Polynesian exploration complex may be viewed as a goal-seeking cultural device. The immediate goal was the discovery of a new niche for settlement. The ultimate goal may be thought of as the biological survival of the migratory group and its long-range self-actualization in a relatively favorable environment (see Grinker, 1956, pp. 72ff.).

Settlement in the New Niche

When the immediate objective of finding a new niche for colonization had been realized, the settlers went about the subsequent goal of its exploration, subdivision, and settlement by using cultural concepts, principles, and tendencies, and also cultural skills and products, which they had brought with them. In due course, certain traditional culture traits, which may be considered part of the goal-seeking complex according to the present conceptual frame, were eliminated in a particular island group on account of climatic unsuitability, aridity, poor soil, etc. In temperate New Zealand, for example, many useful plants which were part of the Polynesian tropical horticulture complex were eliminated. For example, coconut, breadfruit, banana, the paper mulberry from which barkcloth was made (the Polynesians did not have the loom), and pandanus from which mats and baskets were made, did not thrive in New Zealand and were not incorporated into the Maori culture system.

Thus, to compensate for cultural losses and to enrich life in the new environment, there was the discovery, by a process of trial and error, of new useful resources and the invention of new devices to substitute for the old. In New Zealand finger weaving of local flax into cloth displaced barkcloth manufacture. Fern root, local birds, and other local foods were substituted for the pig and fowl which were absent (see Beaglehole, 1944, p. 44; Buck, 1949, pp. 61ff.).

Other goal-seeking cultural devices, for example, ocean-voyage navigation, were lost through disuse, as in Hawaii, or lack of suitable materials, as in Easter Island. With these changes went an alteration in social organization and a shift in cultural emphasis. For example, a change in the function of technological and esoteric specialists was reflected in a change in their respective roles and rank in the social system and a corresponding adjustment in the hierarchical arrangement of ranked gods in the Polynesian pantheon.

Tentative Generalizations regarding Goal-seeking Devices

Reviewing the evidence regarding land discovery and settlement in Polynesia in the context of our theoretical working model, are we justified in formulating any tentative generalizations about goal-seeking cultural devices? At this point, I shall restate and expand a working hypothesis suggested by the Lau study as follows: Settlement of new lands and subsequent local cultural development were guided by the community's need of survival and well-being in the new niche according to its traditionally preferred culture patterns, as well as by the need to change or elaborate those patterns and also to develop new ones in order to transact with the new environment effectively without irreparable damage to natural resources and critical disorganization of the local biotic system. It would seem that, since the group planned to live permanently in the new niche, irreversible changes involving destruction of indispensable resources or irreparable breakdown in homeostatic balance could be tolerated only within the limits of group survival. It may be noted in passing that this point, which is discussed later, suggests one standard for the measurement of "success" in relation to a culture system.

To explore the complex of devices whereby this goal was apparently sought, let us next consider, as a case study, certain aspects of traditional Hawaiian culture.

Hawaii as a Case Study

There was an estimated population of 300,000 in Hawaii on its rediscovery in 1778; the islands were populated almost to the limit of available natural resources within the potentialities of the existing Stone Age technology (Lind, 1938, p. 32). We find skillful farming with laboriously laid-out and irrigated *taro* fields and the use of natural fertilizers such as wild growth

(Handy, 1940, pp. 4–5) and young *hau* branches to restore to the fields the favor of Laka, the goddess of wild wood and growth (see Handy et al., 1933, p. 114). The Hawaiians believed that wild growth contained the vital essences of the land and therefore should never be wasted, a rationalization that we may appropriately consider from the viewpoint of its obvious effectiveness in the conservation of natural resources. We find skillful, carefully regulated, and highly ritualized deep-sea fishing (see Handy et al., pp. 101ff.). It may be noted that coral reefs are poorly developed in Hawaii, a geological fact which favored the development of deep-sea fishing under certain conditions.

As in Lau, there was a pie-shaped land-use division of the islands, which were mainly of volcanic formation (Handy et al., pp. 79ff.). This division of the land gave the inhabitants of each district access to the resources of sea, shore, valley, and mountain forest. In each island or each district within a large island the high chief owned all the land. High production was ensured by his *konohikis* (tribute collectors), one of whose functions was to see that each parcel was used to advantage (Malo, 1903, p. 84). There were also police officers to enforce the tabus which upheld the whole system. Among the tabus was one which forbade washing or bathing except at the mouth of a stream (Handy et al., 1933, p. 82).

As in Lau so also in old Hawaii, the land-use system allowed and indeed fostered a balanced, nutritious diet for every family group. In this case, however, the diet was based on fish and *poi* (baked and pounded *taro* root mixed with water), supplemented by greens, seaweed, yams, etc., and seasoned with sea salt. Males and high-ranking persons were favored by the food-distribution system. Choice foods, such as pork, sea turtle, coconuts, bananas, and certain fish, were tabu to women (Malo, 1903, p. 52). Nevertheless, it appears that most of the people, whether male or female, high or low, had access to a fairly adequate diet. Most food was steamed in the earth oven. A small amount, however, was boiled by dropping hot stones into liquid food in a wooden bowl. Both methods of cooking were unusually efficient in conserving the nutriments.

A good deal of the native technology in Hawaii was highly specialized and ritualized; native herb doctors were trained from fifteen to twenty years by apprenticeship to use about three hundred plants for medical purposes (see Handy et al., 1933, p. 253). Many of these have been found to be of considerable alleviative value (see Handy et al., pp. 256ff.). For instance, *pia,* a fine powder, was used for hemorrhage of the stomach and bowel and for dysentery. *Uhaloa,* a substance producing an effect similar to that produced by aspirin, was used for colds and sore throat, and *kava* (the pounded root of the *Piper methysticum,* strained and mixed with water) was used to induce sleep and dry up secretions (Handy et al., p. 259). The art of massage was carried to a high point and the doctor was also skilled in the practice of controlling pain through suggestion and his own personal influence. Several methods of population control were employed, including abortion and infanticide (Lind, 1938, p. 38).

The significance of this complex of practices and beliefs to native health and welfare seems to be underscored by the effect of their breakdown on native mortality, health, and welfare after European contact. The rapid near extinction of the Hawaiians is well known. Of course their lack of immunity to such imported diseases as measles, smallpox, influenza, and tuberculosis played a major role in this process, but it would appear that the sudden breakdown of the rigidly upheld, authoritarian type of social system had a paralyzing effect on the people and tended to interfere with restorative processes which have operated in the direction of establishing a new, favorable relationship between man and nature in many other Pacific islands (Roberts, 1927, pp. 102ff.).

The importance of the native system of land use and population control within the context of the Hawaiian culture system viewed as a whole was highlighted by the effect of the Great Mahele of 1848 (Handy et al., 1933, p. 78). At that time King Kamehameha III, under pressure from land-hungry Europeans, tried to transfer one-third of the land from his own ownership to the people to be held in fee simple. Only 28,000 acres out of a million made available were actually allotted to the people (Lind, 1938, p. 40), owing mainly to their lack of comprehension of the new land-ownership and arrangement concepts. Soon many of these acres found their way into the foreign plantation-ownership system while the landless natives, most of whom had also lost their fishing rights, died off rapidly. The Great Mahele of Hawaii recalls a parallel case, the Indian Allotment Act of 1887 which was enacted under similar pressures and had similar effects on the lands and welfare of the Indians of the United States (Collier, 1947, pp. 226–227).

Enough has probably been said to suggest that embedded in the native culture system of old Hawaii was a complex of what might be called goal-seeking devices—a complex of institutions, practices, and beliefs—which, viewed in long-range ecocultural context, tended to foster and conserve the natural resources (including the *human* resources) so that the prehistoric native settlers might continue to inhabit their niche without exhausting the essentials to their lifeway.

Effectiveness of Goal-seeking Devices

The discussion so far suggests that if we assume the biological survival of a human community and its long-run self-actualization (including maintenance, reproduction, and completion of the life cycle through the ongoing generations) to be its ultimate aims, we may fruitfully analyze its culture within the effective environmental context in terms of built-in goal-seeking devices, keyed to immediate goals which tend to be oriented in the direction of these ultimate aims.

We have noted the establishment and development of certain native communities in Polynesia from this point of view. The question may also be raised: How effective from the viewpoint of our postulated targets was the goal-seeking complex of each community?

The evidence suggests that, in general, the goal-seeking cultural mechanisms of the several Polynesian communities tended to be highly effective in terms of the ultimate aims postulated above. Not only were the far-flung islands found and settled under extremely hazardous conditions, but Polynesian culture was so planted, cultivated, and pruned as to develop into a number of thriving local variations in several insular environments.

On the basis of the evidence, we may tentatively postulate that the goal-seeking cultural devices of a community *tend* to be predominantly life-promoting and life-conserving within the local environmental context. Once a favorable (or optimal) homeostasis has been developed and institutionalized, we may expect the devices to exert a conservative influence on the culture system in the direction of perpetuating the *status quo* (*Proceedings*, 1954, pp. 252–255).

Goal-changing Devices

But what happens to these communities in situations of stress, such as changes in physical environment or strong pressures by alien cultural groups? I refer especially to a degree and kind of stress in a culture-contact situation which tends to throw the traditional homeostatic system off balance and to necessitate the development of a radically different one if a new one is to evolve at all.

Some aspects of this question have already been mentioned. To explore it systematically, I suggest that an analysis of the several culturally related communities in terms of what might be called their *goal-changing* cultural devices may be useful. By goal-changing devices in this context, I refer to mechanisms, built into a community's culture system, which tend to facilitate change in the direction of the creation and implementation of new immediate goals. If the new goals are functional they will, according to the proposed tentative hypothesis, be keyed to the same ultimate ends as the old ones, namely the survival and long-range self-realization of the community in the local setting.

For example, we might consider the structure of Polynesian society in general, with its emphasis on rank and on specialists in the arts of the priesthood, war, medicine, poetry, and technology, as a goal-changing cultural mechanism. The sacred character and high development of craftsmanship and the prestige attached to fine workmanship, as well as the hierarchy of departmental gods, apparently tended to foster both a thorough exploration of, and experimentation with, the environment and the invention of new forms within the limits of the Stone Age technology.

Following this lead, we note that the cultures of the several Polynesian communities varied in the number and effectiveness of their built-in, goal-changing mechanisms. Where many changes and adaptations were required by the new environment, as in New Zealand, there was an emphasis on sociological and cultural devices which may be termed goal-changing. For example, among the Maori, the chief and his priestly advisor merely suggested important undertakings such as raids; the tribesmen in assembly made decisions and devised means to implement them. The land, whereof there was no scarcity, was the property of the whole tribe and was merely vested in the chiefs. It was worked cooperatively by units composed of several household groups. All chiefs, priests, and heads of families had free speech, and chiefly power was checked by public opinion (Beaglehole, 1944, p. 66).

This arrangement contrasts with that of Hawaii, sketched above, where the sacred and well-nigh all-powerful high chiefs outrightly owned and controlled all the land and resources. It should be emphasized that the flexible Maori system of checks and balances held up more effectively under white pressures than did the near-absolute, authoritarian Hawaiian system (Sutherland, 1940). When under Euro-American influences the Hawaiian islands were united under a single high chief, the traditional control system quickly broke down, and the native culture disintegrated.

Some Generalizations Emerging from the Data

The foregoing "leads" should, of course, be checked for validation with case studies drawn from the cultures of other Polynesian communities. Meanwhile they reinforce the above-stated tentative working hypothesis: In prehistoric Polynesia, the direction of development of local cultures tended toward the establishment and maintenance of a dynamic homeostatic arrangement whereby human communities might survive and continue to live indefinitely in harmony with nature.

These leads also suggest that, whereas a community's goal-seeking cultural devices tend to be effective and conservative in terms of its ultimate aims, its goal-changing cultural devices vary in number and effectiveness. This variability may be expressed in terms of degree of flexibility, or rigidity, of the several culture structures in response to stress. An analysis of phenomena of culture change, in terms of this working model, may be expected to throw light on culture-contact processes. Such an analysis may be especially useful regarding the elucidation of practical problems in human welfare on a group- or community-wide scale. Examples may be found in community development, public health, natural-resources conservation, mental hygiene, and so on.

Furthermore, the present model affords a new way of phrasing problems in applied anthropology. No longer need the applied anthropologist concern himself primarily or exclusively with problems in human engineering—that is, with the manipulation of human relations toward arbitrary goals superimposed from without the cultural group through the exigencies of military or administrative bureaucracy, industrial management, or the proselyting urge of religious, economic, or cultural missionaries. Rather, he may concern himself primarily with the problem of formulating scientifically based relevant goals, in appropriate cultural and environmental context; he may further help to key the immediate goals of the community to such formulated goals in relation to ultimate

aims which are built into the culture of the community itself
and into the psychosomatic organism of each individual member.

Culture as a Goal-management System

Therefore I suggest that from the foregoing analysis
emerges a useful working model of the community, which may
be distinguished from other models because it treats a specific
human culture as a goal-management system. The system
postulated is of the dynamic, open type, wherein each component of the over-all whole is related functionally to every other
component, not primarily in a mechanistic fashion, but according to the basic system of relationships which distinguishes organisms. More specifically, the postulated system
reflects to some extent an ecological model. That is, it reflects
an orderly arrangement of species, including fauna, flora, and
microorganisms, which tends to move, by means of the built-in
self-directive and self-regulative processes of its component
organic species, in the direction of a homeostatic optimum
or open steady state in the context of the effective geophysical
base and climatic conditions.

As postulated, a human community, viewed in long-range
historical and geographic perspective, *tends* under favorable
conditions to develop its culture in the direction of certain
ultimate aims, namely, the self-preservation and self-actualization of the community according to its own inner nature (i.e.,
human nature; see Maslow, 1954, pp. 335ff.) and potentialities,
in transaction with a specific local natural environment. This
environment is viewed as a biotic supersystem which tends to
evolve through time and in relative isolation in the direction of
a homeostatic type of balance with the several species of its
ecological web of life including Homo sapiens, on the one hand,
and its geophysical base, on the other.

Thus, the findings help to document the suggestion of
Alfred Emerson (1954) and others concerning the usefulness
of the biological concept of homeostasis in increasing our multi-

discipline understanding of human-community transactions with one another and with the effective environment, and hence our understanding of human behavior.

It is assumed that the underlying culture process of the community tends to be self-activative, self-directive, and self-restorative. The dynamics of this process may be perceived most clearly by investigating the cultures of definitely bounded human communities which have been relatively isolated over a long time span, preferably millenniums. Hence, isolated island communities, such as those of Polynesia, offer good natural laboratories for experimentation with this approach. Once having isolated and described this basic culture process in a favorable laboratory, however, we may test it elsewhere and appraise its general nature.

According to the present model, movement in the direction of the community's ultimate aims, cited above, is effected by means of the directive and purposive cultural activities of its human members, according to behavior patterns which may be viewed as part of goal-seeking and goal-changing mechanisms, oriented toward immediate goals which are keyed to the ultimate aims. Both ultimate aims and immediate goals may be partly or wholly implicit in the community's culture system. They may be largely unconscious among its members (Herrick, 1956, p. 19). Probably only a small percentage of the directive activities of human organisms are conscious, intentional, purposive or "logical." They seem to be predominately physiological, sensing, aesthetic, or intuitive (Maslow, 1957, pp. 93ff.). Evidently, the dynamics of a culture are of a logico-aesthetic nature. They tend in the long run to integrate the culture structurally, both aesthetically and logically, by means of the symbol system (see Grinker, 1956, pp. 73, 76). This point will be elaborated in the next chapter.

A patent advantage to the present approach is the flexible, multidimensional nature of the conceptual working model which seems to offer a potential niche for all variables or variable sets considered relevant to the problem under investigation. For example, the model affords a flexible instrument for the scientific investigation of the core value system of a community and for the eventual systematic comparison of comparable value systems in relation to explicitly formulated basic assumptions, working hypotheses, and working concepts (see Thompson, 1950b; 1951b). Thus, it may contribute to the objectivity of investigations into human values. Granted the research premises, the investigator may proceed with his observations, analyses, comparisons, and generalizations regarding human value systems in a scientifically acceptable manner.

The model appears to be useful for an inquiry into the culture systems not only of small, isolated, nonindustrialized communities such as those of native Polynesia, but also of modern national groups with complexly organized, composite cultures. But the more complex the community, the less isolated it is, and the more subjected it may be to pressures from alien cultural groups, the more difficult will be the research needed to fulfill the demands of this model (Thompson, 1960).

Conclusion

In sum, the findings suggest that a systems approach in terms of the categories outlined above, combined with the homeostasis concept, may prove effective in the analysis and comparison of the cultures of human communities from the simplest to the most complex. A major advantage of this model may well be its usefulness as a multidiscipline tool toward the development of a unified theory of human behavior and a unified science of mankind.

The greatest value of the model, however, may be its potential as an instrument for the investigation of long-range problems in the applied field, especially medical and psychiatric anthropology, medical sociology, public health, nutrition, resources conservation, population control, education, etc. As noted above, thoughtful students of applied social science are concerned today with the concept of the healthy or therapeutic community. How may a healthy community be defined from the long-range, psychotherapeutic viewpoint? What scientifically based norms or indexes of community health may be set up within this context? How may a given local community work toward the goal of self-improvement of its over-all health?

The present approach sanctions and facilitates the investigation of cultural goals as well as their implementation. It is concerned with ends as well as means. In short, it suggests a methodological lead for converting into scientific problems these crucial practical questions relating to human welfare, with their widely ramifying implications regarding human values and how they may be geared to new and newly recognized human needs and global perspectives. And it holds the hope of their elucidation, and perhaps their eventual solution, by means of the methods of science.

Chapter 10

The Supreme Creation of the Community*

As a working hypothesis, it is here postulated that the advent of Homo sapiens in an isolated biotic supercommunity, and the presence of this new species, does not engender a change in kind regarding the community's most basic dynamics. The isolated community, including man, still tends to evolve in the direction of the ultimate biological goal of all organisms, namely, self-actualization. Ordinarily, through processes of mutual aid, correlativity, symbiosis, accommodation, and competition, each component species in the total arrangement continues actively to maneuver itself into a favorable niche in the life-action supersystem, although, of course, this tendency may be thwarted or diverted under certain conditions to be discussed later. Thus, every human community is confronted with the very real problem of group survival and self-actualization as part and parcel of a complex, biophysical event in a particular geographic context. It represents one species, Homo sapiens, of a number of species transacting with one another and with the geophysical base of the locality, and forming with them an ecocultural supercommunity. The stakes are high. The human group must solve this practical problem or perish.

* The following chapter, in modified form, appeared with permission of McGraw-Hill Book Company, Inc., and the author in the *Publication of the School of Design*, North Carolina State College, 1961, 10, No. 2.

The Human Tendency to Symbolize

Now, great ecosystems which include Homo sapiens as a component differ from those which do not, primarily because of a tendency, unique in the human species, to create and maintain an intermediary system, namely a culture, whereby the human community organizes itself symbolically for more effective pursuit of its ultimate, self-actualization goal. Thus, the presence of man brings a new dimension to a biotic community, viewed as a complex, ongoing event in space-time.

As is well known, only the human species tends to express itself in terms of symbols. By a symbol, we mean "a thing the value or meaning of which is bestowed upon it by those who use it . . . the meaning, or value, of a symbol is in no instance derived from or determined by properties intrinsic in its physical form. . . . The meanings of symbols are derived from and determined by the organisms who use them" (L. A. White, 1949, p. 25). Many animal species communicate by means of signals and signs, but only human beings use symbols as well as signs. Indeed, it is generally agreed that this is the one human trait that distinguishes man from his animal relatives (see, e.g., Howells, 1954, pp. 50–53).

While the human attribute of symbolizing is truly responsible for man's greatness, it should not be forgotten that from it also stem the supremely human problems. M. K. Opler (1956, p. 53) states man's symbolizing dilemma when he writes:

The fact that humans can learn to use systems of symbols and be conditioned to them swells the world of meaning far beyond the mere mammalian level of learning by signs, signals and concrete perceptions. But it promotes the less objectified universe, the gross irrationalities, and, with equal bestowal of the gifts of art, language, science and philosophy, the nonrational use and interpretation of environment, the uncommunicative nonsense, the scourge of war or blight of insanity.

Of man's symbolic systems, language is, of course, the one Westerners most easily comprehend and highly value.

Anthropologists equate the emergence of humanness in the world with the development by members of the genus Homo of a means of communicating with one another through language.

It should be emphasized, however, that according to the present view, the symbolic culture system is not merely man's method of adapting himself more effectively to his environment (Cassirer, 1944, pp. 42–43). As Clyde Kluckhohn (see Romano, 1949, pp. 99ff.) has pointed out, in regard to culture the concept of adaptation is not enough (see also Overstreet, 1949, p. 73; Sinnott, 1955, Ch. 4; Spencer, 1954, pp. 221–248). "We require a way of thinking," states Kluckhohn (Romano, 1949, p. 113), "which takes account of the pull of expectancies as well as the push of tensions, which recognizes that growth and creativity come as much or more from instability as from stability, which emphasizes culturally created values as well as the immediately observable external environment."

The Nature of Human Culture

Accordingly, a human culture is here viewed as a symbolic system originally created, maintained, re-created, and passed on through the generations by a given human community participating as one component of an isolated, biotic super-system, itself transacting as part of a complex, geophysical event. The culture of a local community is that community's distinctively human way of transacting with its total effective environment, and the culture's uniqueness is a function of the unique transactive situation of the human group owing to (1) its own unique genetic and psychosomatic composition; (2) its unique, ongoing culture history; (2) the unique and changing biotic supercommunity, wherein the human community constitutes one component; and (4) the unique and changing geophysical base of the supercommunity, including its changing climate.

Anthropologists agree that the local community is the cradle of race. Every isolated human community, to the extent that it represents a genetic isolate through time, provides a natural laboratory for the evolution of local variations, that is, subspecies or races of Homo sapiens.

I emphasize here that, according to the present thesis, the local community is also the cradle of culture. For a hundred thousand years, the human population of the world lived in small isolated communities under ideal conditions for the creation of unique cultures. Throughout the millenniums of the Paleolithic, Mesolithic, and Neolithic eras, mankind lived in small rural communities, between which communication was limited. Even though towns developed in the Bronze Age, these were relatively small, and the majority of the world's peoples remained rural. Today, despite the urbanization of life in a few great industrial centers, the great bulk of the world's hundreds of millions still live in rural communities. Thus, as noted above, from the viewpoint of an emerging science of mankind, the small, relatively isolated, and deeply rooted local community affords the ideal basic unit of research, the natural laboratory for unifying our knowledge about mankind. It affords a setting for fusing the two main divisions of anthropology, physical and cultural.

A culture cannot be described in an explanatory fashion, according to the present view, except as part of a more inclusive, ongoing supersystem embracing human community, natural ecological community, and relevant geophysical and cosmic events. Especially is a culture incomprehensible apart from the human group which expresses and fosters it. As has been noted, the ethnographer observes the overt behavior of the human community and the products of behavior. It is the human beings themselves—transacting with one another and with the animals, plants, microorganisms, and the elements (earth, sea, sky, sun, moon, and stars, etc.) of their world—it is these that the ethnographer apprehends and/or himself transacts with, as well as the products of human cultural activities (houses, canoes, utensils, baskets, pottery, etc.). From observations and other types of information regarding native behavior, the ethnographer abstracts the culture (Kluckhohn and Kelly, 1945, pp. 79ff.).

Culture as a Dynamic System

It should not be forgotten that the community's culture is in no way a static phenomenon. Human beings, and indeed all organisms, as already noted, are activity systems. Activity is their primary shared characteristic. A nonactive organism is a sick or a dead organism. Thus, the healthy human group—the healthy community—reactivates or creates, or re-creates, its culture every day, every month, every year. Each newborn individual, each new generation reactivates and re-creates it—expresses it anew in an idiosyncratic way. Indeed, the individual is so culture-bound—he builds his culture to such an extent into his muscle and nerve system, even his very bony structure— that he cannot act at all except in terms of it.

A certain spontaneity is a basic ingredient of this culture-reactivation process, which is a component of human community living. It is the type of spontaneity which Moreno has called "activation of the cultural conserve" (Moreno and Moreno, 1944). Just as a dramatic actor reactivates his role, performance after performance, and infuses into the word, repeated by rote, something of himself which is new and idiosyncratic, so each individual in the community infuses into even the most stereotyped cultural role his idiosyncratic version of the culture expressed at his particular point of reference.

It is just at this point—namely, the necessary reactivation of the culture conserve by each individual in the group—that we grasp the inevitability of culture change. Every minute, every day, every year, the culture of a community is being reworked, re-created, rerendered by its component members.

For many years we assumed that certain Stone Age cultures, such as that of the Australian aborigines, had persisted with little or no change from the Paleolithic era to recent times, somewhat after the fashion of archaeological relics. We now know, on the basis of empirical field evidence, that even apparently static cultures are constantly undergoing subtle changes within the framework of the ecocultural supersystem. Elkin (1950) discovered, for example, that the complex Australian eight-class kinship system has spread to new areas within the northwest aborigine territory in recent years.

A relevant question regarding culture reactivation and change is: How is a culture constantly reactivated and reworked? By what processes is it constantly remade?

Observations on Culture Process

According to the present view, human beings tend not only to symbolize, but they tend to symbolize together in communities, and they tend thus to create and re-create complex symbolic systems. But that is not all. They tend to create complex symbolic systems which are moving in the direction of a balanced and harmonious relationship of all the parts with one another and with the effective environmental setting.

A trend toward culture change in the direction of greater harmony of the parts in relation to one another, and to the whole, has long been recognized by some social scientists, but an appropriate explanation of such a trend has tended to elude us. At the turn of the century, Sumner (1906, p. 116) referred to "the strain of the mores toward consistency." In the twenties Edward Sapir (1924, pp. 410, 411, 412) called attention to the fact that some cultures are balanced and harmonious; he called these "genuine" cultures:

The genuine culture is not of necessity either high or low; it is merely inherently harmonious, balanced, self-satisfactory. It is the expression of a richly varied and yet somehow unified and consistent attitude toward life, an attitude which sees the significance of any one element of civilization in its relation to all others. . . . The major activities of the individual must directly satisfy his own creative and emotional impulses, must always be something more than means to an end. . . . A culture that does not build itself out of the central interests and desires of its bearers, that works from general ends to the individual, is an external culture. . . . The genuine culture is internal, it works from the individual to ends.

Redfield wrote in 1941 (pp. 133, 141): "Culture is an organization of conventional understandings manifest in act and artifact. . . . Left undisturbed, the trend of change in the conventional understandings in terms of which a community persists is in the direction of greater harmony and interdependence of parts." He viewed this as related to what he called a "regenerative tendency in culture"; namely, a tendency to reorganize itself by the elimination of "incompatibles" (Redfield, 1941, pp. 146–147).

Also, Sir Julian Huxley (1957, p. 54) discussed what he called "noetic integrators" of culture—"symbolic or conceptual constructions which serve to interpret large fields of reality, to transform experience into attitude and unify factual knowledge in belief." But he noted, significantly, that the general role of such integrators had never been adequately explored.

Malinowski (1944, p. 40) made a suggestion about the nature of the harmonizing process when he stated: "Each culture owes its completeness and self-sufficiency to the fact that it satisfies the whole range of basic, instrumental and integrative needs." The danger in this approach, as Dorothy Lee (1948) has suggested, is that we shall slip into the implicit assumption of stimulus-response, behavioristic psychology that "culture is a group of patterned means for the satisfaction of a list of human needs." Culture is not, according to Lee (1948, p. 390), "a response to the total needs of a society; but rather a system which stems from and expresses . . . the basic values of the society."

It will be recalled that a major finding of the IEPA project was the discovery, by means of empirical field observations and tests, of the key role played by the core value set of variables in the community supersystem. A related finding was that, contrary to the initial assumption of the research staff, the group personality set of variables was not related directly to the social structure set, but rather was related to it indirectly by means of the core value set of variables.

Moving out from an emphasis on core values as subtly and indirectly related to human needs and potentials, I view this tendency toward balance and harmony in a culture system as an expression of the universal dynamics of natural super-community process at the symbolic, cultural level. We have postulated that biotic community process is an expression of the universal directiveness of organic activities at the community level, and from its operation, in geographic isolation and through historic time, emerges the climax or optimum supercommunity in total relevant context. Symbolic community process is here viewed as an expression of the universal directiveness of organic activities at the human level, and from its operation in isolation and through time emerges the balanced and harmonious culture—in other words, the genuine culture.

Symbolic Integration: More Aesthetic than Logical

The sensing process, whereby the human community seeks to harmonize its cultural system transactively with the effective environment, is here viewed as both directive, that is, unconscious, and purposive, that is, conscious. It is both intuitive or aesthetic, and consciously thought out or logical, from the viewpoint of the native conceptual frame. Sorokin (1937, pp. 18ff.) describes the process, but in calling it "logico-meaningful" he explicitly labels only one aspect of it, namely, the logical or conscious aspect. "The logico-meaningful method," he states (1937, p. 24), "has its own common denominator of all relevant phenomena: it is the identity (or similarity) of central meaning, idea, or mental bias that permeates all logically related fragments." However, just as unconscious processes are far more significant than conscious ones in individual creative mentation (Wertheimer, 1945), so the sensing or aesthetic aspect of culture process is obviously far more significant than the logical aspect, according to the present view.*

* My position on this point frequently has been misunderstood as stressing only ideological or logical factors, for example, by Kroeber and Kluckhohn (1952, p. 180) and by Gayton (1946, p. 252).

The tendency in our culture to overemphasize rational and logical processes, when pinpointing man's humanness, is familiar to us all. Pareto (1935, Vol. 4, p. 1,443) long ago warned us against the overemphasis of logical reasoning in studying the organization of the social system. To clarify the point, we quote Sir Julian Huxley (1957, p. 49):

Thinkers discussing the distinctive characters of man have usually laid their main or sole emphasis on intellectual or rational thought, and on language as its vehicle. This is precisely because they were thinkers, not artists, or practical men, or religious mystics, and therefore tended to over-value their own methods of coping with reality and ordering experience. . . . But this intellectual and linguistic over-emphasis is dangerous. It readily degenerates into logic-chopping or mere verbalism. What is more serious, it takes no account of man's emotional and aesthetic capacities, exalts reason and logical analysis at the expense of intuition and imagination, and neglects the important role of arts and skills, rituals and religious experiences in social life and cultural evolution.

I view this logico-aesthetic integrating dynamic as a distinctively human variation of the directiveness which characterizes all organic activities, according to the new biology. It doubtless operates in human groups, mainly at the unconscious level, but also, to varying degrees, at the conscious, or what is here called purposive, level.

As a good example of the process operating mainly on the conscious or purposive level, let us recall a Papago Indian custom, described in Chapter 4. All the adult males of the village met nightly in the village roundhouse to discuss the real problems facing the village community. The Papago village council was an institutionalized goal-seeking and goal-changing mechanism whereby the community regularly, consciously, and purposively faced its practical problems. Little by little, night by night, it changed its culture, voluntarily and by mutual consent, in the direction of symbolic integration both within itself and as part of the great Sonoran ecosystem wherein the tribe had lived successfully for millenniums.

According to the present hypothesis, this inherent, symbol-integrating dynamic is responsible for the tendency of communities, when disturbed under certain kinds and degrees of stress, to develop their culture systems in the direction of a new, more adequate, inner-structural balance in transaction with the effective environment. This tendency is here postulated as a human cultural universal.

Of course, the symbol-integrating process is unlikely to actualize a wholly rational cultural gestalt. It should be emphasized that such a gestalt is not suggested here as the ultimate goal. I merely postulate, as a working tool for research purposes, that the community does tend to move toward immediate cultural goals which are related to the ultimate biological ends of the supercommunity, as defined above. This trend is constantly subjected, of course, to stresses, both from without the community and from within it, so that the group's movement toward its goals is uneven, halting, irregular, and to some extent at least, blocked and compensatory. Indeed, such interference with cultural process is so common as to be viewed appropriately as part of the process itself. But to understand it, we should study compensatory processes, both at the cultural level and at the level of individual personality.

This universal culture process—namely, logico-aesthetic integration—operating at either the unconscious or the conscious level in a human community which expresses and recreates a unique culture system, seems to be responsible for the inference that in every highly integrated culture, the basic structures (or subsystems) of the culture tend to express a common systems model. For example, as already noted, the ecological subsystem, the social subsystem, the psychic subsystem, the somatic subsystem, and the symbolic subsystem—all tend to express the same paradigm.

In other words, regarding genuine cultures, as I attempted to demonstrate in *Culture in Crisis* (1950b) where I used the Hopi culture system as a case study, this working model characterizes both the culture system as a whole and its several subsystems, including their manifestations in overt behavior patterns and in personality structures.

Personality as Self-structured

To dovetail with this working model of culture, our working concept of personality should be one which stresses the innate directiveness of the human organism at the psychic level. In this connection, we note that psychiatrists have quite a lot to say about how the personality is structured. Excellent depth-psychology tests and diagnostic techniques, such as the Rorschach Ink Blot Test, have been devised to probe, describe, and analyze personality structure. But generalizations about the personality-structuring process are frequently formulated in the passive voice.

Positive formulations about how the personality structure emerges within the individual are usually lacking in the literature or are confined to a general description of child-training patterns and experiences as correlated with personality structure, viewed at any one point along the individual's life-development cycle (see, e.g., Greenacre, 1952). Even if one is an extreme cultural or psychic determinist, however, such correlations do not *explain* the emergence of the kind of idiosyncratic organized whole which characterizes even the most psychotic personality, according to findings from depth-psychology tests.

Why, for example, are we (at least most of us) able to predict the behavior of our friends and relatives with sufficient accuracy to use our predictions as a basis for functional conduct? Why, given sufficient training and experience, are psychiatrists able to predict with a high degree of accuracy how a given individual, subject to a sufficient stress, will break down—whether he will become a frank manic-depressive, express the symptoms of schizophrenia, develop anxiety neurosis, etc.?

Actually, directive and self-actualizing tendencies in organic life are currently recognized explicitly by many psychiatrists and psychologists. In the words of Carl Rogers (1951, p. 487), "The organism has one basic tendency and striving—to actualize, maintain, and enhance the experiencing organism." The words used, he states (1951, p. 488), "are an attempt to describe the observed directional force in organic life—a force which has been regarded as basic by many scientists."

In developing a working concept of personality as a group phenomenon, I emphasize the individual's positive tendency in the direction of integrating and building his privately sensed and experienced real world into his own developing psychosomatic organism—into his *neuromuscular system* as well as into his psychic system—toward self-actualization and fulfillment of ultimate biological goals. Each human organism tends to do this, according to the present position, by means of a logico-aesthetic dynamic which is part of his essentially human, biological equipment. This symbolizing dynamic is postulated as the basic process whereby the human organism tries to integrate his experience, as he senses, perceives, and lives through it, in the direction of personality wholeness and balance in transaction with his immediate environment—internal and external, human and nonhuman—as he senses, perceives, and experiences that environment. That this tendency, here postulated as universal, is frequently thwarted and diverted from its goals, we have already noted. Our human heritage may of course be a blessing or a curse, depending on the use we make of it. These points will be discussed further in Chapter 13.

Thus, according to the present position, the need for and the striving for inner integrity are inherent in human nature. Personality integrity is postulated as a positive goal toward which the individual tends to strive as a function of his built-in, logico-aesthetic, personality-integrating dynamic, which is a manifestation at the human level of the universal directiveness of organic life. Neurosis and mental illness spring from the thwarting of this innate tendency and from its diversion into inappropriate channels.

Conclusion

To sum up, a human culture, according to the present working model, is conceived as a symbolic system created, structured, maintained, and re-created by a human community as its idiosyncratically human way of organizing itself, as part of a complex biophysical event in space-time, for the active pursuit of its ultimate goals. A culture is an expression, at the human level, of the goal-seeking tendency inherent in all organic life.

Just as movement in the development of the individual is primary, according to the new neurology, so action in the creation, organization, and re-creation of a culture is primary, according to the new anthropology. Gone with the wind are all varieties of extreme determinism in space and time characteristic of the nineteenth century—economic, psychological, somatological, cultural, or ideological determinism. All yield, according to the new formulation, to the primacy of life-action events in space-time. It is the total-action event in space-time that is conceived as self-transcending.

Gone also is the dogma that events are effected by agents (conceived as simply located in space)—that is, agents which are extrinsic to ongoing, life-action process. Nature is a unity. The scientist's working frame, according to this view, must be extended to encompass what was formerly regarded as "event," on one hand, and "activating agent," on the other.

This position may perhaps be clarified by recalling the anthropologist's frame in his natural laboratory. As noted in our study of Lauan culture, the ethnographer observes the behavior of the ethnic community which constitutes his significant unit of research, and he abstracts therefrom its unique symbolic system, including its postulated natural and supernatural power sources (see Firth, 1936, Ch. 7).

For example, in his *Magic, Science and Religion,* Malinowski (1955) reported on Melanesian religion as a function of the unique culture of Melanesia, in the setting of the Pacific island world. In terms of traditional Melanesian common sense, the natives conceive power immanent in nature as superhuman and impersonal. As noted in our discussion of the Lauan culture, this superhuman, impersonal power immanent in nature is called *mana.* According to this rationale, when *mana* is embodied in a person, or in an animal, plant, weapon, or stone, it can activate that person or object. Hence, the Melanesian believes the person or object to be empowered through the agency of *mana*. Thus, an action-event, wherein a *mana*-full object plays a primary role, is perceived by the native as *mana*-motivated.

To the anthropologist, however, who attempts to encompass both the culture-creating Oceanic community and its conceptual product, *mana*, in a single frame of reference, neither postulated power source, *mana*, nor event postulated as empowered are perceived in sequential cause-and-effect relationship. Rather, the concept of *mana* is apprehended as functionally related to certain kinds of events in native community life —the unusual, the unpredictable, the fortuitous, the strange— according to the natives' efforts to understand and explain their world (Malinowski, 1955, Chs. 1 and 2).

Note that, as in some new perspectives on reality, so in this view of an emerging science of mankind, the familiar Western concept of linear causality in space and time (see Lee, 1950) gives place to that of function in space-time. Note also that, as Bentley (1926, p. v) pointed out long ago, "Space as a barrier, sharply dividing one man from another and demanding that we make a separate unit out of each, has lost its hurtful power. Time has secured a unifying, not a splitting, meaning. Man's society, without the unworkable structures of mass and space and time and hopelessly concrete individuals, can now begin to be interpreted."

Inherent in the present working conception of culture is the notion that every distinctive culture system is created or re-created, maintained, transformed, and transmitted by a group of human organisms who are ultimately biologically oriented. In other words, in the deepest sense, it is a biologically based theory of culture, not a sociological or ideological one. Thus, it holds that human communities tend naturally, although not always successfully, to use their built-in, culture-creating, and culture-maintaining propensities to move actively in the direction of goals of maintenance, reproduction, and self-actualization of the group, as part of a total communal event. It should be emphasized, however, that this tendency is frequently thwarted by influences, emanating from without and within the community, which are experienced as stressful by the human group. The fact that this tendency, as postulated, may thus be obscured or even counteracted by events, however, should not blind us to its universality. The biological goals are keyed to the long-range aims of completing the life cycle of individual components, generation after generation, and thus actualizing and perpetuating the life of the community.

Purpose, unconscious or conscious, is intrinsic to the organization of a community and of its human components, viewed as psychosomatic organisms (see La Barre, 1954, p. 1). And purpose guides both the patterns of perception of the human components and their total patterns of action (Cantril, 1950, pp. 6off.; Murphy, 1947, pp. 345ff., 364ff.).

Chapter 11

Symbolic Integration in Hopi Culture*

To illustrate the point with which we ended Chapter 10, let us consider the traditional culture of the Hopi Indians.

Hopi culture is a genuine culture in Sapir's sense. It fits the environment supremely. But a close study of its subtle aspects suggests that it is characterized by a high degree of the distinctively *human* type of integration discussed above; logical and aesthetic unity reinforces its wholeness at both the conceptual and the sensory levels. Hence, the Hopi community affords an excellent natural laboratory for investigating the symbolic process of cultural integration. In this chapter, we shall consider this logico-aesthetic integrating process as manifested especially in the key unverbalized premises and the explicit concepts which form the covert core of Hopi traditional culture.

A tribe of less than five thousand Indians living in the

* This chapter is taken from my article, Logico-aesthetic Integration in Hopi Culture. *Amer. Anthropologist,* 1945, 47:540–553, reprinted here with permission from *Amer. Anthropologist.* I have described the method of analysis used in a paper currently in preparation (Thompson, in preparation, a). Conditions and social practices are based on field work done in 1942–1943. At the time, Hopi traditional culture was still functioning in somewhat modified form, in eleven out of thirteen villages.

heart of the Arizona desert, the Hopis have developed one of the most internally integrated cultures known to man. Relatively isolated for at least fifteen centuries, this small desert community, without the use of metal tools, succeeded in mastering almost overwhelming environmental odds and, with group survival at stake, built up a truly functional way of life. Arts and artifacts, institutions and customs, myth and ritual have been unified into a complex system, every essential part of which seems to contribute to, and to be conditioned by, the over-all whole. Indeed, as standard psychological tests indicate, even the personalities of Hopi individuals seem to have been sharpened and molded to a complementary pattern (Thompson and Joseph, 1944, pp. 129ff.).

A Nature-Man Cooperative

The Hopis apparently conceive the world as a complex, ordered system regulated by an inherent, logical principle. According to Hopi ideology, all phenomena relevant to Hopi life—including mankind, the animals and plants, the earth, sun, moon, and clouds, the ancestors and the spirits—are interdependent through an innate, dynamic law. By means of this law, the various orders and suborders of the universal scheme work together for the commonweal by exchanging values or services which are essentially equivalent but not identical. Man, the elements, the animals, the plants, and the supernatural powers interact in an orderly fashion, by means of a complex set of correlative interrelationships, for the good of all. Thus the Hopi cosmos is inherently harmonious and cooperative.

The Hopi classify all phenomena relevant to their lifeway according to principles which are similar to those whereon Western science is based. That is, they recognize various classes or species of animals, plants, men, etc. But they also have a system of cross classification, not recognized by Western science, which cuts through the pragmatically based, mutually exclusive orders and relates phenomena from the different classes or species into higher orders, which are believed to function as interdependent wholes in the cosmic scheme. Such a higher order, for example, may include a group of men related by kinship (namely, a clan), one or more species of animals, of birds, of plants, of supernatural beings, of elements, etc. It also may have other attributes, such as direction, color, sex, etc.

Such totemic units are grouped into still higher orders, composed of groups of clans (i.e., phratries) together with all the animal and plant species and other classes of phenomena associated with each component clan. These long-established, cross-classified, higher orders form the backbone of the system of interdependent relationships which structure a sort of super-society. The supersociety is believed to function as a universal nature-man cooperative organization which gives basic form to the universe.

In this supersystem each individual—human and non-human—has its place in relation to all the other effective phenomena, and each has a definite role in the cosmic order. The scheme does not operate mechanically, however, on account of the special role played by man. Whereas, according to implicit Hopi theory, the nonhuman universe is controlled automatically by the correlativity principle, man is a responsible agent who may or may not completely fulfill his function in it. The world of nature is more or less compelled to respond in certain ways to certain stimuli, but man has a margin of choice, and he also has the power to elicit response. Thus, in contrast to the nonhuman world, man can exercise a limited, but positive, measure of control over the universe.

Indeed, the Hopis believe not only that man can positively affect the functioning of the external world of nature to a limited extent, but that in the measure that he fails to do so, the harmonious functioning of the universe may be impaired. To the Hopis, the movements of the sun, the coming of rain, the growth of crops, the reproduction of animals and of human beings depend (to a certain extent at least) on man's correct, complete, and active participation in the fulfillment of the cosmic law.

Moreover, the law requires that, to be effective, man must participate in the universal scheme not only at the overt behavioral level—that is, by performing certain rites at prescribed intervals in certain ways—but he must participate also at the emotional and ideational levels—that is, by a concentration of his psychical energy on praying or willing. In the Hopi language, the word for "to pray" also means "to will." And an appreciation of the Hopi "pray-will" formulation, which has no equivalent in the English language, is crucial in understanding the Hopi culture and character. The individual's success in life, the welfare of the tribe, and to a certain extent, the smooth functioning of the whole cosmic order depend on man's carrying out the rules, in cooperation with his nonhuman partners, wholeheartedly and with an effort of the will.

Hopi unverbalized philosophy, therefore, seems to ascribe to man a purposive, creative role in the universe, a role which is dependent on the development of his volition. The universe is not conceived as a sort of machine at the mercy of mechanical law and blind chance. Nor is it viewed as a system of hostile, competitive forces struggling for existence. It is sensed as a harmonious, integrated system operating on the principle of immanent justice, and in it the key role is played by man's will.

Cosmic Fulfillment

To the Hopis, time is not cut up into segments which can be measured as an hour, a day, or a year can be measured. Rather it is sensed as a duration, wherein the law is being fulfilled. Time is a becoming-later-and-later in which existing phenomena develop or change from one phase to another, each according to its own intrinsic dynamic pattern. In the nature of each phenomenon that manifests itself as a whole entity is the power or energy of its own mode of fulfillment. Some phenomena, like plants, have a growth cycle; others change by means of repetitive or vibratory movements; others take form, diffuse, and vanish; still others, like the earth, develop by a series of metamorphoses (Whorf, 1941, p. 84). Thus there is great diversity in the modes of duration and fulfillment of various phenomena within the unity of cosmic law. And the present manifestation of each phenomenon is one phase of its development, which has been prepared by earlier phases and will be succeeded by later ones now in process of preparation, according to its characteristic inherent dynamics.

Against this ever-becoming-later background of the cosmos, the Hopi conception of history is the unfolding of Hopi destiny according to the law. This unfolding takes place in a sequence of phases. These phases are marked by legendary events, important to the tribe, such as the emergence of mankind from the underworld and the series of settlements along the clan migration routes from the place of emergence to the present site of the tribe.

The Ideal Society

Within this over-all cosmic scheme the Hopis conceive the ideal community as a sort of theocratic pueblo state which reflects, at the social level, the structure and dynamics of the universe. That is, the ideal community is also a unified dynamic whole composed of several parts and subparts, interrelated by a network of correlative obligations and responsibilities on whose fulfillment depends the mutual welfare of all. And each part and subpart of the community system consists not only of human orders and suborders, but also of other categories of phenomena, such as classes of animals, plants, natural elements, and supernatural beings, which may be thought of as intimately associated with, or partners to, the human orders, and which together with them form the nature-man supercommunity.

Moreover, social groups based on kinship—clans—are closely interrelated with social groups based on ritual ties—secret societies—through the equipoise of the female-centered clan system versus the male-centered ceremonial system. The chief priests of the major secret societies, who are also members of certain leading clans, form a "chief's talk" or council. This group is headed by the chief priest of the ranking society who, by virtue of his ceremonial position, is the pueblo chief responsible for the welfare of the pueblo. His main duty is to concentrate on and pray-will for the commonweal in accordance with the law, and he is protected from secular matters and revered as the leader or "father" of the pueblo.

Under this system the religious, judicial, political, social, and economic functions of the pueblo are merged and every part is interrelated and given significance in respect to the whole. Kinship and ceremonial groups are subtly equilibrated through mutual correlativity in a highly integrated and cohesive pueblo theocracy, which reflects the dynamic structure of the cosmos.

Reproduction in this organically conceived community is ideally by means of budding. As the Hopi matrilineal clan grows by adding daughter households to the mother unit, so the pueblo expands by the budding (see E. C. Parsons, 1939, p. 6) of daughter colonies from the original nucleus. Thus ideally, the community is able to segment and completely reconstitute itself.

It should be noted that the Hopis conceive the ideal society in terms of the autonomous pueblo unit, not the tribal unit. The Hopi tribe is not traditionally a formal political unit. It is merely an aggregation of historically autonomous pueblo states of common breed, language, and culture, united by kinship, ritual, economic, and geographic bonds and by a millennium-long tradition of common and similar experiences. Hopi social thought is centered, not on the tribe, but on the pueblo unit of mother and daughter villages.

The Ideal Man

As has been noted, to fulfill his key role in the universal scheme of things, man must actively participate in the law. This means full assumption of personal responsibility by the whole man—including mind, emotions, and body. To the

Hopis, as to modern psychiatrists, man is a complex psycho-physiological whole. Moreover, the Hopis believe that each individual is a responsible agent through the creative develop-ment of his will, and Hopi interest in the whole man centers in the psychophysiological development of the will. Man is a sculptor who can mold himself from within. This assumption seems to be the basic adjustive and generative postulate of their cosmogony.

Traditionally, the ideal man or woman is apparently the individual of maximum effectiveness in the fulfillment of the law. He or she operates at high intensity in his or her own particular place and role in the cosmic scheme. But since every Hopi's place and role is defined in terms of his obligations and responsibilities as a part of the ecocultural whole, the ideal man is envisaged not only within the framework of the cosmos, but also and always very specifically within the setting of the pueblo supercommunity.

A Hopi's ideal is to live, to the utmost of his powers, for the community as envisaged in Hopi terms—i.e., the pueblo unit composed of groups of human beings in association with their nonhuman partners, transacting correlatively in fulfill-ment of the law. And hence the one who approaches most nearly the ideal will be the individual who is most completely socialized (in Hopi terms).

The Hopis have set up a definite standard for the in-dividual, and this standard is expressed by the word *hopi*. The full connotation of the word and its significance in Hopi life seem to be difficult, if not impossible, for anyone who is not a Hopi himself to appreciate. Some of its implications may be grasped if it is realized that this word, which represents the ideal standard for the individual, is used also as a generic term for the whole tribe. Thus it expresses dramatically the concept of the complete identification of the individual and of the group with the ideal.

Whereas much of Hopi ideology is expressed only by impli-cation in the culture, Hopi tradition is explicit on this point.

The word *hopi* is usually translated as "peaceful, good, happy." But so far as can be determined, it also includes all those attributes which, to the Hopi, make up the balanced, law-fulfilling, psychophysiological whole which is man as he should be—that is, it connotes the ideal, dynamic totality at the level of the individual (and hence, of the community). Thus the *hopi* individual is: (1) strong (in the Hopi sense, i.e., he is psychically strong—self-controlled, intelligent, and wise—and he is physically strong); (2) poised (in the Hopi sense, i.e., he is balanced, free of anxiety, tranquil, "quiet of heart," and he concentrates on "good" thoughts); (3) law-abiding (responsible, actively cooperative, kind, and unselfish); (4) peaceful (nonaggressive, nonquarrelsome, modest); (5) protective (fertility-promoting and life-promoting and life-preserving, rather than injurious or destructive to life in any of its manifestations, including human beings, animals, or plants); and (6) free of illness. These are apparently the main positive qualities which make up the subtly balanced, unified (in Hopi terms, "one-hearted") personality which fulfills the law, and hence is good, happy, and healthy.

The Hopi ideal is highlighted in the personality of the village chief. As the human embodiment of the ideal, he is the most revered person in the pueblo. And his word, as the certification and interpretation of the law, is honored and obeyed.

The ideal or *hopi* personality is better understood by contrast to its antithesis, namely, that which is *kahopi*. Whereas the idea complex signified by the term *hopi* represents one pole in the personality potential, that of *kahopi* represents the other. The term *kahopi* includes all those qualities which, to the Hopi, are antisocial in terms of the pueblo community; for example, lack of integrity, quarrelsomeness, jealousy, envy, boastfulness, self-assertion, irresponsibility, noncooperativeness, and sickliness. The personaltiy which represents the *kahopi* pole, the antithesis of the ideal, is sharply drawn in the Hopi concept of the witch. "Two-hearted," the witch personifies all that is antisocial, unlawful, illness-bringing, death-dealing; in a word, all that is "bad."

The Hopi Way

Whereas the nonhuman orders fulfill their obligations more or less automatically under the law, man has definite responsibilities which have to be carried out according to a rather complicated set of rules. These rules embody the immanent, cosmic law reduced to the level of human thought, feeling, and behavior, and they form an unwritten ethical canon known as the "Hopi Way."

The child progressively learns and practices the basic precepts of this code. Each individual, however, is expected to master only those over-all principles and detailed rules which apply to his particular sex, age-grade, status, and ceremonial responsibilities; thus, the learning process is adjusted to the maturation curve. Those selected for high ceremonial office are required, during their period of training and apprenticeship, also to become adept in the more esoteric aspects of the code; the village chief's successor is thus initiated gradually into the most intricate forms and meanings of the whole system as it is related to the over-all law.

The Hopi Way is not only an ethical code for the individual, but is also an unwritten constitution for the pueblo community. It embodies the traditional pueblo legal system —guarded, certified, and interpreted by the village chief. And this functionary, besides his other offices, is the chief judiciary officer of the pueblo.

Hence, Hopi traditional ethics form a unified canon which serves as the ideal standard for the individual and, at the same time, for the community. And since the rules for individual conduct and the laws for the government of the community are part and parcel of the innate, logical principle of the universe, both are sacred and absolute.

The Hopi Way equates the personal and the communal ideal within a cosmic frame of reference and places full and unequivocal moral responsibility for fulfillment of the law on each and every individual in the group as indispensable parts of the whole. Thus, it sets up ideal conditions (in terms of external and internal pressures toward a single goal) for the development of an integrated system of social control. This system functions effectively with a minimum of physical coercion by fostering its internalization within the individual in the form of a conscience which is consistent with the social goal. Traditional sanctions—whether for the group or the individual, whether external or internal—are thus unified by, and directed toward, a single ideal.

The Role of Ritual

In Hopi ideology, complete participation in the law means that man must do more than simply regulate his daily life in accordance with the code. Man must also discharge his full responsibilities in regard to the cosmos. He does this mainly by the performance of an annual cycle of ceremonies, which constitutes the primary business of the pueblo theocracy.

Hopi ritual may be viewed as a complex, but logical and ordered, whole, which expresses symbolically the Hopi conception of the universe, the law, and the life process. It also depicts symbolically the Hopis' view of their life problems and the solutions to those problems. The ritual consists mainly of an annual series of interrelated episodes, the rendition of which, through the media of art and concentrated "will-prayer," is believed to facilitate the harmonious functioning of the universe. The ceremonial is thus an indispensable part of man's fulfillment of the law.

The ritual serves mainly as a mechanism by which the Hopis symbolically forecast and prepare for, and hence participate in and facilitate, the fulfillment of phases of the multidimensional cosmic process, according to the ordered sequence in which they are expected to occur and at various levels relevant to the whole of life. Thus, the ritual is a logical outgrowth of the unverbalized premises regarding the nature of the universe and the concept of time which underlie the Hopi lifeway.

To consider the ceremonial as an instrumentality designed

solely to enable the crops to grow by bringing moisture to the fields is to throw the whole picture of Hopi religion out of focus, and indeed to misinterpret the basic orientation of Hopi culture and character. Each main ceremony, it is true, includes within its rite complex instrumentalities believed to facilitate the coming of rain and the germination, growth, and maturation of the crops. For example, the Powamu or so-called "Bean Dance" in February involves the forced growth of beans and corn in the *kivas* and the arrival of large numbers of *kachinas* (impersonations of ancestor deities associated with rain clouds and other life-promoting power phenomena). It also opens the season for racing, which is believed to speed growth. All these ritual practices obviously are intended to promote the germination and aid the growth of food plants. But this is apparently only one aspect of their over-all significance. The so-called "whipping rite" or first initiation of children is included quadrennially in the Powamu complex, and at this time the four phases of the journey through life are graphically portrayed, and the discipline pattern of the Hopis, as it changes from childhood to adulthood, is dramatized. Thus, it appears that the early growth and psychophysiological development of human beings is also associated with this rite complex. Moreover, the "road of life," as depicted through sand paintings and other media, symbolizes not only the human life cycle, but also the migration of the tribe from the "place of emergence." Viewed at a higher level of abstraction, the road-of-life motif seems to express, with an elegant mastery of the relevant, the Hopi presupposition regarding the unfolding of the law by an intrinsic, multiordinal, episodic process. Thus, it may be inferred from internal evidence that the Powamu ceremonies have multidimensional implications, consistent with the basic structure of Hopi cosmogony.

This extensive character of the Hopi ceremonial is clearly evident in the pivotal Winter Solstice ceremony which inaugurates the annual cycle in December. Although dramatic rites are performed to turn the sun back northward from his winter "house," giving the complex a cosmic focus, as a part of these rites prayer sticks are made for practically every order important to Hopi life—for individual human beings and the ancestors, for nonhuman clan partners, for useful animals and plants, for dwelling houses, fields, shrines, growing crops, and even for points along the traditional migration routes. Thus, while the ceremony emphasizes the yearly cycle of the sun and its significance in the universal scheme, it also apparently expresses the entire Hopi cosmogony, with its stress on correlative interdependence, the emergence of the tribe from the underworld, and the migration to its present site, as well as the cosmic life process. Hence, the Winter Solstice rites also seem to be multidimensional in their underlying significance.

We have noted the Hopis' emphasis on ritual mechanisms directed toward the active promotion of the life process in all its manifestations which they consider important to their life needs. This emphasis is clearly reflected in their formulation of the ideal personality. Also of fundamental importance to the problem under consideration is their focus on the active conservation of life. Emphases on the promotion of life, on one hand, and on its protection, on the other, seem to be complements in a single idea complex.

Interest in the conservation and protection of life is well illustrated in the Hopi hunting ceremonies. The ancient rites involve the propitiation of the specific species of game animal being hunted; the hunters use prayer sticks and entreat the "animal people" not to become angry when killed, but to forgive the Hopis, who take their lives only because of great need (A. F. Whiting, 1939, pp. 6–7). A Hopi should never kill more than he needs and should use every part of the animal, even the bones, hoofs, horns, and skull.

Hopis manifest a similar protective and conciliatory attitude toward the plant world. Children are taught never to destroy a plant needlessly, not even a weed; they are taught to use every plant or part of a plant they gather.

These life-promoting and life-conserving behavior patterns and attitudes underline the fundamental Hopi precept that human beings are actively responsible for maintaining the harmonious nature-man balance, which is indispensable for the welfare of all. Moreover, they are apparently closely related to the Hopi view of premature death. Death from old age is regarded as the natural and proper transition from the last phase of the life cycle to rebirth in the underworld. Premature death, however, seems to indicate to the Hopis some interference with the harmonious unfolding of the life process—some disturbance of the subtly balanced and intricately interdependent life web. There seems to be a definite feeling that the individual himself can develop the power to keep his own life properly balanced to avoid such affliction, and that he displays a lack of concern for others in the community if he fails to do so.

This ideology also seems to play a part in the Hopi attitude toward sickness. Thus, a condition of imbalance in the individual, eventuating from a failure to fulfill the law, may be punished by means of a disease or "whip" inflicted through the agency of a secret society or witch. The sickness may be eliminated by the restoration of the proper balance through various mechanisms—for example, through rites conducted by the society owning the "whip" or by a medicine man or through the sick person's concentration on "good" thoughts and driving away "bad" thoughts.

Ritual as Art

The implications of ceremonial, discussed above, are bound up with the Hopis' unstated concept of art. From the aesthetic point of view, the ceremonial cycle as a whole is a multimediary, polyphonic work of art. It may be thought of as a superdrama which requires a period of one to four years for a complete rendition. This superdrama is composed of a series of dramas or mystery plays, each complete in itself, but an integral part of the whole, and each extending from nine to seventeen days and nights.

Each ceremonial in the ritual whole is in itself a subtly orchestrated unit, combining in a highly stylized manner many creative media—chiefly rhythmic movement, singing, drumming, impersonation, and painting—to express one ever-recurring, master theme. Thus, the cycle forms an exceedingly complex, serialized, fuguelike structure, which each year expresses and reaffirms symbolically the Hopi world view as a whole and in its intricately interwoven details.

The ceremonial cycle, therefore, seems to be an aesthetic formulation of the Hopi creed. It may be viewed as a representation of a configuration of abstract principles. As a whole and throughout the various media used, it seeks to portray not an event or an object which may be perceived through the senses, but a conventionalized concept of such an event or object, whether it be a cosmic event like a solstice, an elementary force like the sun, a plant like corn, or a creature like the butterfly. Hopi art seeks to portray the Hopi idea or ideal of the event, of the force, of the plant, or of the creature, rather than the particularized occasion or object itself. Thus it should be differentiated from the realistic type of art and also from the conventionalized type (such as that of the Eskimo or the Northwest Coast Indians) which seeks stylistically to portray an experience itself rather than an idea or an ideal experience. Hopi aesthetic representations are highly abstract and should be classified as that type of conventionalized art which is primarily abstract.

In this respect, we should bear in mind that in each Hopi creation (such as a sand painting or a pottery design), as well as in each creation complex (such as the Winter Solstice or the Powamu ritual), there seems to be an abstraction of the Hopi world view as a whole. And this holistic quality of each particular design unit will be recognized as an indispensable attribute of highly abstract art throughout history.

It should also be noted that Hopi works of art, in whatever medium or combination of media, are characterized by a particular type of balance. This balance is not based on the principle of symmetry. It is a subtle balance between different artistic factors which have no common denominator and therefore cannot be numerically measured. For example, line is balanced against shade, surface quality against color. It is as if, instead of balancing one black square against another, we counterposed a red circle with a black square. This reflects the organic sort of balance found in nature. To achieve it, the artist must see the problem and at the same time see its solution.

Another outstanding quality of Hopi art is its characteristic rhythm. Hopi designs move both around in a circle and toward the center. That is, the movement is circular and centripetal. For example, take the design on the concave surface of a Hopi bowl. The border design moves around the inside of the rim, while the main central section moves inward toward the center of the bowl. Similarly, the ceremonial cycle moves in a circular or spiral annual orbit, while at the same time it moves inward through various levels of abstraction toward a central creed or core. Viewed within the Hopi concept of time, the main ceremonials would be episodes or occasions in a cyclic event which describes a spiral movement.

Hopi art seems to be, therefore, the symbolic, formalized expression of an idea or an ideal rendered in fulfillment of the law. Each creation forms an organic unit wherein every detail has meaning in relation to the whole, and the whole implies an over-all canon or principle. Hopi art, viewed in its totality, apparently gives a complete representation of the Hopi creed and also an insight into Hopi personality. From this point of view it is a rich, unexplored field which may be expected, upon analysis, to yield objective, internal evidence of those aspects of Hopi culture which are unverbalized and often unconscious.

Education toward the Ideal

Alice Joseph and I (1944) have described the Hopi educative process in detail elsewhere and analyzed its effects on the individual by age-grades from birth to adulthood. Here I wish merely to point out that the Hopis utilize the creative potentialities of the educative process to an extraordinarily high degree. The Hopis conceive of the human life process as a gradual unfolding of the whole human being through four phases of the journey through life; childhood, youth, adulthood, and old age. Education commences at birth and consists in a lifelong process of molding the individual toward the ideal through actual experience which, while effectively meeting the problems of the present life phase, is also preparatory to the life phases that are to come. Through the centuries the Hopis have developed a unique educational system, which tends to orient the individual toward the communal ideal with remarkable effectiveness. It tends gradually to mold the whole person (emotions, mind, and body) toward greatest social usefulness in the fulfillment of the law. The process is directed toward an explicit standard or ideal, namely, that which is *hopi,* or good, in contrast to that which is *kahopi,* or bad; it involves the mastering of a code, the Hopi Way. And the ideal seems to be most assiduously pursued in regard to those destined for the highest ceremonial positions.

An Organic View of the World

This brief survey of the major premises and values of Hopi culture suggests, first, that the Hopis tend to think and to formulate their ideas in terms of complex, abstract, structural wholes, not in a static sense, but in terms of structural wholes that are inherently dynamic. Structure seems to be conceived by the Hopis in the form of subtly balanced, changing relationships. These relationships are between the orders, suborders, sub-suborders, etc., which comprise the whole entities, viewed at various levels of abstraction, and they change according to definite rhythms or periodicities, which vary according to the innate nature of each entity manifesting itself as a structural whole. There seems to be a sense of the unfolding of these diverse, changing structures in fulfillment of the immanent law. And the unfolding of each structural whole is interdependently related to that of every other in the over-all, multiordinal totality.

These findings suggest, secondly, that the Hopis tend to think of cosmic fulfillment as multimodal, in time viewed as a duration. The evolution of each structural whole, mentioned above, seems to be characterized by phases which are marked by events, and these events, viewed as wholes, are epochs in the over-all duration which is time. Time itself is a gradually-becoming-later-and-later which is logically divisible only through the epochal character of events. Thus the cosmic process apparently unfolds through rhythmic, epochal types of evolutionary movement in the duration of time.

And finally, by his insight into this multidimensional cosmic process, man is believed able to foresee and prepare for its harmonious realization. Through concentration on the good, through rite, art, and will-prayer, he can, with the aid of his nonhuman partners, facilitate its fulfillment.

To this end, the Hopi has organized his world into a kind of supercommunity, which cuts across what to Western science are empirically established classes or species. The Hopi has closely related both human and nonhuman phenomena into higher orders, which function ceremonially as interdependent wholes in the cosmic scheme. It is mainly through these cross-classified higher orders (which may be viewed as goal-seeking devices) that man is able to exercise his key role in the cosmos.

Here we recognize an organic view of the universe. The cosmos is formulated as a living whole in which the subtly balanced relationships of the various parts to one another and to the multidimensional totality are similar to those which characterize living organisms. The parts and the whole are believed to transact for the good of all, according to a single, harmonious, immanent law. Man is a psychophysiological whole, differentiated from the rest of nature by his power of volition, which is an integral part of the scheme and is to be used for the commonweal. He cooperates with other men and with his nonhuman partners in fulfilling the law, through kinship and ceremonial groups. And the main mechanisms through which he expresses symbolically the cosmic process are ritual and art, reinforced by concentrated will-prayer. Human life is a developmental cycle which is but one of the many diverse, evolutionary modes of law fulfillment existent in the universe, each with its own intrinsic dynamic pattern, in the ever-becoming-later duration of time.

Thus, the Hopis have extended their harmonious, organic view of the universe logically and aesthetically through the world of nature and also through the world of man at both the personal and the social levels. Combining acute observation and induction with intuition and deduction, they have worked the flux of sensory experience with its multitudinous, apparently unrelated details into a world view, which is a notable achievement not only in pragmatic utility, but also in logic and aesthetics.

Hopi philosophy is not something apart from life; most of it is not even explicitly stated. It is implicitly woven into the very fabric of Hopi life—into institutions, child-training patterns, customs, arts, values, and cosmogony—even into Hopi character and mentality. Under relentless environmental pressures, the Hopi has become a specialist in the arts of thinking, living, and character building. Indeed, he has become an artist of great versatility. He dances, sings, drums, paints; he weaves, makes pottery, and plaits; he even grows corn with the consummate skill of an artist. Though he has raised his achievements in these various media to the creative level of the expert, his focus of attention seems to be not solely on any one of them or a combination of them, but on the mastery of the supreme art of law fulfillment in which all lesser arts play a role.

By relentless concentration on the whole life process as an art, the Hopi has apparently given his culture a high degree of logico-aesthetic integration which is revealed in that crowning attribute of specialism—style. Whitehead's apt remark that style is the particular contribution of specialism to culture is demonstrated here on a multidimensional scale. Through systematic specialization the Hopis have developed a unique style, which not only characterizes their arts but permeates their culture and is expressed even in their personalities. And the Hopi style seems to be an overt manifestation of symbolic integration in the Hopi culture system.

Chapter 12

The Wisdom of the Unconscious

Granted what has gone before, must we not conclude that man has a far vaster potential than is generally assumed, at least by peoples of Western European and American tradition? Indeed, our most precious traditional beliefs persist in holding before us a mirror of man which emphasizes his weaknesses rather than his strengths.

A Power Model of Stone Age Hunters

Many hunting peoples believe in a superhuman force, a Supreme Being who must be propitiated to release his bounty. Without this magic touch even the most skillful hunter will fail to bag his prey (Thompson, 1948a, p. 211). This attitude is well expressed in the world view of the Northern Ojibway Indians, an Eastern Woodland tribe who in former times lived mainly by hunting. Hallowell (1947, p. 884) writes:

[These Indians] . . . take a suppliant attitude toward entities with superhuman powers. Among them [men] . . . are always the "receivers"; the *manitok* are always the ones who give help and "bless" human beings. They pity men and take cognizance of their needs, especially in misfortune. Human beings are conceived as being in constant need of help from birth to death. So essential is such help that no performance of any kind is interpreted as due to an individual's own abilities or efforts. Leadership, too, always is the result of bestowed blessings.

A conceptual model depicting a power arrangement which is structurally similar to the Stone Age hunter's image of his world, described above, seems to be reflected in the concept of man, as related to his power sources,* inherent in many of our basic Western institutions. For example, a superordinate-subordinate power organization characterizes our pre-Reformation, Judeo-Christian religious heritage (see especially Metzenthin, 1924; Muntz, 1913; Oats, 1948; St. Augustine, 1950); our Romanized law (see Declareuil, 1926); our free-enterprise system; our military and government hierarchies; our generally accepted ideal of good organization and good leadership (see, e.g., Likert, 1959).

Anachronistic for Our Complex Era

In the light of recent discoveries regarding the nature of man, the human developmental process, and the human potential, this authoritarian power model seems anachronistic. Nay more. The model appears to be not only obsolete but vicious. For the underlying pattern of power which it expresses tends to hold us, as though in a vise, to a conceptual power model, which is not only inappropriate but also unfruitful for our complex times. As long as we view man, even halfheartedly and ambivalently, as weak, sinful, and impotent except when empowered by some external power force—e.g., a Supreme Being traditionally located outside the individual himself—we shall fail to understand, even superficially, the nature of human nature, and the vast, untapped human potential revealed by modern sciences (see, e.g., Murphy, 1958).

Sometimes it seems as though modern Western man is pushing farther and farther into outer space and straining his resources in a herculean effort to conquer and control the universe, so that he will not have to push inward, face, and con-

---

* By the term "power source" I refer here to all sources of power as conceived by man through the ages, supernatural as well as natural; social, economic, and political as well as religious.

trol his own psyche and his own culture. We are becoming even more divorced from our essential human nature.

The mounting incidence of mental illness, especially schizophrenia, and the signs of increasing social disorganization—delinquency, crime, alcoholism, drug addiction, resources wastage, etc.—all give evidence of the deeply schizoid condition of modern man. Obviously, we need a new model for depicting the relationship between man, community, cosmos, and Deity —a model which reflects the new view of man's vast potential.

Actually, of course, the orthodox Christian view of an indulgent Father, or Son, or Mother, who, if properly approached and supplicated, will forgive transgressions and wipe them clean away (including the guilt they engender), is a more comforting belief than that of the iron laws of nature and of human nature revealed by modern science. In nature's system of built-in rewards and punishments, any transgression, as well as any fulfillment, of the cosmic law, contains within itself its own eventuality just as a seed contains within itself its own future development (subject of course to the contingencies of environment). Such a system requires of the individual a clear-eyed, down-to-earth maturity, and a responsibility for his own actions, which is not for the weak, childish, or romantic. It also holds a promise of self-fulfillment far beyond our usual dreams.

Realism of the Northmen

As a case in point, it is not generally known that the so-called "barbarians" of the Baltic, our northern European ancestors, contained within their pagan religion this type of realism (see, e.g., Wax, 1955). Indeed, life in that cold region in the immediate postglacial era (when we assume they created their culture), apparently tolerated fewer extravagances in basic attitudes, from the present viewpoint, than life in less rigorous milieus.

According to the Northmen, nature was all powerful. In the unequal struggle against catastrophes and death, man was always the loser. Sooner or later death overtook him. These Northmen did not expect a favorable outcome to events. They usually phrased a moral decision, not as a choice between two alternatives, one good and the other evil, but as a choice between two alternatives, both of which were disagreeable or evil. This type of choice situation is exemplified in *Hamlet*.

But man, the Northmen believed, could triumph over fate, and even over death, by sheer gallantry of spirit. He could win by refusing within himself to be vanquished (Grönbech, 1931, Vol. 1, Intro.). The genius of the Northmen lay, I believe, in their belief that man, through sheer manliness, could win regardless of circumstances. Man could triumph with all the odds against him if, even in the supreme moment of death, he remained brave, strong, and heroic (Phillpotts, 1931, pp. 93–94; see also Gordon, 1927, p. xxx).

Traditionally, the Northmen apparently did not conceive of an Absolute in any form. They retained, well into the era of conversion to Christianity, a flexibility of outlook and a respect for the laws of nature. It is interesting to note that their world view included the concept of a basic principle of turbulence. According to Dame Phillpotts (1931, pp. 28–29), the world view of the Northmen was characterized by incessant movement.

With penetrating insight into the acculturation process, Phillpotts also noted that the abounding vitality of the Northmen tended to transform whatever they borrowed from more static cultures to the south. In analyzing the carved wood panels in an excavated Viking ship from Oseberg, Phillpotts (1931, p. 29) suggested that the lion's mane and tail became twisting and coiling snakes, and even the parchment scrolls, imitated by the Northmen in borders of Runic inscriptions, sprang into life as encircling serpents.

This view of the world seems to have had considerable survival value in the rigorous, changing climatic conditions of the far North in the postglacial era. Indeed, the modern Icelanders still retain elements of so-called "northern pagan realism" in their basic values and attitudes toward life. As one of my Icelandic informants expressed it: "All Scandinavia differed from the rest of Europe in that it did not take so much of Christianity, nor take it so thoroughly, as the rest." This realism accounts, in my opinion, for no small part of the Icelanders' success in regaining their independence from Denmark in 1944. It stands the people in good stead in their unique role of a tiny sovereign nation of some 150,000 people poised between the two great world power poles (see Thompson, 1960b).

I mention the realism of the Northmen merely as one example of the wealth of information regarding historical and contemporary religious attitudes and beliefs which modern man has at his disposal to broaden his own perspective. It is just one case among many which may be studied and compared in our search for enlightenment and a world view adequate to our era. I do not, of course, intend to suggest that any one historic outlook on life should be adopted or embraced by modern man, whose problematic situations are in many ways peculiarly his own.

Wanted: An Appropriate Model for Modern Man

If we Westerners are to retain our religious roots in Near Eastern and Mediterranean religious traditions and still function successfully in the moden world (from the viewpoint of supercommunity balance and well-being), we may have to revise our ideal regarding the basic relationship pattern between man and his Deity. We may have to change it from one of slave and master (according to St. Paul's doctrine), or one of subordination and superordination (according to sociological terminology) (Simmel, 1955), to one of mutual aid and correlativity.

Man needs his God, but mature Western man needs a mature relationship to a maturely conceived Deity. In other words, in order to meet our real problems successfully, we may have to revise our version of Christianity in the direction of a grown-up religion suited to the needs of mature, responsible adults facing their practical problems and changing their cultures for the sake of their own healthy community living and sanity.

As Mukerjee (1950, p. 494) has noted, "The mind of humanity now gropes after a more complete ideal image or myth of man as it ponders over the tragedy, mutilation and degeneration that have come in the way of the inadequate and perverse images."

Indeed, according to the present thesis, the new model of man, consistent with our new knowledge not only of personality but also of culture, community, and cosmos, must go beyond traditional anthropology. It must even go beyond traditional psychology and psychiatry. Man must be for himself (Fromm, 1947). Yes, but much more. Man cannot be for himself unless he is also for his world, since he is inextricably and transactionally a part of this world. With it, his destiny is profoundly intervolved. To achieve self-realization, man must be for all of nature, including himself and his fellow men.

Personality Process

This brings us to a consideration of what we mean by *personality*.

In the present context, human personality in process of formation (which continues throughout the life of the human organism) may appropriately be conceived as the genetic relation between occasions of biosocial experience of a developing human organism with other organisms; it may be conceived as part of a complex biocultural communal event in which the organism directs itself toward the immediate goals of self-maintenance, reproduction, and self-realization (Murphy, 1947, Ch. 39; Thompson, 1950b, p. 16; Whitehead, 1933, pp. 239ff.). The personality-creating organism is thus conceived as one component in the supercommunity's effort to complete its group life cycle through the generations. Each human individual tends to work and rework through his own experiences himself and to systematize them. He tends to fashion them into a logico-aesthetic whole which moves toward a homeostatic type of balance as part of a complex geophysical, biologic, and cultural event. He does this by means of his uniquely human, symbolizing potential, which operates mainly at the unconscious level (in other words, at the sensing or aesthetic level), but also, of course, at the conscious level (that is, the cognitive or logical level). According to the present thesis, this ordering and re-ordering by each individual of his own inner world in relation to his outer socioecological world occurs in space-time (see Whitehead, 1933, pp. 242ff.).

Thus, the individual's personality is here viewed as *self-structured* to a high degree. The healthy individual himself must be the active, positive agent in a basically *unconscious* process which operates in the direction of his own structural wholeness and self-realization. If he is not active in this way, he ceases to remain healthy.

The psychoanalyst Karen Horney (1950, p. 17; see also pp. 37–38) illuminated the point when she wrote:

> You need not, and in fact cannot, teach an acorn to grow into an oak tree, but when given a chance, its intrinsic potentialities will develop. Similarly, the human individual, given a chance, tends to develop his particular human potentialities. He will develop then the unique alive forces of his real self: the clarity and depth of his own feelings, thoughts, wishes, interests; the ability to tap his own resources, the strength of his will power; the special capacities or gifts he may have; the faculty to express himself, and to relate himself to others with his spontaneous feelings. In short, he will grow, substantially undiverted, toward *self-realization*.

Culture and Personality Built into the Neuromuscular System

But we human beings are innately conservative regarding personality and culture. We are habit-bound. Indeed, we actually cannot change our culture-rooted habits, and our organism-rooted habits, easily or extensively. It will be recalled that life systems are here viewed primarily as action systems.

Culture is conceived as built into the human individual's neuromuscular system through his own actions from birth or even before.

According to modern child-development theory, our neuromuscular systems are developed within and geared to the cultures wherein we are reared, as inculcated by traditional child-rearing practices. These practices differ markedly from culture to culture. As human beings, we cannot function except through our culture. We are not only habit-bound; we are also muscle-bound and nerve-bound (Birdwhistell, 1952; Grinker, 1953, p. 85; Greenacre, 1952).

The evidence suggests that the basic attitudes, values, and tensions of the community's culture system are built into the psychomotor system of each individual growing up in the community, especially through child-training practices and "social-climate" patterns. These gradually become an integral part of each individual's organism, and especially of his neuromuscular system. He expresses these culturally conditioned attitudes and tensions in behavior. He expresses them in every movement— facial expressions, gestures, speech, everyday behavior, and ritual. Indeed, he cannot fail to do so since his movements are controlled by his conditioned psychomotor system. Thus the expressions and movements of the individuals belonging to a given cultural community—their speech, gestures, dance forms, musical style, art patterns, and ceremonies—tend to reveal a certain functional integration which is logical as well as aesthetic. The logico-aesthetic integration process, therefore, underlies the phenomenon we call "style" in the individual, as well as in the community.

Successful Psychotherapy

From the present viewpoint, successful psychotherapy may be described as a process whereby the symbolic personality-integrating mechanisms of the individual, which function habitually mainly at the unconscious level to keep his personality structure in homeostatic balance with the surround (e.g., the eco-socio-symbolic event whereof he is an integral part), move from a more unconscious to a less unconscious (or from a less conscious to a more conscious) level. In this way, the patient, whose neurotic illness was blocking his appropriate functioning (or his sensing mechanism of adjustment) regarding the realities of his world, is enabled to move—ever so slightly—toward a homeostatic balance with those realities. He accomplishes this mainly by means of (1) improved functioning of his unconscious (sensing or aesthetic) mechanisms for integration and adjustment through release of blockage, etc., and (2) conscious logical analysis.

If this position is valid—if there is indeed an innate need for, and tendency to strive toward, a condition of inner integrity in every human being—then the implications of this process should be explored culturally. What kind of integrity is sought? Is recognition given this process by teachers, religious leaders, business executives, statesmen? What is the meaning of the process in regard to the problem of human goals and norms?

Significance of the Unconscious

Actually, what we recognize here is not merely the "wisdom of the body," as defined by Canon (1932) and others. We are, indeed, recognizing that, but also much more. We are especially emphasizing the *wisdom of the unconscious*.

The discovery of the human unconscious by Janet, Freud, Jung, and many others may well prove to be the most momentous discovery of all time about human beings. It is so crucial to our understanding of ourselves that even the most advanced thinkers since Freud have probably failed to grasp its full significance, not only for the development of a mature science of the psyche, but also and especially regarding the development of a mature, unified science of man, his culture, personality, and place in the cosmos. Indeed, one may even predict that, until we assimilate the full meaning of this discovery for anthropology and related disciplines centering on man, we shall not be able to break through the present impasse in the social sciences.

At present only a handful of workers are exploring the frontiers of this dimension of human science (see La Barre, 1958). But led by a few scholars, sophisticated in both anthropology and the psychic disciplines, we are making rapid progress in extending our basic hypotheses about man and his cultures to include the new scientific discoveries.

Perhaps the most significant outcome of this movement is the increased respect, and indeed growing awe, with which those with sophisticated multidiscipline training and experience in the psychic disciplines, as related to broad-based anthropology, view the human potential. We are only beginning to glimpse the astonishing wisdom of the human unconscious as it reveals itself in the symbolizing process in personality and culture. But the glimpse is enough to change our sights forever, and to imbue those with eyes to see with a deep sense of the magnificence of the human potential, both latent and expressed in cultures and personalities throughout the ages.

Chapter 13
Community Systems under Stress

Why have we had trouble in defining the basic principles of culture-personality process? Perhaps it is because so many communities in the modern world are in a state of disorganization, imbalance, and chronic crisis. Stresses from man-made problems have been so continuous, varied, and devastating that thousands of communities throughout the world have been thrown off balance and have failed to reestablish a healthy, flexible relationship with the surround. They have not succeeded in reestablishing a functional type of supersystem in relation to their environments, tendencies, and ultimate goals.

It is obvious that many so-called "civilized communities" are in this partially disorganized condition. With the geometric increase of twentieth-century missions to industrially underdeveloped communities, we may expect that a large proportion of primitive and folk communities will likewise become disorganized. Spurred by the aggressive power struggle of our age, community disequilibrium, cultural disorganization, and its inevitable concomitants—personality disturbance and mental illness—may be expected to spread throughout the world like a plague.

Favorable Laboratories

In these disorganized communities the dynamics of culture-personality process tend to become obscure. Hence they are not ideal laboratories for its discovery and exploration. Only by taking a cue from Darwin and selecting relatively isolated communities as natural laboratories have anthropologists and other students of organic life begun to discover the nature of community process. We have had to investigate functioning local communities in life-action situations, where all the relevant factors are present, including the human species. Favorable laboratories have been found in isolated island communities such as southern Lau, Iceland, the Mariana Islands, Hawaii, and New Zealand. Other useful laboratories have been found in isolated desert, semidesert, oasis, forest, lowland, and mountain communities, such as the Hopi and Zuni pueblos and the Papago communities. As already noted, such communities have had to be investigated with a broad-based, multidiscipline approach, which included tools for acquiring a perspective on the ecological, geophysical, culture-history, sociological, and depth-psychology dimensions of the local supersystem.

Communities under Stress

Such investigations suggest that the usual penalty for travesty of the principles of culture-personality process, in the context of ongoing environmental realities, is that the local community's homeostatic balance, the product of centuries, if not millenniums, of evolution, will be thrown so far out of kilter that the group cannot reestablish a truly functional relationship with the surround. In less extreme cases, the community may succeed in developing a new cultural homeostasis. We have noted how the Papago Indians, by means of somewhat altered, traditional goal-changing mechanisms, such as the village council, and new goal-changing mechanisms, such as the tribal council, may have succeeded in developing a rather satisfactory modern lifeway on the traditional, dual-organization base.

A community may also work out a new adjustment by drawing a sort of "magic circle" around the core of its traditional culture. A good example of this type of adjustment is found among the Zuni Indians (Leighton and Adair, Ms.). The Zunis' "seven cities of Cibola," which were located directly on the route from Mexico City to the American Southwest, were the first Southwestern pueblos encountered by the Coronado expedition of gold-seeking and soul-seeking explorers. These Indians have kept the core of their ceremonial complex inviolate, while allowing, and even fostering, change in other parts of the culture system. Test results of the IEPA project at Zuni suggest that these people have paid a heavy price for their acculturation compromise. Today, their habitual mental approach to practical problems is characterized, according to the test findings, by a shattered field which emphasizes small details. There is little evidence of the complex holism which characterizes the mental approach of their pueblo neighbors, the Hopis (Thompson and Joseph, 1944, pp. 18ff.), and apparently was preferred by prehistoric Zunis, to judge from their art and ceremonial forms.

If the community cannot integrate the new elements with the old system in a genuine structural synthesis at all relevant levels, including that of the central value system at the core of the culture, it apparently cannot achieve a reconstituted cultural optimum. The component members may continue to function as a community, however, in low gear from the viewpoint of personality hygiene and social morale. The results of psychological tests suggest that in such cases many of the community members never attain a balanced or optimal development of personality in relation to the ecocultural realities. Rather, their development tends to be arrested at a preadult level.

Communities under Intolerable Pressures

In more extreme cases wherein the cultural matrix from which the new has emerged tends to be structurally incompatible with the traditional system, the community may fail to establish any kind of new balance. It may remain disorganized institutionally, its human components regressing personality-wise to a less mature level and in time exhibiting a relatively high degree of neurosis or psychosis. This I consider to be diagnostic of chronic cultural crisis.

An acute crisis reaction is exhibited by the Hopi pueblo of Hotevilla. The people of Hotevilla on Third Mesa constitute the most extreme antiwhite community of the Hopi tribe. They are reacting to aggressive, alien cultural pressures by trying rigidly to preserve their ancient "tradition" intact (Thompson 1950b, pp. 80–82). Every community must build into its culture system a minimum degree of flexibility requisite for a functional relationship to the environment in order to survive *in situ*. Therefore, according to the present approach the extent to which the Hotevillans succeed in crystallizing their traditional culture measures their cultural doom, and indeed also their personal survival as a culturally distinct group.

The Saipanese: a Case Study

One of the most meticulously documented studies of a community whose culture shows the symptoms of acute crisis is reported by Joseph and Murray in *Chamorros and Carolinians of Saipan* (1951). This small island (47 square miles) lies directly in line between Guam and the Japanese islands to the north. The two psychiatrists spent six months on Saipan in 1947; they studied native personality and culture against a background of the history, prehistory, and geography of the area.

In 1944 Saipan was bombed heavily by United States invading forces. The battle raged for several weeks. Many of the natives were killed or wounded and all of them lost their homes and possessions. For the first two years of American occupation, until the Japanese settlers on the island were repatriated, the Saipanese were kept behind barbed wire in semiconfinement. This change in the jurisdiction of Saipan was the fifth such change in the government of the island since its "discovery" over four hundred years ago. First, after a decimating thirty years' war of defense against the Spaniards, Saipan, as part of the Mariana Islands, was dominated for over two centuries by Spain and Mexico. This regime was followed by fifteen years of German colonial government, and then thirty years of Japanese rule under a League of Nations mandate. Eventually the island was occupied by American military forces; and finally, it became a United Nations trust territory under the United States.

The personality picture which emerged from the Saipan investigation was one of "a profoundly frustrated people who, against overpowering forces, strive for survival and self-esteem" (Joseph and Murray, 1951, p. 293). The testing program revealed the conspicuousness, pervasiveness, and intensity of anxiety of the native personalities studied, probably rendered more acute by the postwar period of shock, physical privation, and malnutrition. The results suggest that the level of Saipanese accomplishment had been significantly lowered under the circumstances. They highlight the types of reactions and defenses which the people have built up.

It is interesting to note the difference in reaction to frustration between the two major ethnic groups who inhabit postwar Saipan, the native Chamorros and the intrusive Carolinians (Joseph and Murray, 1951, p. 293). The former have been subjected to pressures from dominant aliens much longer and more intensively than the latter. Among the Chamorros, frustration appears to be chronic and profound; it is accompanied by a virtual atrophy of spontaneous and productive responses to everyday experiences. In the Carolinian newcomers from the Micronesian islands to the south, frustration is more acute but less crippling in its effects on personality.

Protection of the Community's Essential Structures

The reason why sudden, man-made interference with the essential structures of a community frequently proves to be so disastrous to an ecocultural supercommunity—both human and biotic—now becomes clear. By the term "essential structures," I refer to the community's institutions and attitude patterns, and above all, to its core value system—the subsystems of the culture which root the human community in its natural setting. These include, of course, the community's ecological organization, and the reflection of the latter in the social system, including its symbolic sanctions, and especially its religious beliefs and ethical principles.

Recall the inner structural harmony between ecologic arrangements, social organization, and social sanctions in the communities of the traditional Hopi Indians, the Papagos, the Lauans, the traditional Hawaiians, and the Maoris. Many others might be cited from the vast evidence available through anthropological field work. In many cases, the natives of such communities have fought with every means in their power against harmful disturbance of their ecocultural balance by alien pressures. For example, over thirty years of warfare—long enough to exhaust or kill off a whole generation—were necessary to break the armed resistance both of the Old Saxons (about A.D. 804, see Cambridge Medieval History, 1936, p. 613) and of the Chamorros of the Marianas (A.D. 1698, see Thompson, 1947a, p. 58), and only then, in each case, were the aggressors assured of victory by the slaughter of a large proportion of the male population and by the exile or migration of many others. Thousands of Saxons were moved by force to the territory of the Franks (in the years from 795 to 804; see Cambridge Medieval History, 1936, p. 613). In the Marianas case, hundreds of Chamorros migrated by choice to the Caroline Islands.

In the Lau Islands, the natives ostensibly accepted the religion and native regulations of the dominant power, but they continued covertly to activate traditional practices, as well as traditional roles related to them (the master fisherman, the custodian of crops, etc.), which were essential to their ecocultural web of life.

By way of illustration, we have historical evidence that both the Hopis (post-Spanish) and the Icelanders (ancient and modern) employed strategy to further their ecocultural institutionalized needs. In each case, the native peoples worked out a compromise with the dominant powers: the Hopis, with the

United States government; the Icelanders, with Norway and later with Denmark.

It seems that, in response to external man-made pressures, human communities tend to use available cultural devices, at both the conscious and unconscious levels, to protect the essential structures of their cultures and to keep their ecocultural supersystems in balanced working order, within the limits of the changing geophysical environment. The main cultural mechanisms employed for this purpose, in the cases cited above, were (1) defensive warfare, (2) covert resistance with outward compliance, and (3) compromise, including partial acceptance of the alien new, especially those aspects which seemed least harmful to traditional arrangements. Clean-cut examples are the Icelanders' partial acceptance of Roman Catholicism (Bryce, 1901, p. 295; Gjerset, 1925, pp. 63–64; Stefansson, 1939, pp. 10ff.; Sveinsson, 1953); the Zunis' magic-circle technique of protecting their most esoteric lore; and the Hotevillans' crystallization device for preserving their tradition.

Reactions to Pressures from the Natural Environment

Now, what may we say regarding (1) the reaction of an isolated community to pressures from slow, natural environmental changes—e.g., warming up, cooling off, desiccation, moistening, soil erosion, changes in shore lines, changes in land elevation, shifting of ocean currents, changes in salt content of bodies of water, changes in the habits of fish and wildlife; and (2) community reaction to violent natural catastrophes—e.g., epidemics, earthquakes, hurricanes, droughts, volcanic eruptions, land innundations, and conflagrations?

These questions open up an area of problem which needs a thoroughgoing review and appraisal of the available evidence (Rayner, 1957). Without systematic research, any conclusions we may reach will remain quite tentative. The evidence suggests, however, that the isolated communities mentioned above, at least, have responded to such natural environmental pressures in a fashion similar to their response to man-made pressures. They have tried to maintain the traditional ecocultural super-system as long as possible, have changed it only when they could find no alternative, and then only as little and as superficially as possible.

However, there seems to be a significant difference between the changes made by the community in response to stresses from the natural environment and those pressed on the community by alien cultural influences. As seen in our study of the Papago Indians, changes of the former kind seem to have developed or evolved actively and voluntarily from within the community itself, on the basis of its institutionalized, goal-changing cultural devices in the direction of long-range ultimate goals. Changes of the latter variety, however, were superimposed from without. Such exotic cultural changes may prove to be incompatible with the institutions, roles, and symbols of the community, as well as with its long-range purposes and values.

For example, formerly when a hurricane ruined the crops in southern Lau, the natives, using traditional social groups (clans) and traditional roles (clan chiefs), actively coped with the emergency by increasing the collection and use of wild edible bush plants, such as *yangava*. Now when sudden disaster strikes, they wait for British officials to provide government rations through the recently created official channels of provincial commissioner and village chief. Fewer wild food plants are used in the native diet, and famine has become a greater threat to native security (Thompson, 1940a, p. 5).

Evidence of the persistence of the traditional ecocultural pattern, despite environmental change, is found in late Paleolithic archaeological sites of European hunting communities. As the climate improved, the great ice sheet melted, and its southern limit retreated northward. Big game, which was adjusted to the glacial cold, moved toward the Arctic with the retreating ice, and the human hunters migrated along with their prey (Coon, 1939, pp. 69ff.). Some groups moved as far north as possible, to Scandinavia. They did not radically change their traditional culture—i.e., from a late Paleolithic type to a Mesolithic type—until there was nowhere else to go, and life offered no alternative. It was change or perish.

The goal-changing devices of the New Zealand Maori, discussed above, provide another case in point. It will be recalled that the Polynesian settlers, who moved southward from the tropical Society Islands to New Zealand, changed their culture only as much as was necessary to cope with the markedly cooler climate of their new home, with its predominantly temperate flora and fauna.

If we may, at this point, hazard a second tentative generalization regarding the nature of culture process, let us consider the following: By means of goal-seeking and goal-changing devices and of symbolic integrating devices, the human community tends to develop its culture toward a balanced system in transactive relation to the environmental setting. Once a satisfactory relationship has been attained—ideally, a symbolically harmonious culture system—the community strives to maintain this relationship with as little change as possible. Indeed, it tends to change its ecoculture organization only when life offers no alternative, and then only as little and as superficially as possible.

Similarities between Culture and Personality Dynamics

Here we glimpse a structural similarity, frequently overlooked, between ecoculture process and personality dynamics. Our generalization obviously resembles that of Gardner Murphy noted in Chapter 3, regarding the human perception process. It seems to be in the nature of a human being to attempt to develop his personality in the direction of a whole which is structurally harmonious with his ecocultural environment, and to preserve that organization with as little change as possible until life offers no way out except to change or perish.

Most people throughout the history of the human race have had to master only one culture—that of the ecocultural community wherein they were born and reared. In this connection, we should not forget that any essential change in one's culture involves a change not only in one's behavior and thought habits, but also a change in one's neuromotor activity patterns. Modern research reveals that there is a definite limit to the kind and degree of change any one individual's psychosomatic system can tolerate without serious strain leading to deterioration or breakdown (see, e.g., Leighton and Clausen, 1957; M. K. Opler, 1956). Thus every individual, no matter how balanced and healthy, has a limit of stress tolerance (Grinker and Spiegel, 1945). However, our present knowledge in this area is limited.

We know that human beings are by no means like potter's clay; they cannot be molded to any specified form at the whim of some dominant power—parent, leader, or governor. The notion that people can be so molded is related to our traditional contents-and-container linguistic stereotype, which, as we have seen, tends to warp the facts. It seems to stem from our traditional Mediterranean-Near East power orientation. Even at birth, a child has a whole arsenal of idiosyncratic hereditary potential. Indeed, from the first moment of life, even before birth according to many psychoanalysts (see, e.g., Greenacre, 1952, Ch. 1), the child, through the development of his neuromuscular system, begins to be conditioned to certain outlets for self-expression and to certain culturally induced pressures toward conformity. Thus, the culture pattern is built into his psychosomatic system from the beginning.

It seems that personality conservatism and culture conservatism are related and that we should search for the connection between the two in this psychosomatic area of problem. Further research is needed to fill in details of process and product (see Grinker, 1953, Ch. 7).

A Principle of Limited Possibilities

It is clear that scientific investigations have revealed insights into the dynamics of culture-personality organization and change. Specifically they suggest the presence of a principle of limited possibilities of change in the sphere of culture and in that of personality. Anthropologists, e.g., Goldenweiser (1913; 1933, pp. 33–55), long ago sensed the presence of such a principle.* But we have not yet succeeded in defining its scope and mode of operation.

Fortunately, we are now in a position at least to ask relevant questions which may expand our knowledge of a principle of limited possibilities of change in the culture of a community and in the personalities of its components. For example, what kinds and degrees of stress can a designated local community (viewed as a supersystem) tolerate, while still able to recover an optimal homeostatic balance in its particular setting? Conversely, what kinds and degrees of stress are demonstrably intolerable to the given community to the extent that it has not shown itself able to recover itself. That is, instead of recovering, it has been thrown into a condition of chronic cultural crisis or even into a condition of social disorganization tending toward its extinction?

Hallowell's brilliant investigations of three Ojibway Indian communities, under differing degrees of stress from the pressures of expanding Western civilization, have given us valuable insights into this problem. By means of a multidiscipline approach, which included depth-psychology tests such as the Rorschach, Hallowell (1950) found that northern Ojibway adults in the least acculturated community studied, Berens River, had retained their traditional core value system and were on the whole quite well adjusted and healthy mentally. On the other hand, many adults in Lac du Flambeau, the most acculturated community studied and the one under greatest pressure from without to change its traditional core value system, revealed a frustration of emotional maturity to the extent that their test performances resembled those of Berens River Ojibway children.

Thus, such investigations also yield new insights into the dynamics of personality formation in relation to the cultural

* The idea was probably borrowed from classical economics.

milieu. A principle of limited possibilities apparently applies equally to personality structure and to culture structure. Since personality organization is to a considerable extent a function of culture structure, when the latter becomes disorganized such disorganization tends to be reflected in the group or modal personality structure of the community members. This relationship was clearly revealed by the findings of the IEPA project and related projects, such as Joseph and Murray's Saipan investigation and Lewis's Tepoztlan study (Lewis, 1953). The findings from such researches suggest new fruitful questions and point toward more precise predictions in the so-called "culture-personality" area.

A Principle of Reemergence

Illumination concerning a principle of limited possibilities and its operation in ecocultural supercommunity process throws light on another aspect of cultural dynamics, namely, the phenomenon of *reemergence*.* Cultural reemergence or reconstitution was recognized long ago by anthropologists of the American Historical school (see, e.g., Kroeber, 1944, p. 798).

The sociologist Sorokin describes a similar process as the "resurrection of cultural systems." In connection with this process Sorokin (1947, pp. 712-713) states: "Truly great cultural systems and supersystems are virtually indestructible. They may be enfeebled, suppressed, or temporarily extinguished; but ultimately most of them reassert themselves and renew their development until they have achieved their creative mission."

Recently this cultural phenomenon has received little attention from anthropologists. And indeed, reemergence phenomena described in the literature are frequently interpreted merely as examples of the process of culture change. From the

---

* Reemergence also characterizes the genetic process, according to geneticists. Carlton Coon (1939, p. 680) has defined reemergence in this sphere as "the reappearance of an older racial entity through the vehicle of a mixed population by the mechanism of differential selection."

present viewpoint, however, the process of reemergence takes its place as a major ecocultural process, inherently linked with the principle of limited possibilities of ecocultural and group personality formation and change in relation to a given environmental context.

Rejection of the Anglican aristocracy, and the development of Nonconformist organization in Wales in the eighteenth century, may be viewed as an example of the reemergence of the traditional native Celtic culture of the area. According to Rees (1951, p. 164):

The repudiation of the aristocracy and the "Church of England" and the retardation of acculturation during the past two centuries was the negative side of a renaissance of the native culture which began with the religious awakening and then spread to the realms of learning, literature, music and politics. Viewed externally, this transformation emerged from the ultimate acceptance of Puritanism. But its acceptance was no ordinary case of cultural diffusion by which an overt element is borrowed and gradually integrated with the pre-existing elements through being endowed with function and meaning. Nonconformity and chapel-building were the unforeseen *consequences* of a spiritual experience and a regrouping of emotional attachments at the core of the culture. The external forms of Nonconformist organization were for the most part copied, but the meaning and emotive energy emerged from within.

Indeed, the European Reformation movement may be interpreted, from this viewpoint, as expressing a reemergence of *indigenous* northern European preferred relationship patterns, in modified form. I refer to native organization systems—of Germanic, Celtic, or Slavic types, for example—which developed north of the Near East–Mediterranean culture area. At the time of the Reformation, these indigenous European systems had undergone strong pressures for several centuries from Roman Catholic strictures and institutions introduced from southern Europe.

Another striking example of the principle at work may be found in the reemergence of the traditional Hopi culture after these Indians, with the help of other pueblos, defeated and

drove out the Spanish Roman Catholic priests and their retainers, who had tried for half a century to superimpose an
alien organization pattern on the Hopi communities (Thompson, 1950b, pp. 29–30).

The culture history of Israel also reveals, across millenniums, the persistence of a traditional value system, expressed in
its recurring reemergence after having been suppressed by alien
pressures.

The meaning of the phenomenon of reemergence, within
the context of the changing ecocultural supercommunity, now
becomes clear. Just as there seems to be a natural tendency for
the biotic community, when disturbed, to move toward the
reestablishment of a certain optimal organization of species
within the particular environmental context of culture, geophysical base, water supply, kind and degree of solar radiation,
etc., there also seems to be a built-in tendency for the human
community, deep-rooted in a particular locale, to establish (and
if disturbed to reestablish) a particular optimal culture structure. This may be thought of as an extension, in human terms,
of the organization of its ecological base. Note that it is not the
so-called "content" but rather the structure or organization of
the culture, viewed as a system, which tends to reemerge.

Multilevel Community Process

The evidence suggests that modern man, with all his
technological inventions and know-how, and with his limited
control of the environment, has not yet succeeded, and perhaps
never will succeed, in controlling this persistent tendency of the
human community to establish, in the long run, an appropriate
culture profile on a given soil, climate, and biotic base. The
process, which after all is here postulated as merely a tendency,
is obscured, of course, in local communities whose cultures are
in a state of chronic crisis. Especially is it blurred in modern
urban communities, divorced as they are from their natural
environments by man-made barriers.

I am not referring to a gross phenomenon similar, for

example, to a zoning of culture types according to gross, global climatic zones. Not at all. I am referring to a multilevel, transactional built-in process, so subtle and multifarious as to have escaped the notice of most observers: namely, the tendency of human communities in isolation and through millenniums to create, in transaction with a given environmental action process, a certain idiosyncratic climax type of culture appropriately structured, from the transactional viewpoint, in terms of the total milieu.

For example, let us consider the democratic sociocultural forms of the early Baltic communities, wherefrom, of course, stem the indigenous democratic institutions of Scandinavia, of the Lower Saxons of northwest Germany, and of the Anglo-Saxons of southern and central England. The latter are, we agree, the prototypes of many traditional American democratic institutions. These early Baltic social forms were apparently integral parts of a supercommunity organization manifest in small, isolated, forest-dwelling communities which were products of a slow evolution toward a climax in the postglacial epoch (see, e.g., Childe, 1931).

Within this hypothetical frame, we also may explain why the influx of exotic cultural forms from the Mediterranean region was so disastrous, culturally, to these small, scattered, northern European communities, and why their peoples, especially the Old Saxons on the southern margin of the Baltic culture area, fought against intrusions from the south with every means in their power. Indeed, as already noted, the Lower Saxons succumbed to pressures from southern Europe only when they were unconditionally defeated, according to terms which allowed them no alternative.

The lesson which culture history, so interpreted, teaches once again is that human beings and their cultures cannot be cast into any prescribed form and made to accept alien, nonfunctional goals imposed arbitrarily from without. Attempts to treat either people, or their ways of life, as though they were malleable in this way fail sooner or later, apparently because of the operation of a principle of limited possibilities of culture and personality development and change in a given natural setting. The evidence suggests that failure to respect this principle and the realities of human culture and personality process tend in the long run to breed disorganization, imbalance, stress, and resources depletion—natural and human—at the local community level. Concomitantly, ignoring this cultural and psychological principle tends to foster psychosomatic disorders, mental illness, and disease in its human members and, if the pressure is sufficiently powerful and/or prolonged, their eventual death, and thus the extinction of their lifeway.*

Finally, we may now be moving, on an empirical basis, toward a refinement in our concept of what may constitute a "healthy" community. According to the present position, a healthy human community would be one that was actively integrating and reintegrating its culture in terms of its basic structures and in relation to its transacting ecological and geophysical setting. Moreover, it would be a community whose human component, when thrown off balance, manifested self-recovery powers built into personality structure and institutional organization. By the term "self-recovery" in this context, I have in mind recovery of the capacity to develop a new optimal balance in effective environmental context, which allows and directs the community's human component to move in the direction of the ultimate, biologically based human goals.

Summary

I shall now attempt briefly to draw together our findings resulting from the search for an appropriate theory and methodology for the solution of practical problems pertaining to the total health, welfare, and self-actualization of human communities.

The appropriate unit of research regarding such problems was found to be the whole ecocultural supercommunity viewed

---

* Here might be marshaled a cogent argument against purposive pressures toward change in the direction of the values of superimposed authoritarian systems.

as an ongoing concern—i.e., as an organic type of action system with historical depth in a definable, effective, changing, environmental setting. This kind of community supersystem fits into our emerging working model of reality (see Chap. 5) as a system of order in space-time, which, with the development of appropriate scientific methodology, should eventually yield to mathematical formulation.

Phrased in terms of our emerging working concept of reality, a community supersystem may appropriately be viewed as tending processually toward self-perpetuation and self-recuperation, but also as constantly interpenetrating with other such supersystems. If stress on the supersystem under investigation, engendered by interpenetration with other units, develops beyond the point of stress tolerance, that supersystem may be expected to fail to recover its balanced wholeness and, eventually, to dissipate into statistical disorder or turbulence. Out of such disorder, however, other community supersystems may be expected to emerge. Thus, the community supersystem under investigation, presumed to be an ordered part of a predominantly turbulent cosmos, is here viewed as containing within itself the seeds of its own self-fulfillment.

Conclusions

The central problem is that of human behavior,
shaped and guided in complete awareness of the
process of the living community, world-wide, of
which man is inescapably the dominant participating organism.

Paul B. Sears

Chapter 14
Planning and Human Goals

The foregoing working hypothesis concerning the nature and dynamics of the living community (involving both its organic and inorganic components, inside and outside, so to speak) has one significant advantage over most other hypotheses about man, personality, community, and culture. As mentioned above, it contains a ready-made frame for handling the planning problem in relation to human goals, a problem which has puzzled social planners through the ages. Once the present hypothesis is understood as a multidimensional working model for use in investigating the comprehensive community, based on a twentieth-century view of reality, it eliminates the need to search further, at this time, for a theory of social planning and human goals. The basic assumptions of our hypothesis may be formulated as an emerging philosophy of mankind.

An Emerging Philosophy of Mankind

The urgent need for an operational philosophy encompassing the new knowledge which anthropologists and others have been accumulating about mankind has long been the subject of widespread discussion among those who realize the potency of emotionally charged ideas (see Whitehead, 1933). Finally, by slow stages and through the efforts of thousands of workers in many disciplines, fruitful formulations are beginning to emerge. Goettingen's philosopher of anthropology, Hermann Wein (1952), attributes this phenomenon, as yet hardly noticed in the United States, mainly to certain contemporary anthropologists and philosophers.

The new philosophy of mankind should probably be classed as neonaturalistic—that is, as one of those philosophies which attempts to discover rules for human conduct in the laws of nature (Hartmann, 1953, pp. 35ff.). Its relation to current phenomenological and existential developments is obvious (see, e.g., May, 1958). When fully formulated, it may find a place among other philosophies in the naturalistic tradition, created by men in their endless search for self-understanding and social reconstruction in the direction of goals appropriate to their needs, aspirations, and circumstances.

The Role of Little-known Cultures

The idea of searching for illumination of our contemporary planning and goals problem outside the ideologies and cultural traditions of Western man, and even outside the high civilizations of the Orient, is new, I suspect, in our time. But I believe that this idea is proving to be germinal to discovery, for the present formulation obviously contains components borrowed from many sources, especially from unfamiliar value systems and preferred organization patterns of peoples who have developed their unique cultures in small, comparatively isolated communities across millenniums before they came into contact with Western civilization. From countless little-known peoples, who are our contemporaries, we may learn much about our own cultural limitations and dilemmas. We can, if we will, gain through them a broader perspective on practical human problems which in our day have expanded to global scope and indeed to interplanetary proportions. They can help us to recognize and define, not only the particular, but also the universal in mankind. Yet more, they can help us to appreciate and charter man's as yet untapped potential.

If we add background studies of little-known, indigenous

cultures of Western Europe as manifested in contemporary rural communities,* people of West European and American tradition may in time develop a sound comprehensive basis for scientific self-understanding from the points of view of modern comparative culture-history, psychiatry and ecology.

A Theory of Planning and Human Goals

What then is the theory of planning and human goals implicit in the present working hypothesis?

If we assume the biological survival of the community and if we assume the community's long-run self-actualization (including maintenance, reproduction, and completion of the life cycle through the ongoing generations) to be its ultimate aims, we may fruitfully analyze its culture and personality systems, as part of a complex biophysical event in space-time, in terms of built-in, goal-seeking, and goal-changing devices—as inherent planning mechanisms directed toward immediate goals, which tend to be oriented in the direction of such ultimate aims. Once the culture system of a designated human community has been described as a goal-management system in an explanatory fashion (rather than a general fashion), and its pattern of dynamics has been identified, the community's built-in goal system may be reinforced or altered through traditional or introduced goal-orienting devices in the direction of appropriate man-made goals. Such man-made goals may be keyed to long-range, universal biological ends, in the context of the changing world-wide web of interpenetrating community supersystems, viewed as complex, multifaced events in space-

* These background studies include those made of such communities as the Andalusian (Pitt-Rivers, 1954, etc.), the Basque (Caro-Baroja, 1944; 1949; Coon, 1939, pp. 501–504; Ripley, 1899, pp. 180–204; Strong, 1893, etc.), the Highland Scots (Chadwick, 1949; Childe, 1935; Darling, 1955, etc.), the Irish (Ancient Laws of Ireland, 1865; Arensberg, 1937; Arensberg and Kimball, 1940; Grinnell, 1894; Movius, 1942; O'Grady, 1892, etc.), the Scandinavian (Chap. 12), the Walloon (Turney-High, 1953, etc.), the Welsh (Rees, 1951; Rhys and Byrnmor-Jones, 1923; Vinogradoff, 1920, etc.).

time. The planning and implementation process, therefore, consists in finding the means—traditional, if possible, introduced, if need be—whereby this may be accomplished successfully with a minimum of stress to the community members and institutions from the culture-personality point of view.

Planning is indeed a formidable task, as anyone knows who has tried to implement successful social-action research at the local community level. By so stating the planning problem, I do not mean to minimize it. I merely wish to emphasize the following point: What is usually regarded as a first stage and major task of the social planner—that is, development of an appropriate blueprint to be implemented later (see, e.g., Mannheim, 1940)—has been eliminated in the research design.

No blueprint stage is contemplated, according to the present approach. Planning and implementation are not conceived as two separate operational phases of a grand design or strategy of planning. Indeed, it is recognized that to approach the planning problem by means of a blueprint actually rules out the achievement of an appropriate solution, as I have attempted to demonstrate in regard to the Hopis and other Indian tribes (Thompson, 1946b; 1950b; 1951b).

Tapping the Community's Reservoir of Psychic Energy

Such an approach tends to throttle the genius of the community. It stifles creativity by closing the door to the unconscious. It rules out or neglects about 99 per cent of the group's productivity potential.

The Hopi Indians have an opening in the floor of every *kiva* (ceremonial chamber used by a men's club for religious and other creative activities). This aperture, which they call the *sipapu*, is believed to be the group's lifeline to superhuman helpers in the underworld, with whom the Hopis maintain an active, correlative relationship of mutual aid. From the present approach, we may view the Hopis' *sipapu* as symbolizing the door to their unconscious world; dream, fantasy, the afterlife, the beforelife, their reservoir of essentially human creative power.

The Hopis have learned through the millenniums always to keep the aperture to their power source open. In view of recent empirical findings regarding the nature of the creative process and the potency of the unconscious, we may well take a lesson from the Indians. Especially in a large-scale, community-wide planning project, which to be successful requires the appropriate marshaling of man's essentially human, creative resources, it is of utmost importance, I believe, to open the *sipapu* to the unconscious and actively to foster the creative process in both individuals and groups. Thus may the wisdom of the group's unconscious psychic energy be harnessed by its members for the benefit of the local community, the nation, and the world.

Field Research in Planning

Our formulation of the planning problem, then, suggests that if we wish to illuminate this area by the methods of science, we may do so by systematic field research. For example, we may seek out and study small, naturally isolated, relatively stable human communities whose ecocultural roots and traditional goal patterns and goal-management institutions have not been greatly upset by the impact of modern industrial civilization.

It is interesting to note that important insights along these lines have come from city and regional planners (see Mayer, 1958). For example, E. A. Gutkind (Thomas, 1956, pp. 21–27) suggests that man's use of space throughout history expresses implicitly several different attitudes toward the environment. Many primitive communities express fear and longing for security. Others manifest a growing self-confidence and increasing observation leading to a more rational adaptation of the environment to differentiated needs. Many modern industrial settlements express aggressiveness and conquest leading to un-limited exploitation on an expanding frontier. And finally, some contemporary architectural forms suggest a spirit of responsibility and unification in a world of closing frontiers.

Systematic application of the new anthropology would activate the latter attitude. But I wish to underline Gutkind's suggestion that Western man, in attempting to face current realities, may well investigate contemporaneous and historic communities which manifest what he refers to as "growing self-confidence and increasing observation leading to a more rational adaptation of the environment." Here modern man may find leads regarding the contemporary planning problem in its manifold local expressions. For, as suggested above, small isolated communities have achieved throughout the ages, by means of wise goal-management and symbolic integration, a high degree of what we now seek by means of a scientific approach.

Our researches suggest that such investigations might well use multidiscipline community analysis. Accordingly, not only the socio-cultural dimensions, but also the ecologic and psychic dimensions of a community would be analyzed as though they represented basic components of a single supersystem, operating as a complex event in space-time.

A Model for Inquiry into Goal-management Systems

A patent advantage of the present working model of the supercommunity, already mentioned, is that it facilitates the empirical investigation of cultural goals and the means whereby they may be implemented. It guides the fieldworker toward a concern for ends as well as means.

Razor-edge types of small, relatively isolated communities with limited natural resources and economies of scarcity—desert-encircled oases, seagirt "famine" societies, icebound northern fjords—offer particularly favorable conditions for exploration of this area of problem. They offer ideal laboratories for testing the hypothesis. But once the multidiscipline, team approach is mastered, the working model may be used for investigating the goal-management systems not only of small, simply structured communities with integrated cultures, but also of complex industrialized nations with highly organized, composite cultures. However, the more subjected the community has been to pressures from historically alien culture systems and the more composite its culture, the more arduous will be the research needed to fulfill the demands of the model.

New Standards of Community Health and Mental Hygiene

It should be noted that this type of multidiscipline, supercommunity analysis gives us a refocused perspective on traditionally accepted values, especially in the field of social organization and institutional structures. Group-dynamics findings (Lewin, 1945) and personality-research findings (Murphy, 1947), combined with multilevel research on ancient, isolated communities, afford new insights regarding types of balanced sociocultural systems which foster favorable conditions for nourishing healthy personalities.

We have noted that many students of applied social science are concerned today with the concept of the healthy community. The present approach maps the investigation of problems in this area of concern, involving both cultural goals and their implementation. Our working model sets the stage and prejudices the investigator in the direction of the acquisition of the kind of empirical information about a community needed by applied anthropologists and others whose function is to elucidate the problems of community health and sanity. It is a fruitful theory, I believe, from the viewpoint of the major practical problems which confront practitioners of the applied disciplines which focus on social man.

Indeed, we are beginning to establish, I think, universal, sociopsychological norms of community balance, health, and sanity, far removed from the traditional values implicit in the common-sense thinking which dominates classical historical research. I refer, for example, to values implicit in nineteenth-century concepts of progress, unilinear cultural evolution, backward peoples, etc.

We Westerners are also questioning our traditional notions of the ideal personality. These include, to mention a few favorite stereotypes: (1) the rigidly strong character; (2) the self-sacrificing martyr; and (3) the aggressively independent individual who scorns mutual aid. Modern psychotherapy reveals the suppressed hostility, narcissism, masochism, and sadism —frequently also the latent homosexuality—which, in many such personalities, may operate vigorously just below the level of consciousness (English and Pearson, 1945, Ch. 15; Fromm, 1941; Horney, 1950; Reik, 1941; for a contrary view, see La-Pierre, 1959). We have begun to strive for a healthy, actualized type of personality—characterized by a nicely equilibrated balance of psychic forces. We seek to cultivate a built-in control system, the reward of a delicately tuned, spontaneous process involving both the release and the control of psychic energy. We strive for fulfillment of the whole human being—male or female—as an ongoing process in the context of family, community, and cosmos.

These developments are making way for a new type of objectivity in many academic fields, including most of the social, psychological, and historical disciplines—as well as many clinical fields, such as mental hygiene and community development. No longer need the modern investigator into mankind's perennial problems be shackled by widely held, traditional assumptions regarding the superiority of any one form of cultural achievement, based on a very limited knowledge of the great variety of human culture systems—contemporaneous and historical.

We now have the knowledge, the methodological procedures, and the conceptual tools for asking new and more relevant questions in relevant contexts regarding group cultural achievement. The relevant question now does not seem to concern the absolute cultural achievement of a community at a single point in absolute historical time and geographical space (such as Athens in the fifth century B.C., Florence during the Renaissance, the Incas at the time of discovery, or the Hebrews of the Moses epoch). On the contrary, the relevant question regarding the cultural achievement of a human community, in the light of modern research, appears to be: How adequately from the viewpoint of the conservation of its total resources, human and nonhuman, has a human community, viewed as integral to an ongoing life-web event in space-time, solved its living problems and fulfilled itself in the course of its existence, generation after generation?

This question opens up new problems in the field of research into human cultures and cultural values. It challenges the anthropologist, in cooperation with the ecologist, the psychiatrist, the psychosomatic physician, the sociologist, the culture historian, the archaeologist, etc., to sharpen his understanding of the total human-resources conservation problem by means of the new multidiscipline methodologies. Applied to whole communities, deep-rooted historically and geographically, and to the global web of communities of our contemporary human world, it challenges all of us—scientists, scholars in the humanities, artists, technicians, and laymen alike—to ponder on our new and growing insights into cultural values and their relevance to our own cultural dilemma. It opens up vistas, as broad as the world itself and as deep as the human race's span, to give us new perspectives on the values crisis of our time. And it points to a new, scientifically based goal—universal resources conservation, human as well as natural resources—which holds hope of providing a scientific foundation for a universal, cross-cultural code of ethics which may help to resolve that crisis.

Chapter 15

Toward a Science of Mankind

Our review of recent advances in anthropology toward a mature scientific formulation suggests that four basic steps have been necessary forerunners to the present position. In enumerating these steps, however, I do not mean to exclude others which may be equally fundamental. These are the four which, in my own experience, have proved axiomatic.

A Biologically Based Science of Mankind

The first is the assumption that a mature science of mankind must be biologically based.* The proposition that Homo sapiens is a social animal, a member of the animal kingdom, with deep-rooted genetic affinities must, I believe, be kept constantly in mind by the student whose goal is to further the development of this science.

Thus, a major chore that lies ahead is the formulation of a unified biocultural anthropology, a fusion of the fundamentals of the two major subdivisions of anthropology—sociocultural and physical anthropology—with findings and fruitful hypoth-

* It is in biology that we shall find a firm scientific foundation for the new anthropology (Hartmann, 1953; Howells, 1954; LaBarre, 1954; Malinowski, 1944; Montagu, 1957; for a different view, see Radcliffe-Brown, 1957).

eses of modern biology, ecology, biosocial psychology, psychiatry, psychosomatic medicine, nutrition, etc.

A firm foundation to the new unified anthropology is now being laid, and its full development and maturation may be expected before too long. Then the basic role of the new anthropology in bridging the gap between the life sciences, the social sciences, and the humanities will be clarified, and the existing confusion between anthropology and other social disciplines, such as sociology, will be dissipated.

As has been noted throughout this book, the clinical disciplines believed to prove of major significance in contributing to the development of the applied branch of this new anthropology are also biologically based. They are, on the one hand, applied ecology, e.g., natural-resources conservation and regeneration; and on the other, clinical-psychic disciplines, e.g., psychiatry, psychoanalysis, and psychosomatic medicine. The classic social disciplines, such as sociology, economics, political science, and law, seem to have a limited immediate relevance. Thus, the basic affinity of an emerging unified science of mankind is primarily with the biological sciences and medicine, rather than with the social sciences.

Until biology began to outgrow its mechanistic orientation, however, it could not co-sire the infant science of mankind. Biology itself had to mature and had to accept, with all its implications, the proposition that the basic types of systems that may be used appropriately to characterize living organisms as wholes differ in kind and quality, and not merely in degree or quantity, from those that may validly reflect the inorganic world. Axiomatic to this difference is the goal-directed nature of protoplasmic behavior, as compared with inorganic activity. As noted above, in the last twenty years many leading biologists have favored and advanced this proposition. A new biology has emerged capable, not only of a general description, but also of an explanatory description of organic activities. In this kind of description, we now have a scientific basis for predicting the behavior of organisms.

It is not generally realized how crucial this development in biology has been as a forerunner to the emerging unified science of mankind. Its significance has, I hope, become clear to the interested reader who has had the patience and temerity to follow the thesis of this book.

I am fully aware, of course, that organismically oriented, functional biology is still viewed askance by many biologists and other students of living organisms. The hypothesis is still regarded as unorthodox (Sinnott, 1955, pp. viiff.). This fact, however, is irrelevant to its heuristic influence on the development of a mature science of mankind. To anthropology, and especially to clinical anthropology, this hypothesis is a new and fruitful working tool.

For example, the new biological concept that structure and behavior are not separate and distinct, but are merely two aspects of the organization of organisms with their built-in, goal-seeking proclivities serves directly as a building block for a basic working concept of clinical anthropology. I refer to the concept that the human organism and human culture, which is created by a community of human organisms, are not separate but transactive. Culture is not superorganic (for another view, see Kroeber, 1917). Structure and behavior are aspects of biological organization and the goal-seeking propensities of living organisms.

Multidiscipline Research

The second basic step which, according to the present thesis, is proving axiomatic to the development of a mature science of mankind is multidiscipline research.

Only recently have anthropologists and other students of man learned how to pool their approaches, methods, empirical data, and generalizations, and to organize this body of tools and findings into a genuine synthesis. I do not refer to so-called "interdisciplinary research" or "cross-discipline research" wherein only a superficial juxtaposition of fields and findings has been achieved. Rather, as noted above, I have in mind long-range research endeavors involving a genuine cross-fertilization of several distinct disciplines, such as cultural anthropology, functional ecology, and psychiatry. A multidimensional synthesis of many disciplines at the conceptual level, as well as in the field and laboratory—the most difficult accomplishment to date—appears a necessary forerunner to the development of a mature and unified science of mankind. It remains a necessary condition for further growth at every level. Much of this volume, of course, has been devoted to the significance of and the problem areas of multidiscipline research focusing on human community problems.

The Clinical Situation as Self-corrective

The third basic step, which I view as an indispensable building stone in the development of a science of mankind, is the use of the clinical situation as a self-corrective device for the improvement of theory and method (Collier, 1945; Thompson, 1959; 1960a; for a different view, see Spencer, 1954, p. 298).

In rejecting armchair theorizing in favor of empirical, world-wide field investigations, anthropologists have brought to the social sciences a healthy tendency, which is gradually invading the more conservative social disciplines such as sociology, political science, and even economics. The clinical approach is transforming our body of knowledge regarding mankind from prejudice and speculation to empirical facts and inductive generalizations of universal relevance.

This approach is exerting a similarly healthy influence in applied social research and other applied human disciplines, including social work, group work, and community organization. In attempting to apply his field findings to the elucidation of practical problems, the applied anthropologist, consistent with his empiricist tradition, tends to reject quick, easy solutions based on traditional norms and goals and on one-culture, ethnocentric moral codes. Rather, he favors painstaking clinical diagnosis of the actual life situation viewed in the context of the round of daily activities of an ongoing community observed over a long period of time in the local setting.

Indeed, the applied anthropologist is gradually learning the primary lesson of the basic, clinical life disciplines, such as medicine, psychiatry, psychoanalysis, and clinical psychology, and also of resources conservation, forestry, and animal husbandry. The lesson which the clinical life disciplines have to teach is that when their goal is therapy and long-term good health (whether of the human organism or an eroded area or a forest from which healthy sustained yield is desired), success is measured pragmatically (Thompson, 1959).

Charles S. Peirce (Wiener, 1958, p. 181) pointed out long ago that pragmatism applies the sole principle of logic recommended by Jesus: "Ye may know them by their fruits." Treatment is judged good or bad in the measure that it does, or does not, stimulate change in the direction of the desired goal —namely, the increased well-being, health, and balance of the unit in context under consideration. Therapy submits to and wins by the pragmatic test. Does it work? This is the relevant criterion of all basically clinical disciplines, whether reference is made to medicine, psychiatry, or natural-resources conservation.

In other words, the event usually precedes its understanding. Activity moves toward discovery, not vice versa. The analysis of actual events in the context of a situation in real life, not in a contrived laboratory, lays the basis for their understanding. The disadvantage of the contrived laboratory —especially regarding problems wherein whole human communities are the significant units of research—is that the most relevant factors regarding solution of the problem may be just those left out of the experiment. On the other hand, in the clinical situation, all factors are necessarily present, including ecological and historical ones. Thus, as noted above, success depends to a considerable extent on whether the scientist selects those factors or factor sets that are relevant.

Since a real-life situation is observed and analyzed— whether it be a psychosomatic human organism transacting in the life situation, or an ongoing local community expressing a distinctive culture, or a whole ecological arrangement such as an isolated island community, a forest, or an oasis—there emerges from the clinical experience the conception of a culture as a whole dynamic process (see Benedict, 1934, p. xii). The human organism is viewed as a going concern which is in transaction with its entire effective environment (Frank, 1951).

The soil conservationist, who is of course an applied biological ecologist, views an eroded area as a whole changing biotic unit which tends to move in the direction of a homeostatic balance or optimal arrangement of species in relation to specific changing geophysical conditions. If this unit is disturbed by some sort of stress such as overgrazing, he sees it as tending to restore itself when the stress is removed, and as tending to reestablish a new climax or optimum structurally similar to the former one if conditions remain the same. Corrective measures which the conservationist takes regarding the area—e.g., removal of herds to reduce the stress, fencing to protect the area, filling in gullies and planting shrubbery to arrest critical erosion—are taken in the light of the above concept of an ongoing biotic system. By his success in fostering conditions which favor a reversal of the destructive process and a restoration of movement in the direction of a new optimum, the conservationist measures the fruitfulness of his working hypothesis. Thus, clinical experience serves as a corrective to theory.

Similarly, our concept of man emerges from the clinical experience keyed to therapy as a whole human organism or ongoing life process participating transactionally with the social and ecophysical environment through his culture. Thus, the applied anthropologist is notably sharpening his focus regarding which units of research may appropriately be treated as significant in relation to the community-welfare and mental-hygiene problem.

An Existential View of Reality

The last basic step regarded as indispensable to the development of a mature unified science of mankind is the emergence of a heuristic phenomenological model of reality based on certain empirical discoveries in the biological and physical sciences about nature and man. This step also involves the emergence of an empirical approach to logic. The philosopher of anthropology, Hermann Wein (1952, p. 632), writes: "Our problem of categorical systematics derives not from a logical deduction but from focusing our attention on an order in the existing world." And again Wein writes (1952, p. 633): " 'Order,' and ultimately 'world' or 'cosmos,' are names for this discovered, structural unity among things experienced."

In sum, a unified science of mankind is emerging, according to the present thesis, on the basis of new perspectives on reality which seem to be implicit in the findings of modern scientific research in the life sciences. An attempt has been made to formulate some significant aspects of these perspectives. Such a science could not be born until social scientists, seeking solutions to urgent human problems, began to question anachronistic models and to alter the assumptions implicit in their working hypotheses in keeping with the conceptual revolution which has transformed modern physics and mathematics and which is leavening the life sciences.

Of course, the very notion that we can, and even should, search the findings of science for new perspectives on reality which may be useful to our research into the nature of mankind is rather new and by no means universally accepted (see Wiener, 1958, pp. 142ff.). It is, nevertheless, part of the thesis of this book that theories regarding the nature of man, and his relations to other men and to the universe, which are proving fruitful for our time, tend to be rooted in emerging conceptions of reality which are proving functional in helping to solve major problems in the physical and biological sciences.

After all, the scientist is not seeking absolute truth or the nature of reality. He is looking for fruitful formulations which are nothing more than working hypotheses—formulations that may serve as the basis for research yielding findings which may prove useful and valid for his time. That is all that may be expected of a scientific theory. It is in the nature of a scientific theory, viewed in long-range perspective, that it is ephemeral. Its effective life history ends when it becomes obsolete and is discarded because of the discovery of a new and more fruitful theory which supersedes it. This fact about the tentative, exploratory nature of scientific endeavor and scientific findings should be kept constantly in mind, especially when discussing the development of a mature, unified science of mankind.

Bibliography

Allee, W. C., et al.
   1949 *Principles of animal ecology.* Saunders, Philadelphia and London.
Ancient Laws of Ireland
   1865 *Introduction to Senchus Mor and Law of Distress.* Longmans, London. Vol. I.
Arensberg, Conrad M.
   1937 *The Irish countryman.* Macmillan, New York.
   1955 American communities. *Amer. Anthropologist,* 57:1143–1162.
Arensberg, Conrad M., and S. Kimball
   1940 *Family and community in Ireland.* Harvard Univer. Press, Cambridge, Mass.
Asher, Robert E., et al.
   1957 *The United Nations and promotion of the general welfare.* The Brookings Institution, Washington, D.C.
Axelrod, Daniel I.
   1959 Poleward migration of early angiosperm flora. *Science,* 130 (3369):203–207.
Barnett, H. G.
   1953 *Innovation: the basis of cultural change.* McGraw-Hill, New York.
   1956 *Anthropology in administration.* Row, Peterson, Evanston, Ill.
Bates, Marston
   1950 *The nature of natural history.* Scribner, New York.

1952 *Where winter never comes: a study of man and nature in the tropics.* Scribner, New York.
1953 Human ecology. In A. L. Kroeber (Ed.), *Anthropology today.* Univer. of Chicago Press, Chicago.

Beaglehole, Ernest
1944 The Polynesian Maori. *J. Polynesian Soc.,* 49:39–67.

Beckwith, Martha W.
1951 *The Kumulipo, a Hawaiian creation chant.* Univer. of Chicago Press, Chicago.

Benedict, Ruth
1934 *Patterns of culture.* Houghton Mifflin, Boston and New York.

Bennett, Hugh H.
1939 *Soil conservation.* McGraw-Hill, New York.

Bennett, John W.
1946 The interpretation of Pueblo culture: a question of values. *Southwestern J. Anthrop.* 2:301–374.

Bentley, Arthur Fisher
1926 *Relativity in man and society.* Putnam, New York.

Bergson, Henri
1911 *Creative evolution.* A. Mitchell (Trans.), Holt, Rinehart and Winston, New York.

Bettelheim, Bruno
1943 Individual and mass behavior in extreme situations. *J. abnorm. soc. Psychol.,* 38:417–452.

Bidney, David
1947 Human nature and the cultural process. *Amer. Anthropologist,* 49:375–399.
1949 The concept of meta-anthropology and its significance for contemporary anthropological science. In F. S. C. Northrop (Ed.), *Ideological differences and world order.* Yale Univer. Press, New Haven, Conn. Pp. 323–355.
1953 *Theoretical anthropology.* Columbia Univer. Press, New York.

Bierstedt, Robert
1949 A critique of empiricism in sociology. *Amer. sociol. Rev.,* 14:584–592.

Birdwhistell, Ray L.
1952 *Introduction to kinetics: an annotation system for analysis of body motion and gesture.* Univer. of Louisville, Louisville, Ky.

Boas, Franz
    1940   *Race, language and culture.* Macmillan, New York.
Bohr, Niels
    1933   Light and life. *Nature,* 131:421–423, 457–459.
    1950   On the notions of causality and complementarity. *Science,* 111:51–54.
Bridgman, P. W.
    1928   *The logic of modern physics.* Macmillan, New York.
Brown, G. Gordon, and A. M. Hutt
    1935   *Anthropology in action: an experiment in the Iringa District of the Iringa Province, Tanganyika Territory.* International Institute of African Languages and Cultures, Oxford Univer. Press, London.
Bryan, Edwin H., Jr.
    Ms.   Preliminary report on the Lau group, Fiji (1924). Bishop Museum, Honolulu.
    1948, 1960   Personal communications.
Bryce, James
    1901   *Studies in history and jurisprudence.* Oxford Univer. Press, New York.
Buck, Sir Peter H. (Te Rangi Hiroa)
    1938   *Vikings of the sunrise.* Stokes, Philadelphia.
    1939   *Anthropology and religion.* Yale Univer. Press, New Haven, Conn.
    1945   An introduction to Polynesian anthropology. *Bull.* 187, Bishop Museum, Honolulu.
    1949   *The coming of the Maori.* Whitcombe and Tombs, Wellington.
Bunzel, Ruth Leah
    1929   The Pueblo potter: a study of creative imagination in primitive art. *Columbia Univer. Contr. Anth.,* 8. Columbia Univer. Press, New York.
Burkitt, M. C.
    1929   Archaeology. In *Encyclopaedia Britannica* (14th ed.). Encyclopaedia Britannica, Inc., Chicago.
Cambridge Medieval History
    1936   H. M. Gwatkin (Ed.). Macmillan, New York. Vol. 2.
Cannon, Walter B.
    1932   *The wisdom of the body.* Norton, New York.

Cantril, H. A.
    1950 *The "why" of man's experience.* Macmillan, New York.
Capell, A., and R. H. Lester
    1941–1942 Local divisions and movements in Fiji. *Oceania,* 11:313–341; 12:21–48.
Caro-Baroja, Julio
    1944 *La vida rural en Vera de Bidasoa (Navarra).* Talleres graficos, Madrid.
    1949 *Los Vascos. Ethnologia.* Biblioteca Vascongado de los Amigos del País, San Sebastian.
Carson, Rachel
    1955 *The edge of the sea.* Mentor, New York.
Carter, George F.
    1945 Plant geography and culture history in the American southwest. *Viking Fund Publications in Anthropology.* no. 5, New York.
    1950 Ecology—geography—ethnobotany. *The Scientific Mon.,* 70:73–80.
Cassirer, Ernst
    1944 *An essay on man.* Yale Univer. Press, New Haven, Conn.
Chadwick, H. M.
    1949 *Early Scotland: the Picts, Scots and Welsh of southern Scotland.* Cambridge Univer. Press, London.
Chapple, E. D., in collaboration with C. M. Arensberg
    1940 Measuring human relations: an introduction to the study of the interaction of individuals. *Gen. Psychol. Monogr.,* 22:3–147.
Chapple, E. D., and C. S. Coon
    1942 *Principles of anthropology.* Holt, Rinehart and Winston, New York.
Childe, V. Gordon
    1931 The forest cultures of northern Europe. *J. R. anthrop. Inst. Great Britain and Ireland,* 61:325–348.
    1935 *The prehistory of Scotland.* Kegan Paul, Trench, Trubner & Co., London.
Clark, J. G. D.
    1936 *The mesolithic settlement of northern Europe.* Cambridge Univer. Press, London.

1951   Folk Culture and European prehistory. In W. F. Grimes (Ed.), *Aspects of archaeology in Britain and beyond: essays in honor of O. G. S. Crawford*. Edwards, London. Pp. 49–65.

1952   *Prehistoric Europe: the economic basis*. Philosophical Library, New York (Methuen, London).

Collier, John

1945   The United States Indian administration as a laboratory of ethnic relations. *Soc. Res.*, 12:265–303.

1947   *The Indians of the Americas*. Norton, New York.

Conferences on a Unified Theory of Human Nature

1953   *Proceedings*, April 18–19. Michael Reese Hospital, Chicago (mim.).

1954   *Proceedings*, March 27–28. Michael Reese Hospital, Chicago (mim.).

Coon, C. S.

1939   *The races of Europe*. Macmillan, New York.

1948   *A reader in general anthropology*. Holt, Rinehart and Winston, New York.

Darling, F. Fraser (Ed.)

1955   *West Highland survey: an essay in human ecology*. Oxford Univer. Press, New York.

Darwin, Charles

1859   *The origin of species*. Modern Library, New York.

1871   *The variation of animals and plants under domestication*. J. Murray, London. Vol. I.

Declareuil, Joseph

1926   *Rome the law-giver*. Knopf, New York.

Dewey, John, and A. F. Bentley

1949   *Knowing and the known*. Beacon Press, Boston.

Dixon, R. B.

1928   *The building of cultures*. Scribner, New York.

Dobbs, H. A. C.

1947   *Operation research and action research*. Foreword by John Collier. Institute of Ethnic Affairs, Washington, D.C.

Dollard, John, et al.

1939   *Frustration and aggression*. Yale Univer. Press, New Haven, Conn.

Dorner, Alexander
1949 *The way beyond "art." The work of Herbert Bayer.*
Wittenborn, Schultz, New York.
DuBois, Cora
1944 *The people of Alor: a social-psychological study of an
East Indian island.* Univer. of Minnesota Press, Minneapolis.
Einstein, Albert, and L. Infeld
1942 *The evolution of physics: The growth of ideas from
early concepts to relativity and quanta* (first published
1938). Simon and Schuster, New York.
Elkin, A. P.
1949 The rights of man in primitive society. In UNESCO
(Ed.), *Human rights, comments and interpretations: a
symposium.* Allan Wingate, London and New York.
1950 The complexity of social organization in Arnhem land.
Southwestern J. Anthrop., 6:1–20.
Elton, Charles
1935 *Animal ecology.* Sedgwick and Jackson, London.
Embree, John
1939 *Suye Mura: a Japanese village.* Introduction by A. R.
Radcliffe-Brown. Univer. of Chicago Press, Chicago.
Emerson, Alfred E.
1954 Dynamic homeostasis: a unifying principle in organic,
social, and ethical evolution. *Scientific Mon.,* 78:67–85.
Emory, Kenneth
1953 A program for Polynesian archaeology. *Amer. Anthropologist,* 55:752–755.
English, O. S., and G. H. Pearson
1945 *Emotional problems of living: avoiding the neurotic
pattern.* Norton, New York.
Evans-Pritchard, E. E.
1940 *The Nuer, a description of the modes of livelihood and
political institutions of a Nilotic people.* Oxford Univer.
Press, New York.
1946 Applied anthropology. *Africa,* 16:92–98.
1951 *Social anthropology.* Free Press, Glencoe, Ill.
1956 *Nuer religion.* Oxford Univer. Press, New York.

Festinger, Leon
    1957 *A theory of cognitive dissonance.* Row, Peterson, Evanston, Ill.

Firth, Raymond W.
    1929 *Primitive economics of the New Zealand Maori.* Preface by R. H. Tawney. Dutton, New York.
    1936 *We, the Tikopia: a sociological study of kinship in primitive Polynesia.* Preface by B. Malinowski. American Book, New York.
    1939 *Primitive Polynesian economy.* Routledge, London.

Forde, C. Daryll
    1934 *Habitat, economy and society: a geographical introduction to ethnology.* Methuen, London.

Frank, Lawrence K.
    1951 *Nature and human nature: man's new image of himself.* Rutgers Univer. Press, New Brunswick, N.J.

Freeman, Otis W. (Ed.)
    1951 *Geography of the Pacific.* Wiley, New York.

Fromm, Eric
    1941 *Escape from freedom.* Holt, Rinehart and Winston, New York.
    1947 *Man for himself: an inquiry into the psychology of ethics.* Holt, Rinehart and Winston, New York.

Fry, Roger
    1924 *Vision and design.* Brentano, New York.

Gamow, George
    1952 Turbulence in space. *Scientific Amer.*, 186 (6):26–45.

Gatty, Harold
    1958 *Nature is your guide: how to find your way on land and sea by observing nature.* Dutton, New York.

Gayton, A. H.
    1946 Culture-environment integration: external references in Yokuts life. *Southwestern J. Anthrop.* 2:252–268.

Gesell, Arnold
    1945 *The embryology of behavior: the beginnings of the human mind.* Harper, New York.

Giedion, Siegfried
    1949 *Space, time and architecture: the growth of a new tradition.* Harvard Univer. Press, Cambridge, Mass.

Gillin, John P. (Ed.)
1954 For a science of social man: convergence in anthropology, psychology, and sociology. Macmillan, New York.

Gjerset, Knut
1925 History of Iceland. Macmillan, New York.

Goldenweiser, A. A.
1913 The principle of limited possibilities in the development of culture. J. Amer. Folklore, 26:259–290.
1933 History, psychology and culture. Knopf, New York.
1937 Anthropology: an introduction to primitive culture. Appleton-Century-Crofts, New York.

Gordon, Eric V.
1927 An introduction to Old Norse. Oxford Univer. Press, New York.

Greenacre, Phyllis
1952 Trauma, growth and personality. Norton, New York.

Grinker, R. R.
1953 Psychosomatic research. Norton, New York.

Grinker, R. R. (Ed.)
1956 Toward a unified theory of human behavior. Basic Books, New York.

Grinker, R. R., and J. P. Spiegel
1945 Men under stress. McGraw-Hill–Blakiston, New York.

Grinnell, Lawrence
1894 The Brehon laws. T. Fisher Unwin, London.

Grönbech, V. P.
1931 The culture of the Teutons. Trans. from the Danish 1909–1912. Humphrey Milford, London. 3 vols. in 2.

Gutkind, E. A.
1952 Our world from the air: an international survey of man and his environment. Chatto & Windus, London.

Hack, J. T.
1942 The changing physical environment of the Hopi Indians of Arizona. Reports of the Awatovi expedition no. 1, Peabody Museum Papers 35. Harvard Univer. Press, Cambridge, Mass.

Hailey, Lord
1938 An African survey. Oxford Univer. Press, London and New York. Rev., 1956.

Hall, Edward T.
1959   *The silent language*. Doubleday, New York.
Hallowell, A. I.
1947   Myth, culture and personality. *Amer. Anthropologist*, 49:544–556.
1950   Values, acculturation and mental health. *Amer. J. Orthopsychiat.*, 20:732–743.
Handy, E. S. C.
1923   The native culture of the Marquesas. *Bull. 9.*, Bishop Museum, Honolulu.
1940   The Hawaiian planter. *Bull.* 161, Bishop Museum, Honolulu. Vol. I.
Handy, E. S. C., et al.
1933   *Ancient Hawaiian civilization: a series of lectures delivered at the Kamehameha Schools.* Kamehameha Schools, Honolulu.
1934   Outline of Hawaiian physical therapeutics. *Bull.* 126, Bishop Museum, Honolulu.
Hartmann, Nicolai
1953   *New ways of ontology.* R. C. Kuhn (Trans.), Regnery, Chicago.
Haury, Emil
1950   *The stratigraphy and archaeology of Ventana cave.* Univer. of Arizona Press, Tucson, Ariz.
Havighurst, Robert J., et al.
1946   Environment and the Draw-A-Man test: the performance of Indian children. *J. abnorm. soc. Psychol.*, 41:50–63.
Havighurst, Robert J., and Rhea R. Hilkevitch
1944   The intelligence of Indian children as measured by a performance scale. *J. abnorm. soc. Psychol.*, 39:419–433.
Havighurst, Robert J., and B. L. Neugarten
1955   *American Indian and white children: a sociopsychological investigation.* Univer. of Chicago Press, Chicago.
Hawley, Amos H.
1950   *Human ecology: a theory of community structure.* Ronald, New York.
Henry, William E.
1947   The thematic apperception technique in the study of culture-personality relations. *Genet. Psychol. Monogr.*, 35.

1956   *The analysis of fantasy: the thematic apperception technique in the study of personality.* Wiley, New York.

Herrick, C. Judson
1949   *George Ellett Coghill, naturalist and philosopher.* Univer. of Chicago Press, Chicago.
1956   *The evolution of human nature.* Univer. of Texas Press, Austin, Tex.

Herring, Pendleton
1947   The social sciences in modern society. *Soc. Sci. Res. Council Items,* 1:5. Social Science Research Council, New York.

Herskovits, M. J.
1936   Applied anthropology and the American anthropologists. *Science,* 83:215–222.
1940   *The economic life of primitive peoples.* Knopf, New York.
1952   *Economic anthropology, a study in comparative economics.* Knopf, New York.

Hilgard, Ernest R.
1948   *Theories of learning.* Appleton-Century-Crofts, New York.

Hocart, A. M.
1929   Lau Islands, Fiji. *Bull.* 62, Bishop Museum, Honolulu.

Hogbin, H. I.
1934   *Law and order in Polynesia.* Introduction by B. Malinowski. Harcourt, Brace & World, New York.

Homans, George C.
1950   *The human group.* Harcourt, Brace & World, New York.

Horney, Karen
1950   *Neurosis and human growth: the struggle toward self-realization.* Norton, New York.

Howells, W. W.
1954   *Back of history: the story of our own origins.* Doubleday, New York.

Huntington, Ellsworth
1907   *The pulse of Asia.* Houghton Mifflin, Boston and New York.
1945   *Mainsprings of civilization.* Wiley, New York.
1951   *Principles of human geography.* Wiley, New York.

Huxley, Sir Julian S.
  1942   *Evolution, the modern synthesis.* Harper, New York.
  1955   Evolution, cultural and biological. In W. L. Thomas
         (Ed.), *Yearbook of Anthropology,* Wenner-Gren Founda-
         tion for Anthropological Research, New York. Pp. 3–25.
  1957   *New bottles for new wine.* Harper, New York.
Joseph, Alice, et al.
  1949   *The desert people: a study of the Papago Indians of
         Arizona.* Univer. of Chicago Press, Chicago.
Joseph, Alice, and Veronica F. Murray
  1951   *Chamorros and Carolinians of Saipan.* Harvard Univer.
         Press, Cambridge, Mass.
Kardiner, Abram
  1939   *The individual and his society: the psychodynamics of
         primitive social organization.* Columbia Univer. Press,
         New York.
Kelly, W. H.
  1954   Applied anthropology in the Southwest. *Amer. Anthro-
         pologist,* 56:709–719.
Keur, John Y., and D. L. Keur
  1955   The deeply rooted: a study of a Drents community in
         the Netherlands. *Monogr. Amer. ethnol. Soc.,* 25.
Kluckhohn, Clyde, and W. H. Kelly
  1945   The concept of culture. In R. Linton (Ed.), *The science
         of man in the world crisis.* Columbia Univer. Press, New
         York. Pp. 78–106.
Kluckhohn, Clyde, and Dorothea C. Leighton
  1946   *The Navaho.* Harvard Univer. Press, Cambridge, Mass.
Kluckhohn, Clyde, and O. H. Mowrer
  1944   Culture and personality: a conceptual scheme. *Amer.
         Anthropologist,* 46:1–29.
Kluckhohn, Florence R.
  1950   Dominant and substitute profiles of cultural orienta-
         tions: their significance for the analysis of social stratifi-
         cation. *Soc. Forces,* 28:376–393.
Koffka, K.
  1924   *The growth of the mind.* R. M. Ogden (Trans.), Har-
         court, Brace & World, New York.
Köhler, W.
  1925   *The mentality of apes.* E. Winter (Trans.), Harcourt,
         Brace & World, New York.

Kraus, W. H.
　1959　Review of T. Hodgkin, *Nationalism in colonial Africa.*
　　　　Science 130 (3367):94.
Kroeber, A. L.
　1917　The superorganic. *Amer. Anthropologist,* 19:163–213.
　1939　Cultural and natural areas in native North America.
　　　　Univer. Calif. Publ. Amer. Archaeol., Ethnol., 38, Berke-
　　　　ley, Calif.
　1944　*Configurations of culture growth.* Univer. of California
　　　　Press, Berkeley, Calif.
Kroeber, A. L., and Clyde Kluckhohn
　1952　Culture: a critical review of concepts and definitions.
　　　　*Papers of the Peabody Museum of American Archaeology
　　　　and Ethnology,* 47 (1). Harvard Univer. Press, Cam-
　　　　bridge, Mass.
Kropotkin, P.
　1902　*Mutual aid: a factor of evolution* (rev. ed.). Heinemann,
　　　　London.
La Barre, Weston
　1948　The Aymara Indians of Lake Titicaca Plateau, Bolivia.
　　　　Mem. Amer. Anthropol. Assoc., 68:1–250.
　1954　*The human animal.* Univer. of Chicago Press, Chicago.
　1958　The influence of Freud on anthropology. *Amer. Imago,*
　　　　15:275–328.
Ladd, Harry S.
　1934　Geology of Vitelevu, Fiji. *Bull.* 119, Bishop Museum,
　　　　Honolulu.
Ladd, Harry S., and J. Edward Hoffmeister
　1945　Geology of Lau, Fiji. *Bull.* 181, Bishop Museum, Hono-
　　　　lulu.
Landsberger, Henry A.
　1958　*Hawthorne revisited: management and the worker, its
　　　　critics, and developments in human relations in industry.*
　　　　Cornell Univer. Press, Ithaca, N.Y.
Lantis, Margaret
　1959　Alaskan Eskimo cultural values. *Polar notes: occasional
　　　　publications of the Stefansson Collection.* Hanover, N.H.,
　　　　1:35–48.
LaPierre, R. T.
　1959　*The Freudian ethic.* Duell, Sloan & Pearce, New
　　　　York.

Laporte, Paul M.
1948   The space-time concept in the work of Picasso. *Magazine of Art*, 1:26–32.

Larrabee, Harold A.
1945   *Reliable knowledge*. Houghton Mifflin, Boston.

Lee, Dorothy
1948   Are basic needs ultimate? *J. abnorm. soc. Psychol.*, 43:391–395.
1950   Lineal and nonlineal codifications of reality. *Psychosom. Med.* 12:89–97.

Leighton, Alexander H., et al.
1957   *Explorations in social psychiatry*. Basic Books, New York.

Leighton, Dorothea C., and John Adair
Ms.   *People of the middle place: a study of the Zuni Indians*. Indian Education, Personality and Administration project, U.S. Office of Indian Affairs.

Leighton, Dorothea C., and Clyde Kluckhohn
1947   *Children of the people: the Navaho individual and his development*. Harvard Univer. Press, Cambridge, Mass.

Lewis, Oscar
1951   *Life in a Mexican village: Tepoztlan restudied*. Univer. of Illinois Press, Urbana, Ill.

Likert, Rensis
1959   An interview in *The Nation's Business*, August.

Lind, Andrew W.
1938   *An island community: ecological succession in Hawaii*. Univer. of Chicago Press, Chicago.

Linton, Ralph
1923   The material culture of the Marquesas Islands. *Mem.* 8 (5) Bishop Museum, Honolulu.

Lowie, Robert H.
1935   *The Crow Indians*. Holt, Rinehart and Winston, New York.
1937   *The history of ethnological theory*. Holt, Rinehart and Winston, New York.

Macgregor, Gordon
1946   *Warriors without weapons: a study of the society and personality development of the Pine Ridge Sioux*. Univer. of Chicago Press, Chicago.

Malinowski, Bronislaw

1922   *Argonauts of the western Pacific: an account of native enterprise and adventure in the archipelagoes of Melanesian New Guinea.* Preface by Sir James Frazer. Routledge, London.

1935   *Coral gardens and their magic: a study of the methods of tilling the soil and of agricultural rites in the Trobriand islands.* American Book, New York.

1944   *A scientific theory of culture and other essays.* Univer. of North Carolina Press, Chapel Hill, N.C.

1945   *The dynamics of culture change: an inquiry into race relations in Africa.* Phyllis M. Kaberry (Ed.). Yale Univer. Press, New Haven, Conn.

1955   *Magic, science and religion and other essays.* Doubleday, Anchor Books, New York.

Malo, David

1903   *Hawaiian antiquities.* N. B. Emerson (Trans.), Hawaiian Gazette Press, Honolulu.

Mandelbaum, David (Ed.)

1949   *Selected writings of Edward Sapir in language, culture and personality.* Univer. of California Press, Berkeley, Calif.

Mannheim, Karl

1940   *Man and society in an age of reconstruction.* Harcourt, Brace & World, New York.

Maslow, A. P.

1954   *Motivation and personality.* Harper, New York.

1957   *Intuition versus intellect.* Life Science Press, Valley Stream, N.Y.

May, Rollo (Ed.)

1958   *Existence: a new dimension in psychiatry and psychology.* Basic Books, New York.

Mayer, Albert, and associates

1958   *Pilot project, India.* Univer. of California Press, Berkeley, Calif.

Mead, Margaret

1928   *Coming of age in Samoa.* Morrow, New York.

1930   *Growing up in New Guinea.* Morrow, New York.

1935   *Sex and temperament in three savage societies.* Morrow, New York.

Mead, Margaret (Ed.)
    1937 *Cooperation and competition among primitive peoples.*
          McGraw-Hill, New York.
    1953 *Cultural patterns and technical change: a manual pre-*
          pared by the World Federation for Mental Health.
          UNESCO, Paris.
Menninger, Karl A.
    1942 *Love against hate.* Harcourt, Brace & World, New York.
Metzenthin, E. C.
    1924 The Heliand: a new approach. *Stud. Philol.*, 21:502–539.
          Univer. of North Carolina Press, Chapel Hill, N.C.
Miller, N. E., and J. Dollard
    1941 *Social learning and imitation.* Yale Univer. Press, New
          Haven, Conn.
Montagu, Ashley
    1941 The nature of war and the myth of nature. *Scientific*
          Mon. 54:342–353.
    1952 *Darwin: competition and cooperation.* Schuman, New
          York.
Moreno, J. L., and F. B. Moreno
    1944 Spontaneity theory in its relation to problems of inter-
          pretation and measurement. *Sociometry,* 7:399–355.
Morgenbesser, Sidney
    1958 Role and status of anthropological theories. *Science,*
          128:285–288.
Moulyn, Adrian C.
    1957 *Structure, function and purpose: an inquiry into the*
          concepts and methods of biology from the viewpoint
          of time. Foreword by Y. H. Krikorian. Liberal Arts Press,
          New York.
Movius, H. L., Jr.
    1942 *The Irish Stone Age: its chronology, development and*
          relationships. Cambridge Univer. Press, New York.
Mukerjee, Radhakamal
    1950 *The dynamics of morals: a sociopsychological theory of*
          ethics. Introduction by Gardner Murphy. Macmillan,
          London.
Muntz, W. S.
    1913 *Rome, St. Paul and the early church. The inflence of*
          Roman law on St. Paul's teaching and phraseology and
          on the development of the church. J. Murray, London.

Murdock, George P., et al.
1945 *Outline of cultural materials.* Yale Univer. Press, New Haven, Conn.
1954 *Outline of world cultures.* Human Relations Area Files, New Haven, Conn.
Murphy, Gardner
1947 *Personality: a biosocial approach to origins and structure.* Harper, New York.
1958 *Human potentialities.* Basic Books, New York.
Northrop, F. S. C.
1947 *The logic of the sciences and the humanities.* Macmillan, New York.
Oats, Whitney J. (Ed.)
1948 *Basic writings of Saint Augustine.* Random House, New York.
O'Grady, M. Standish
1892 *Silva Gadelica.* Williams & Norgate, London.
Opler, Marvin K.
1956 *Culture, psychiatry and human values: the methods and values of a social psychiatry.* Foreword by T. A. C. Rennie. Charles C. Thomas, Springfield, Ill.
Overstreet, H. A.
1949 *The mature mind.* Norton, New York.
Packard, Vance
1957 *The hidden persuaders.* McKay, New York.
Pareto, Vilfredo
1935 *The mind and society.* Harcourt, Brace & World, New York. 4 vols.
Parker, G. H.
1919 *The elementary nervous system.* Lippincott, Philadelphia.
Parsons, E. C.
1939 *Pueblo Indian religion.* Univer. of Chicago Press, Chicago. Vol. I.
Phillpotts, Dame Bertha Surtees
1913 *Kindred and clan in the Middle Ages and after.* Cambridge Univer. Press, London.
1931 *Edda and saga.* The Home Univer. Library, London.
Piaget, Jean
1957 The child and modern physics. *Scientific Amer.,* 196 (3): 46–51.

254   BIBLIOGRAPHY

Pitt-Rivers, Julian A.
  1954   *The people of the Sierra.* Introduction by E. E. Evans-Pritchard. Weidenfeld & Nicolson, London.
Polanyi, Karl
  1944   *The great transformation.* Holt, Rinehart and Winston, New York and Toronto.
Polanyi, Karl, et al.
  1957   *Trade and market in the early empires: economics in history and theory.* Free Press, Glencoe. Ill.
Radcliffe-Brown, A. R.
  1922   *The Andaman islanders: a study in social anthropology.* Cambridge Univer. Press, New York.
  1930   Applied anthropology. *Rep. Australian and New Zealand Assoc. Advancement Sci.,* Section F, Sidney, Australia, 20:267–280.
  1957   *A natural science of society.* Foreword by F. Eggan. Free Press, Glencoe, Ill.
Radin, Paul
  1933   *The method and theory of ethnology: an essay in criticism.* McGraw-Hill, New York.
Ratzel, Friedrich
  1921–1922   *Anthropogeographie.* J. Engelhorns, Stuttgart. 4 vols.
Rayner, Jeannette F.
  1957   Studies of disasters and other extreme situations: an annotated selected bibliography. *Human Organization,* 16:30–40.
Redfield, Robert
  1941   *The folk culture of the Yucatan.* Univer. of Chicago Press, Chicago.
  1953   Relations of anthropology to the social sciences and to the humanities. In A. L. Kroeber (Ed.), *Anthropology today.* Univer. of Chicago Press, Chicago. Pp. 728–738.
  1955   *The little community: viewpoints for the study of a human whole.* Univer. of Chicago Press, Chicago.
Rees, Alwyn D.
  1951   *Life in a Welsh countryside.* Univer. of Wales Press, Cardiff.
Reik, Theodor
  1941   *Masochism in modern man.* M. H. Beigel and G. M. Kurth (trans.), Grove Press, New York.

Rhine, Joesph B.
   1953   *New world of the mind.* Sloane, New York.
Rhine, Joseph B., and J. G. Pratt
   1940   *Extra-sensory perception after sixty years.* Holt, Rinehart
          and Winston, New York.
   1957   *Parapsychology: frontier science of the mind.* Charles
          C Thomas, Springfield, Ill.
Rhys, J., and D. Brynmor-Jones
   1923   *The Welsh people.* Macmillan, London.
Ripley, W. Z.
   1899   *The races of Europe: a sociological study.* Appleton-
          Century-Crofts, New York.
Roberts, Stephen H.
   1927   *Population problems of the Pacific.* Routledge, London.
Roethlisberger, F. J., and W. J. Dickson
   1939   *Management and the worker.* Harvard Univer. Press,
          Cambridge, Mass.
Rogers, Carl R.
   1951   *Client-centered therapy: its current practice, implication,
          and theory.* Houghton Mifflin, New York.
Romano, John (Ed.)
   1949   *Adaptation.* Cornell Univer. Press, Ithaca, N.Y.
Russell, E. S.
   1945   *The directiveness of organic activities.* Cambridge
          Univer. Press, New York.
Saint Augustine
   1950   *The city of God.* M. Dods (Trans.), Modern Library,
          New York.
Sapir, Edward
   1924   Culture, genuine and spurious. *Amer. J. Sociol.,* 29:401–
          429.
Schapiro, Meyer
   1957   The liberating quality of avant-garde art: the vital role
          that painting and sculpture play in modern culture.
          Art News, 56:36–42.
Sears, P. B.
   1939   *Life and environment: the interrelations of living
          things.* Teachers College, Columbia Univer. Press, New
          York.
   1949   Integration at the community level. *Amer. Scientist,*
          37:235–242.

1955   Changing man's habitat: physical and biological phenomena. In W. L. Thomas (Ed.), *Yearbook of Anthropology*, 1955. Wenner-Gren Foundation for Anthropological Research, New York.

Seligman, C. G.
1928   The unconscious in relation to anthropology. *Brit. J. Psychol.*, 18:373–387.

Sherrington, Charles
1941   *Man on his nature.* Cambridge Univer. Press, New York.

Shils, Edward A., and H. A. Finch (Trans. and Ed.)
1949   *Max Weber on the methodology of the social sciences.* Free Press, Glencoe, Ill.

Simmel, Georg
1955   *Conflict.* K. H. Wolff (Trans.). *The web of group-affiliations.* R. Bendix (Trans.). Foreword by E. C. Hughes. Free Press, Glencoe, Ill.

Simmons, Leo W., and H. G. Wolff
1954   *Social science in medicine.* Russell Sage, New York.

Sinnott, Edmund W.
1955   *The biology of the spirit.* Viking, New York.

Snow, C. P.
1959   *The two cultures and the scientific revolution.* Cambridge Univer. Press, New York.

Sorokin, Pitirim A.
1937   *Social and cultural dynamics.* American Book, New York. Vol. I.

1947   *Society, culture, and personality.* Harper, New York.

Spencer, R. F. (Ed.)
1954   *Method and perspective in anthropology. Papers in honor of Wilson D. Wallis.* Univer. of Minnesota Press, Minneapolis.

Spicer, E. H. (Ed.)
1952   *Human problems in technological change: a casebook.* Russell Sage, New York.

Spoehr, Alexander
1957   *Marianas prehistory; archaeological survey and excavations on Saipan, Tinian, and Rota.* Chicago Natural History Museum, Chicago.

Stefansson, V.
1939   *Iceland, the first American republic.* Doubleday, New York.

Steward, Julian H.
  1933 Ethnography of the Owens Valley Paiute. *Univer. Calif. Pub. Amer. Archaeol., Ethnol.*, 33 (3). Univer. of California Press, Berkeley, Calif.
  1955 *Theory of culture change: the methodology of multilinear evolution.* Univer. of Illinois Press, Urbana, Ill.
Strong, William T.
  1893 The Fueros of northern Spain. *Polit. Sci. Quart.*, 8:317–334.
Sumner, W. G.
  1906 *Folkways: a study of the sociological importance of usages, manners, customs and mores.* Ginn, Boston.
Sutherland, I. L. G. (Ed.)
  1940 *The Maori people today.* Oxford Univer. Press, London.
Sveinsson, Einar Ol.
  1953 The age of the Sturlungs: Icelandic civilization in the thirteenth century. J. S. Hannesson (Trans.), *Islandica*, XXXVI. Cornell Univer. Press, Ithaca, N.Y.
Tax, Sol
  1945 Anthropology and administration. *America Indigena*, 5:21–33.
  1952 Action anthropology. *America Indigena*, 12:103–109.
Taylor, T. Griffith
  1936 *Environment and nation: geographical factors in the culture and political history of Europe.* Univer. of Chicago Press, Chicago.
Thomas, W. L., Jr. (Ed.)
  1956 *Man's role in changing the face of the earth.* Univer. of Chicago Press, Chicago.
Thompson, Laura
  1938 The culture history of the Lau islands, Fiji. *Amer. Anthropologist*, 40:181–197.
  1940a *Fijian frontier.* Introduction by B. Malinowski. Institute of Pacific Relations, New York.
  1940b Southern Lau, Fiji: an ethnography. *Bull.* 162, Bishop Museum, Honolulu.
  1941 Report of the Social Scientist. In Elizabeth Collins (Ed.), *Community survey of Education in Hawaii*, Territory of Hawaii, Honolulu. Pp. 126–142.
  1945a Logico-aesthetic integration in Hopi culture. *Amer. Anthropologist*, 47:540–553.

1946   The Hopi crisis: a report to administrators. U.S. Office of Indian Affairs, Washington, D.C. (mim.).

1947a   *Guam and its people* (3d ed.). Princeton Univer. Press, Princeton, N.J.

1947b   The problem of "totemism" in southern Lau. *Oceania,* 17:211–225.

1948a   Attitudes and acculturation. *Amer. Anthropologist,* 50: 200–215.

1949a   Relations of men, animals, and plants in an island community (Fiji). *Amer. Anthropologist,* 51:253–267.

1949b   The basic conservation problem. *Scientific Mon.,* 68:129–132.

1950a   Action research among American Indians. *Scientific Mon.,* 70:34–40.

1950b   *Culture in crisis: a study of the Hopi Indians.* Harper, New York.

1951a   Operational anthropology as an emergent discipline. *Etc. A Review of General Semantics,* 8:117–128.

1951b   *Personality and government: findings and recommendations of the Indian Administration Research.* Instituto Indigenista Interamericano, Mexico, D.F.

1959   The clinical situation in psychotherapy, dependency government, and applied anthropology. *Human Organization,* 18:131–134.

1960   Core values and diplomacy: a case study of Iceland. *Human Organization,* 19:82–85.

Ms.   Field notes on Iceland (1952, 1960).

In preparation
        a. A documentary approach toward the analysis and comparison of core value systems
        b. *Peoples I have known*

Thompson, Laura (Ed.)

1942a   Field guide to the study of the development of interpersonal relations for staff and consultants, Research on Indian Education. U.S. Office of Indian Affairs, Washington, D.C. (mim.).

1942b   Guide to the authority system of each tribe. Research on Indian Education. U.S. Office of Indian Affairs, Washington, D.C. (mim.).

Thompson, Laura, and Alice Joseph
1944   *The Hopi way.* Univer. of Chicago Press, Chicago (reprinted Univer. Microfilms, Inc., Ann Arbor, Mich., 1959).

Thurnwald, Richard
1932   *Economics in primitive communities.* Oxford Univer. Press, London.

Titiev, Mischa
1944   Old Oraibi: a study of the Hopi Indians of Third Mesa. *Papers of the Peabody Museum,* 22 (1). Harvard Univer. Press, Cambridge, Mass.

Turney-High, Harry H.
1949   *Primitive war: its practice and concepts.* Univer. of South Carolina Press, Columbia, S.C.
1953   *Chateau-Gérard: The life and times of a Walloon village.* Univer. of South Carolina Press, Columbia, S.C.

Underhill, Ruth
1939   Social organization of the Papago Indians. *Columbia Univer. Contr. Anthropol.,* 30. Columbia Univer. Press, New York.
1946   Papago Indian religion. *Columbia Univer. Publ. Anthropol.,* 33, Columbia Univer. Press, New York.
Ms.   a. Acculturation at the village of Santa Rosa (1942).
Ms.   b. Papago morality (1942).
Ms.   c. The individual in Papago society (1942).

van der Haag, Ernest
1959   Applications of social science. *Science,* 129:1399–1444.

Vinogradoff, Sir Paul
1920   *The growth of the manor* (3d ed.). G. Allen, London.

von Bertalanffy, L.
1952   *Problems of life.* Wiley, New York.

Warner, W. Lloyd
1937   *A black civilization: a social study of an Australian tribe.* Harper, New York and London.
1946   *The social systems of American ethnic groups.* Yankee City Series. Yale Univer. Press, New Haven, Conn. Vol. 3.

Warner, W. Lloyd, and J. O. Low
1947   *The social system of the modern factory. The strike: a social analysis.* Yankee City Series. Yale Univer. Press, New Haven, Conn. Vol. 4.

Warner, W. Lloyd, and P. S. Lunt
  1941 *The social life of a modern community.* Yankee City
        Series. Yale Univer. Press, New Haven, Conn. Vol. 1.
  1942 *The status system of a modern community.* Yankee City
        Series. Yale Univer. Press, New Haven, Conn. Vol. 2.
Wax, Rosalie, and Murray Wax
  1955 The Vikings and the rise of capitalism. *Amer. J. Sociol.,*
        61:1–10.
Wein, Hermann
  1952 The categories and a logic of structure. *J. Phil.,* 49:
        629–633.
Weiss, Paul
  1960 Knowledge: a growth process. *Science,* 131:1716–1719.
Weltfish, Gene
  1960 The ethnic dimension of human history: pattern or pat-
        terns of culture? In A. F. C. Wallace (Ed.), *Selected
        papers of the Fifth International Congress of Anthro-
        pological and Ethnological Sciences.* Univer. of Pennsyl-
        vania Press, Philadelphia.
Wertheimer, Max
  1912 Experimentelle Studien über das Sehen von Bewegungen.
        Z. Psychol. 61:161–265.
  1945 *Productive thinking.* Harper, New York and London.
Weyl, Hermann
  1922 *Space, time and matter.* H. Brose (Trans.), Methuen,
        London.
White, Leslie A.
  1949 *The science of culture: a study of man and civilization.*
        Farrar, Straus and Cudahy, New York.
Whitehead, A. N.
  1926 *Science and the modern world.* Macmillan, New York.
  1933 *Adventures of ideas.* Macmillan, New York.
Whiting, A. F.
  1939 Ethnobotany of the Hopi. *Bull. Museum north. Arizona,*
        15. Flagstaff, Ariz.
Whiting, John W. M.
  1941 *Becoming a Kwoma: teaching and learning in a New
        Guinea tribe.* Foreword by J. Dollard. Yale Univer. Press,
        New Haven, Conn.

Whorf, B. L.
1941 The relation of habitual thought and behavior to language. In Leslie Spier et al. (Eds.), *Language, culture and personality: essays in memory of Edward Sapir.* Sapir Memorial Publ. Fund, Menasha, Wis. Pp. 75–94.

1956 *Language, thought and reality; selected writings.* John B. Carroll (Ed.). Foreword by Stuart Chase. Technology Press, Cambridge, Mass.

Whyte, Lancelot Law
1949 *The unitary principle in physics and biology.* Holt, Rinehart and Winston, New York.

Wiener, Philip P. (Ed.)
1958 *Values in a universe of chance: selected writings of Charles S. Peirce (1839–1914).* Stanford Univer. Press, Stanford, Calif.

Wissler, Clark
1912 *North American Indians of the plains.* American Museum of Natural History, New York.

1922 *The American Indian; an introduction to the anthropology of the New World* (2d ed.). Oxford, New York.

1923 *Man and culture.* Crowell, New York.

Yerkes, Robert Mearns, and A. W. Yerkes
1929 *The great apes: a study of anthropoid life.* Yale Univer. Press, New Haven, Conn.

Name Index

Adair, J., 52, 61, 203, 250
Allee, W. C., 29, 85n., 99, 130, 238
Arensberg, C. M., 16, 27, 223n., 238, 241
Asher, R. E., 45, 238
Axelrod, D. I., 129, 238

Bachofen, J. J., 9
Barnett, H. G., 13, 47, 83, 238
Bates, M., 13, 99, 103, 104, 128, 129, 238
Beaglehole, E., 146, 152, 239
Beckwith, M. W., 143, 239
Beigel, M. H., 254
Belshaw, C., 27
Bendix, R., 256
Benedict, R., xii, 31, 235, 239
Bennett, H. H., 239
Bennett, J. W., 39n., 239
Bentley, A. F., 81, 82, 85, 239, 242
Bergson, H., 80, 239
Bettelheim, B., 135, 239
Bidney, D., xxiv, 239
Bierstedt, R., xxvi, 239
Birdwhistell, R. L., 198, 239
Boas, F., 9, 30, 31, 240
Bohr, N., 78, 79, 240
Bridgman, P. W., 78–80, 240
Brown, G. G., 48, 240
Bryan, E. H., Jr., 107, 109, 110, 112, 143, 240
Bryce, J., 207, 240
Brynmor-Jones, D., 223n., 255
Buck, P. H., 142–144, 146, 240
Bunzel, R. L., 30, 240

Burkitt, M. C., 5, 240

Cannon, W. B., 129, 240
Cantril, H. A., 50, 172, 241
Capell, A., 111, 241
Caro-Baroja, J., 223n., 241
Carroll, J. B., 261
Carson, R., 87, 88, 241
Carter, G. F., 29, 241
Cassirer, E., 160, 241
Chadwick, H. M., 223n., 241
Chapple, E. D., 17, 18, 20, 24, 241
Chase, S., 261
Chesky, J., 52, 61
Childe, V. G., 215, 223n., 241
Clark, G., 128
Clark, J. G. D., 28, 241
Clausen, 210
Coghill, E. G., 78, 92, 93
Collier, J., xii, 49, 53, 150, 233, 242
Collins, E., 257
Coon, C. S., 16, 18, 20, 24, 208, 212n., 223n., 241, 242

Darling, F. F., 223n., 242
Darwin, C., xii, 130, 132, 202, 242
Declareuil, J., 192, 242
de Coulanges, F., 9
Dewey, J., xii, 81, 82, 85, 242
Dickson, W. J., 34, 255
Dixon, R. B., 5, 242
Dobbs, H. A. C., 66, 242

263

Subject Index